Defending the Book of Mormon

Proceedings of the 2023 FAIR Virtual Conference

Edited by:

Scott Gordon
Trevor Holyoak
Jared Riddick

FAIR
2025

Defending the Book of Mormon: Proceedings of the 2023 FAIR Virtual Conference

Edited by Scott Gordon, Trevor Holyoak, and Jared Riddick

Proceedings from the Defending the Book of Mormon Conference, held September 22nd and 23rd, 2023, at American Fork, UT.

Cover Image: "Praying at Cumorah" by Patrick Spencer.
Cover Design: Jared Riddick
Interior Design and Typesetting: Jared Riddick
Copyediting: Jared Riddick

ISBN: 979-8-9993242-0-7 (Paperback)
Library of Congress Control Number: 2025942698
First edition: August 2025, second printing

Published by:
FAIR
PO Box 491677
Redding, CA 96049
United States
fairlatterdaysaints.org

Produced and published in the United States of America

For permissions, academic inquiries, or bulk orders, contact: dbeck@fairlatterdaysaints.org

Table of Contents

Introduction

Trevor Holyoak

I believe the original idea of having a virtual conference was from DeLayna Beck, FAIR's Operations Manager. In August 2020, at the height of the COVID 19 pandemic, we had put on what was essentially a virtual conference, since we could not allow anyone to actually physically attend our annual conference that year. But then, in 2023, we had our own little studio and had the ability to hold a virtual conference in a single room, and we (Scott Gordon, DeLayna, and I) thought we would give it a try.

If we held it in the fall, we reasoned, there would be time to get it together after our traditional annual in-person conference. We decided to make this different from our typical conferences by issuing a call for papers, instead of inviting particular people to speak. Little did we realize that doing so would complicate our simple vision beyond our imaginations. I ended up sending out acceptance and rejection emails during our August conference at the same time I was producing the live stream.

As yet another element to set this virtual conference apart, we wanted to have a theme. We looked at the calendar and remembered that on September 22, 1827, Joseph Smith received the gold plates. This seemed like the most significant event in the fall, and it was connected to a major topic for Latter-day Saint apologetics - defending the Book of Mormon. Later we recalled that the Book of Mormon would also be the theme for "Come, Follow Me" for the following year. Everything seemed to click into place, as if little rays of inspiration combined to become a pillar.[1]

1. Alexander Dushku, "Pillars and Rays", *Liahona,* April 2024, online at churchofjesuschrist.org.

We received a gratifying number of submissions, encompassing multiple aspects of the study of the Book of Mormon and the Gold Plates. We were introduced to some new people this way, which has prompted us to continue this pattern for subsequent virtual conferences. The eminent Latter-day Saint historian Richard Bushman kindly agreed to give our keynote, based on his then-recent book, *Joseph Smith's Gold Plates*, which fit perfectly with the September 22nd date on which his presentation began the conference.

Other presentations included topics such as archaeology, doctrine, theology, geography, and even nautical science. They were streamed via our YouTube channel, where they are still available to watch. This book contains the papers represented by those presentations, along with three that were not presented at the conference.

This book has been a long time in coming – it turned out to be a bigger project than we first anticipated. But we are now set up to more quickly publish future volumes. And we have learned something each year about improving the submission process. We appreciate everyone's patience as we have navigated the learning curves.

We would also like to thank Joshua Halverson, Sarah Allen, Brant Gardner, David Smith, and Elisabeth Bentley. And we are extremely grateful for the support of Janna Holyoak, Sheri Gordon, and Jeff Beck.

The overall theme of this conference is that the Book of Mormon is scripture, originally inscribed on gold plates by prophets, translated by a prophet, and is defendable as such. We hope you enjoy and are edified by the papers contained in this volume.

Trevor Holyoak
FAIR Vice President
June 12, 2025

1

Joseph Smith's Gold Plates

Richard Lyman Bushman

This conference keynote address was given on September 22, 2023. The transcript has been edited for clarity from the original video presentation.

It is a pleasure to be connected with FAIR again. I have always admired its work and benefited from it personally.

Today, I would say a little about how my recent book, *Joseph Smith's Gold Plates,* came to be, how I think of it, and then some of the stories that emerge from the book. I think of it as a collection of stories about how the plates have been treated and understood.

The idea for a book on the Gold Plates came to me in 2010 while I was teaching at Claremont Graduate University. It simply occurred to me one day that it would be interesting to write a book about the plates. I didn't get to work on it much until about 2016 but then worked pretty steadily until the manuscript went to Oxford about a year ago. I really don't know why the Gold Plates came to mind. I had long been intrigued by them. They have no real predecessors and no real successors; they sit there as an exotic, mysterious object. I wrote in a kind of playful mood. I didn't have any heavy-duty scholarly points to make. I did not set out to prove the reality of the plates. I simply wanted to explore them and to figure out how they had been treated over the years.

On the other hand, saying that the book is light-hearted does not mean that the plates are unimportant. They are heavy with implications, both for Joseph Smith and for us. Looking at Joseph Smith's early life, his vision of two heavenly beings in 1820 had a huge impact on him, but it was not particularly distinctive. I once did a study of visionary experiences in the United States recorded in print between 1785 and 1820, and there are over 33 of them. Through all of Christian history, many people have seen angels, God, and Christ.

If Joseph Smith's basic claims rested on the First Vision alone, he would have been one more visionary in a long history of visionaries. People would have ridiculed him as the Palmyra villagers did, but his experience would be perfectly understandable. On the other hand, to say that he had discovered gold plates in a hill was unbelievably fantastic. The plates turned him into a fraud. From being one more visionary, he became a charlatan and impostor, likely trying to cheat people of their money.

The plates had a huge impact on Joseph, but they also have an impact on those who believe in him. It is one thing to say you believe in God and that God speaks to us, but to say you believe in the Gold Plates means that you believe in a world where there are angels and invisible events going on beyond our sight, where there are powers at work in the universe that we only partially glimpse. In other words, you reenchant the world. Human existence is situated in the midst of complex and energetic supernatural forces.

I think that is one reason why the witnesses are not given more credence when they testify that they saw the plates. It is a perfectly good testimonial but of events so far beyond the ordinary it is hard to accept. It changes the nature of the world, and, credible as they are, the witnesses are just not enough to swing people into a new orientation toward life.

So the plates are important; a lot hinges on them.

When you write about the plates, as I did, everyone will want an answer to one question: "Do you believe in the plates?" Whatever you say on the matter, you are going to lose half your readers. The Latter-day Saints want to know: "Are you a believer? Are you one of us?" If I assure them I am, my scholarly colleagues will think: "Really, Richard, how can you?" Those are the conditions under which I began to write this book.

The subtitle is "A Cultural History." That means it is not a history of the plates: how Joseph got them, what he did with them, and how he disposed of them after twenty-two months. I talk about such things, but when I say cultural history, I mean how the plates were imagined, how they have sat in human minds down through the years? I talk about how they were conceived when they first were mentioned in the newspapers, down to today in our lesson manuals, our missionary instruction, and the scholarship about the plates.

That's the background of what I'm trying to do. For the remainder, I am going to tell you a few of the stories that came out of my studies. I found them interesting and hope you will, too.

One of them is about the initial reactions when word circulated in Palmyra that Joseph Smith claimed that he had gold plates. The first in-print mention of the plates was in June of 1829 in a Palmyra newspaper. There they were called the "Golden Bible," and the phrase stuck. It was picked up by other newspapermen around the country. Eber D. Howe included the words "Golden Bible" in big type on the title page of the 1834 edition of *Mormonism Unvailed.* I think of the June 1829 newspaper report as the first public attempt to conceptualize the plates. The phrase wasn't used by Latter-day Saints themselves – they usually referred to the plates as "the record." They are not even described as gold in the Book of Mormon itself. The Plates of Ether were, but not the Plates of Nephi. Moroni called them gold during his first visit to Joseph Smith, and I surmise that Joseph Smith, Senior, a person involved in treasure-seeking, used the term when he told Palmyra people about the plates.

Whatever its origins, the term showed up in this early newspaper account. So what is implied by the characterization of the plates as the "Gold Bible?" Gold is a highly ambiguous word. It is a term that exalts. It is the color of God. The Ark of the Covenant is papered in gold. There's the Gold Book, which lists the names of the Italian nobility. Gold is the gold standard. It's something noble, strong, and lasting. But it's also greed, as in the "Gold-Bug," Edgar Allan Poe's story of the discovery of Captain Kidd's treasure, or the Gold Rush. Lewis Bidamon, Emma Smith's second husband went west for the Gold Rush, a get-rich-quick scheme which gripped the imagination of Americans at mid-century and has been a mythic passage in our history ever since. All that hovers over the word "gold." "Bible," on the other hand, is the sacred word of God. It is scripture, godliness, obedience to heavenly commandments, spirituality rather than materialism, qualities quite at odds with gold as greed. The polarity captures an underlying tension in American society: materialism, wealth, the Almighty dollar on one hand, and the word of God, humility, obedience, and religion on the other. Perhaps not coincidentally, it is also the over-riding issue in the Book of Mormon. The ongoing question in Nephite society is what are the Nephites to be: a worldly, people who pursue wealth and until class struggle takes over their society and they lose God's protection? Or are they going to be the people of God? Eventually, it is this strain and the Nephites' inability to stick with God that leads to their destruction. All that is embedded in the words "Gold Bible." The casual epithet, coined by an unknown newspaper reporter to account for the gold plates, resonated with cultural issues running through American society and is the overriding tension in Nephite history.

Another configuration of meaning hovering over the plates comes out of the stories about how the Book of Mormon was obtained and how Joseph Smith handled the plates. Of all these stories--going to the hill, getting the plates, retrieving them, hiding them, translating them, showing them to witnesses--of all this you can ask a question: are the plates heavenly or are they earthly?

They certainly have a heavenly cast to them. An angel guards them, an angel informs Joseph Smith they are there, and the angel is the one who allows Joseph Smith to obtain the plates. It is a holy book. The plates tell a story of prophets speaking for God. Joseph translates the plates by the gift and power of God. They are forbidden to look upon – like the face of God in the Hebrew Bible. The plates are wrapped in the heavenly.

On the other hand, the plates were not just given to Joseph Smith by the angel. He didn't bring them down out of heaven to present to the prophet. Joseph Smith had to get up, walk two miles to the Hill Cumorah, look around on the hill, find a stone, pry it up, pull away the dirt, and then lug the plates home, dislocating his thumb on the way. Besides the recovery, there are all the stories of keeping the plates: making a box, hiding them under a floor board, in a barrel of beans, under the bed, wrapping them in cloth. They are very, very earthly in that they are a heavy, material object that had to be cared for.

The plates then are this hybrid. They are something so holy that you are forbidden to look upon them, and yet they are earthy too. That division marks the experience with the witnesses as well. The Three Witnesses are shown the plates by the angel; the word of God comes to them, admonishing them to serve God. The experience of seeing the plates and being enveloped by the spirit of God was heavenly. On the other hand, the Eight Witnesses hold the plates in their hands, turn the pages, pass them on to the next person, and use the word "heft" to say how they held them.

This strange contrast surrounds the plates. Are they holy exalted things of God, or are they earthy? Part of their fascination is their dichotomous nature. We sometimes complain, "Why couldn't Joseph Smith hold on to the plates and show them to people? Why not put them in a museum where they would be accessible?" But the moment you did that you would strip them of their heavenly aura. They would become an artifact, something for archaeologists and metallurgists to examine. People could turn over the individual plates and touch them. They would no longer have this magical grip on our imaginations, being both heavenly and earthly at the same time. Linguists would translate the characters not a prophet. The text would be a subject of science not a gift of God.

Those are a couple of the stories that occurred to me while working through the gold plates sources. Beyond these, the plates themselves as an artifact are perplexing. What are they like? There are stone tablets but no examples of inscribed metal plates in the Bible. Sonia Hazard has suggested that copper stereotyped plates used by printers may have suggested gold plates to Joseph Smith, but she found no evidence that he saw such an object.[1] The plates themselves do not really have a natural antecedent in nineteenth-century America. If you think or hear about the plates, what else would you think of? What in Joseph Smith's environment was like these gold plates with ancient writings, telling the history of a people, and calling out for translation?

Translation is even more difficult to explain. Why in the world would Joseph Smith undertake – or believe he could undertake – to translate ancient writing? Translation was a common skill, but it was the skill of learned men. Educated children would learn Latin grammar in school, and study it in college. Very learned men would know Greek, and an even smaller number would learn Hebrew. But this is at the high end. Common farm boys did not translate. When Joseph Smith wanted help with translation, he doesn't just ask around in Palmyra. He sent to New York City and to learned men. Translation is beyond the realm of Joseph Smith's experience and certainly his skill. He could not do such things.

1. For Bushman's discussion of Hazard's theory, see Richard L. Bushman, *Joseph Smith's Gold Plates: A Cultural History* (Oxford University Press, 2024): 155-156. For the original article, see Sonia Hazard, "How Joseph Smith Encountered Printing Plates and Founded Mormonism." *Religion and American Culture* 31, no. 2 (2021): 137–192.

The only translation that Joseph was likely to be aware of was the King James Version of the Bible, but that is translated by learned men in England, and it took years and years. Again, quite beyond his experience. And yet translation becomes part of his identity. He starts his prophetic career as a translator; it becomes integral to his story. Where in the world he got the idea of being a prophet-translator – a seer – is hard to explain.

That interests me and not only because it is a puzzle for a historian – figuring out where the idea came from – but it would be a problem for Joseph Smith himself. How did he ever think he was to translate? Having a heavenly being who appears in his room tell him he is to translate is not going to help. That's like saying, "You will jump over the moon." It was totally out of range of possible experiences.

Looking closely at the stories, I think that at first Joseph did not understand what was expected of him. He himself says in his 1832 account when he couldn't get the plates that he doubted his own vision. He thought it was a dream, something that appeared in his mind but with no reality.[2] Oliver Cowdery says that when Joseph Smith went to the hill, he was torn, asking is this a holy record, something I have to care for, or is it a treasure, like all the treasures my father has been seeking?[3] Still in the grip of the treasure-seeking mentality when he got to the hill, Joseph decided it was a treasure. When he couldn't get the plates, he started thinking about Abracadabra and the stories he had heard of guardian spirits denying access to treasures. It took three or four years before the Smith family realized that this was not a treasure but a holy record.

That was a major first step, but then Joseph had to figure out translation. How does he decide he is going to translate? Because of conflicting evidence in the sources, it is hard to know when exactly Joseph accepted his role. The late accounts, written in 1838 and which were affected by intervening historical events, suggest that he was told in 1823, but his 1832 account gives no indication of translation or of any interest in the Urim and Thummim, which goes unmentioned in the 1832 version.

I offer the argument – and it must remain a hypothesis, as there is not enough evidence to prove it – that it was not until Joseph actually had the plates that he realized translation was involved in possessing them. In the account of his good friend Joseph Knight, when Joseph Smith brought

2. History, circa Summer 1832, p. 4, online at josephsmithpapers.org.
3. Oliver Cowdery, "Letter VII" *The Latter Day Saints' Messenger and Advocate* 1, no. 10 (July 1835): 155–59.

the plates back from the hill, he exclaimed "I want them translated."[4] That is the first truly clear statement. It is as if holding the plates, seeing the engravings, and having the Urim and Thummim suddenly drove home the fact that they had to be translated.

There is also a problem in knowing when he realized that he was to be the translator. There is a disagreement in the sources about when he actually began. Did he do a little translating in the fall of 1827 after he had received the plates from Moroni, or was he delayed? I think the preponderance of evidence, which comes from Joseph Knight, Lucy Smith, and others, is that at first he did not realize that he was to translate. He sent Martin Harris to New York to obtain a translation of the characters he copied from the plates hoping to develop a lexicon that he could use to figure out what was on the plates.

I don't know when he realized he was to do the impossible and translate the characters himself. He hesitated through the fall and early winter of 1827-28. But in the winter of 1827-28, as he says in his 1832 history, reading Isaiah 29 in view of Martin Harris's visit to Charles Anthon persuaded him. He was the unlearned man who was to translate the plates.[5] Suddenly, the words of the text started pouring from his mouth.

Not only did Joseph start dictating the Book of Mormon, in the summer of 1828 a few months after he began, he had the first revelation where he spoke in the voice of God. It was no longer just Joseph Smith saying, "God told me this." The voice of God speaks in Doctrine and Covenants section 3, and it goes on from there. Somewhere in that period, in those few months, something was triggered within him, and he became a spokesman. He became, for the first time I think, a prophet who spoke for God. The Book of Commandments contain one revelation after another spoken in the voice of God. Though the words come from Joseph Smith's lips, they were in the voice of God.

That's my second story about translation, a baffling one in my opinion. I do not know how to understand it, but there it is in the record.

My final story moves forward in time. In the book, I discuss the Kinderhook Plates, James J. Strang and his plates, novels touching on the plates, and criticisms by historians.

4. Joseph Knight, 1772-1847. Joseph Knight reminiscences, online at catalog.churchofjesuschrist.org.
5. History, circa Summer 1832, p. 5, online at josephsmithpapers.org.

Then comes the 20th century and the post-manifesto Church, which is so deeply concerned about how it presents itself to the world. Can it escape its image as a backward people who oppress women and live under a theological dictatorship? With polygamy behind it, the Church becomes self-conscious about the presentation of itself to the world. That concern manifests itself at the Chicago World Fair and continues through the next century. It eventually involved the plates, because in the late 1920s, the Church buys the Hill Cumorah, and wants to develop it, just as they had developed Joseph Smith's birthplace, by placing a monument. They want a monument to Moroni and the Gold Plates to go with the shaft on the Hill Cumorah.

Soon after the turn of the century, a sculptor named Torleif Knaphus left Norway after his conversion as a young man and came to Utah where he was put to work doing the carving in various temples. Thinking he should seek to sculpt the Cumorah monument, Knapfus developed various designs to present to Church authorities. In the middle of the night on top of Ensign Peak, he prayed for direction. He later said an angel appeared and pointed to one of his sketches. The next day when he went to the General Authorities, they chose the same sketch.[6] Knapfus took care with the placement of the statue. He wanted it high on the hill but in sight of Route 21, where drivers passing by could see it. He had ambitions to present Mormonism to the world and wanted a Moroni who would tell the story as he felt that the Church should tell it.

To achieve his goal Knapfus created a Moroni that broadly redid the angel's actual history. His Moroni is a gold figure, ten-feet-tall, standing on the top of a pillar, holding the plates with his arm raised as if he were preaching. It is a striking figure, but there is nothing in the record that depicts Moroni in his latter-day mission doing either of these: holding the plates in his arm or preaching. Knapfus seems to be seeking to connect Moroni with the angel in Revelation 14, who brings the everlasting gospel and preaches it to all the earth. Knaphus's way of telling the Book of Mormon story was to turn Moroni into a character from the Bible. In a time of concern about the image of Mormonism in the public mind, a biblical Moroni made sense.

---

6. Allen P. Gerritsen, "The Hill Cumorah Monument: An Inspired Creation of Torleif S. Knaphus." *Journal of Book of Mormon Studies* 13, no. 1-2 (2004): 127-128.

Another adaptation of the Moroni story was offered by John Henry Evans, the author of *Joseph Smith, an American Prophet*, a very well-received book published by Macmillan. Like Knapfus, Evans wanted to present a view of Mormonism that would make sense in the larger world. Evans even refers to the Knaphus statue, as if he believed it was linked to his own work.

Evans was a faithful Latter-day Saint. He had published a book that was accepted as a Mutual Improvement Association manual for teaching purposes. But in his version of Joseph Smith, Moroni and the Gold Plates are not mentioned. He says that Joseph Smith left his home in Palmyra when he was a young man and when he came back, he had a new wife on one arm and a manuscript sheaf in the other. Then the Book of Mormon story follows. No Moroni makes an appearance. At the very back, in an appendix with source material in it, he quotes Joseph Smith's story, but he himself does not talk about it, and even uses statements such as "if an angel actually appeared to him," as if it was uncertain if an angel appeared or not. It is a strange tactic, but what Evans is trying to do is to present Joseph Smith as an admirable character on his own, without the divine dimension. Evans emphasized that Joseph built a city, published a compelling religious philosophy, and attracted thousands and thousands of followers. He deserved respect apart from any visitors from heaven. Evans book is of a piece with an image of Brigham Young that emerges in this period as the great colonizer. It is not Brigham Young, the Prophet of the Lord, who was establishing Zion. He was the man who helped settle the West. He is absorbed into American history, and the prophetic side of him is played down.

Contrasting views of Joseph Smith and the plates then prevailed in the same decade. Knapfus linked Joseph to the Bible as the angel in Revelations who restores the gospel, and Evans sees him as a city-builder and creator of a great religion, an American hero rather than a prophetic figure. Of these two, the Joseph Smith of the Bible is the one to prevail. The systematic missionary teaching programs built on the Knaphus assumption that Moroni was a biblical figure. The Gold Plates of the Book of Mormon are blended with the stick of Joseph mentioned in Ezekiel 37, becoming an ancient Hebrew scroll. At mid- century the Knapfus version became official. LeGrand Richards' *A Marvelous Work and a Wonder* elaborated the biblical references in Ezekiel, Isaiah, and Revelations for use in missionary presentations. In the hands of Knapfus and Richards, the plates became either the Stick of Joseph or the book carried by the angel flying through the midst of heaven, in both cases biblical artifacts.

Through the course of the 20th century the biblical version of the plates gradually evolved. Faith in the Bible, the assumption that made references to Ezekiel and Revelations effective, was fading. Missionaries could not count on investigators being Bible believers, making it difficult for the missionaries to use scripture to prove the Book of Mormon. Instead, they urged people to pray for revelation about the truth of the book. The Gold Plates almost disappear from the missionary lessons. There is no effort to conceal the existence of the Gold Plates; their existence is never the issue. They have just receded.

Does this mean that the Gold Plates will fade as we pay less attention to our early history? At one point, while I was working on the book, I wrote to twenty scholarly friends to ask them how they felt about the Gold Plates.[7] This group showed no tendency to discard the plates or deny them, but they seem to be becoming less to the point. Judging from the reactions in my tiny sample, people do not think much about the plates. They are not an active part of our religious life. I don't think they will disappear. They are an essential part of the founding story which we do not dwell on, but we still embrace. As history in general fades in our self-presentation, the plates will fade a little too, but they will never disappear entirely.

To close I wish to read my own view of the plates as laid out in the first pages of *Joseph Smith's Gold Plates*. Like all Latter-day Saints, I was taught about the plates as I was growing up. So far as I was concerned, they were just part of history. But how did they hold up as I matured?

"A logical path for a Latter-day Saint growing up in the modern world, especially one who became a historian, would be to grow out of my childhood beliefs. The plates would be spiritualized and their meaning made allegorical. But my life did not follow that course. The plates have continued to have a hold on me, and the same is true for other Mormons. Polls show that more than three-quarters of American Mormons believe that 'the Book of Mormon is a literal historical account,' a likely indicator of belief in the plates. This makes a big difference in

7. A discussion of the responses from this list were later published in Richard L. Bushman, "What Are We to Make of the Gold Plates." *BYU Studies* 64, no. 1 (2025): 97-113.

one's outlook on the world. With the plates comes an angel and divine intervention in ordinary human lives. The plates imply a world where God is an active agent in human affairs in opposition to the skepticism that has eroded religion for the past two hundred years."[8]

That is the world I was brought up in and the one in which I still live.

Questions and Answers

Scott Gordon

Thank you so much for your remarks, Richard. I think they were enlightening. Certainly things I hadn't thought about the Gold Plates, how much people talk about them or don't talk about them. I know I did talk to a paint manufacturer once to ask if they even had gold paint back then, because I had a critic say that it was obviously just gold paint on the plates. And the paint manufacturer said, no, there was no such thing as gold metallic paint back in the 1830s. We did have some questions that people have sent to me to ask you. And the one question was not about the plates, per se, but about the translation process, of which I know we know very little. But there was confusion with the Nephite interpreters being called the Urim and Thummim, and then the seer stones. So in your opinion, were the seer stones also referred to as the Urim and Thummim, or do we know, or what do you think?

Richard Bushman

There's a lot of disagreement, and the reason there is, is because the sources are not watertight on what's going on there. My own version of that is that they were initially called spectacles. That's what Joseph Smith calls them in 1832. But in 1834, a very severe blow is dealt to the Church by E.D. Howe and *Mormonism Unvailed*, where all of Joseph Smith's and his family's money-digging ventures are brought against them. These are depicted not just as silly, they are mistrusted because they are money diggers. From then on, there is a wish to, not absolutely deny, but to cover up or push to the background, those money-digging ventures, which at the time, they didn't think were such a big deal. Everyone was doing it, so it wasn't hard at all, but it became a source of shame after 1834 or so. From then on, the word seer stones – or the spectacles – is replaced by Urim and Thummim. The same urge that was generated later when they

8. Bushman, *Joseph Smith's Gold Plates,* ix.

were trying to find the place of the plates. It gives them a biblical base, even though the Urim and Thummim in the Bible is not much like the Urim and Thummim that Joseph had, but it gave them a big base.

So, what I did was to compare revelations in the Book of Commandments, which were all given before 1832 or so, with revelations in the Doctrine and Covenants, which were 1835, after *Mormonism Unvailed* was published. And what happened is the word Urim and Thummim was put into the revelations themselves. The word was added, and it also was put into the headings. So, the seer stone becomes the old treasure-seeking Smith family and is sort of suppressed. And the Urim and Thummim becomes the biblical Joseph Smith family, and that takes over.

Scott Gordon

Another question we got. Joseph Smith, as he talks about the plates, talks about the Large Plates of Nephi and the Small Plates of Nephi. In your opinion, were these all the same gold plates? All these different plates were in the one set of plates? Or were there more than one set of plates that Joseph Smith actually dealt with?

Richard Bushman

I don't think that's easy to figure out. I'm kind of impressed by the argument that there was another set of plates given to Joseph Smith when he went to Fayette.[9] He just had the Large Plates when he was translating it first, and then the other plates were given to him later. But again, I don't see enough evidence to really nail that down.

Scott Gordon

So finally, my last question then is, you've been studying Joseph Smith for a long time. I would say you probably know more about Joseph Smith than just about anybody else on the planet. You've seen the good, you've seen the bad, you've seen the ugly that has been brought out. As you spent time studying Joseph Smith, have you found that your testimony of the gospel has been strengthened or weakened?

Richard Bushman

It's remained pretty steady. I don't really have troubles believing in the gospel. It all seems right, and true, and good to me. There have been times when I got a little impatient with Joseph Smith. As I say in *Rough*

9. For more on this argument, see Bushman, *Joseph Smith's Gold Plates*, 172-173.

Stone Rolling, he did have a temper, and I don't like people who blow up at others, which he did from time to time. But he was a massive personality whose emotions were on the surface, and the emotion of anger was there, but also of love. He would just charm people. He was just filled with such energy, emotional energy, and love was part of it. As a person, I might have trouble always being around him, but I certainly admire him. I immensely admire his resilience. As for being a revelator, I think he's unmatched in world history - anyone we know of. All the things he revealed, new initiatives of all kinds. He was a religion-maker, as has been said. I'm thrilled by those revelations. I think the Book of Mormon is a constant source of new insight and larger understanding. I've had no troubles remaining in the Church. I love the Church. I love Joseph Smith. I love his revelations. I think they tell us more about God than about anything that we have available to us.

2

The Book of Mormon and Archaeology

Challenges, Questions and Perspectives

Matthew Roper

Questions relating to archaeology and the Book of Mormon can sometimes pose challenges to readers. On the one hand critics sometimes frame the evidence as one that is almost entirely hostile to the belief that the Book may be an authentic historical record. On the other hand, Latter-day Saints may sometimes entertain unrealistic expectations about what archaeological information can or cannot say about the text. In this presentation I will discuss several challenges that archaeologists face in addressing questions about the archaeology of animal and human remains, ancient weapons, metals, chariots, and lost scripts. An understanding of these challenges can help us to correct mistaken assumptions, adjust our expectations, and provide clearer perspectives as we seek for better information as well as answers.

Introduction

Critics of the Book of Mormon often frame the subject of archaeological data as one that is almost entirely hostile to the belief that the volume may be an authentic historical record. On the other hand, some Latter-day Saints perhaps entertain unrealistic expectations about what archaeological information may or may not be able to say about the text. In some of these discussions about archaeological evidence or the lack of such, what is often missing is an appreciation for some of challenges in archaeology as they might be applied to questions about the Book of Mormon. In my presentation today, I will address a few examples of these.

I am not an archaeologist, so in an attempt to understand things better I appreciate and try to follow what archaeologists have said about their endeavor and to seek understanding and wisdom out of "the best books" and the best work available (Doctrine and Covenants 88:118). I would like to share a few perspectives that have helped me as I approach some challenges that relate to this significant book.

In each of the examples given below, I will first reference a challenge to the Book of Mormon offered by critics past or present. Then, I will offer some perspectives based on statements from informed scholars of archaeology and related fields who have addressed similar or relevant questions in their own work. The purpose of this is to illustrate how these kinds of perspectives can inform our inquiries about Book of Mormon questions.

Challenge #1: Animal Remains and Archaeology

From the 1830s up until today, some readers of the Book of Mormon have considered the description of animals known to the Jaredites and the people of Lehi as problematic.[1] One recent critic stated "Horses, cattle, oxen, sheep, swine, elephants ... did not exist in Pre-Columbian America."[2] If the Book of Mormon were true, it is asserted, evidence for the existence of such animals during the time of the Book of Mormon ought to be plentiful today.

Growing evidence, including data from new discoveries, shows that some ancient American species, including some mentioned in the Book of Mormon, may have survived into more recent times. This is encouraging, although we still have ways to go in terms of what the Book of Mormon presents. Meanwhile, as we look forward to new discoveries, several points should be kept in mind.

Perspective: The Material History Past Animal Life

First, there is a huge gap between what animals once existed in any given location and what the archaeologist or paleontologist can identify and study. This is not a revolutionary insight, but still an important one that can ground our expectations of evidence.

---

1. See for example H. Stevenson, *A Lecture on Mormonism* (Newcastle: J. Blackwell and Co., 1839), 9-11.
2. Jeremy Runnells, *CES Letter* (2017), 11.

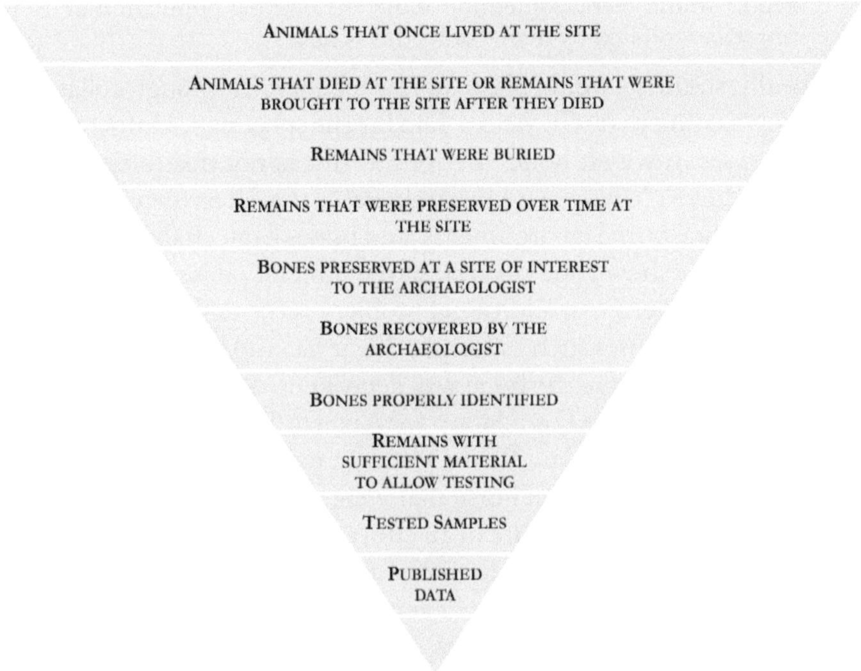

Animals that once lived at the site

Animals that died at the site or remains that were brought to the site after they died

Remains that were buried

Remains that were preserved over time at the site

Bones preserved at a site of interest to the archaeologist

Bones recovered by the archaeologist

Bones properly identified

Remains with sufficient material to allow testing

Tested Samples

Published data

Most information that could inform our understanding about past animal life is lost over time, with many of these factors entirely out of the control of the scientists involved. Elizabeth Reitz and Elizabeth Wing note, "The remains of all animals used by people living at the site will not be recovered from the site, because either their remains were discarded beyond the excavated portion of the site, or their remains did not survive deposition."[3] Other factors are influenced by the researchers, and careful scholars will do their best to take such factors into account when that is possible. Simon Davis, a specialist in Zooarchaeology observes:

> A long chain of events occurs between the original collection and slaughter of animals in antiquity, their incorporation within an archaeological site, their ending up on the faunal analyst's workbench, and their final publication. One sometimes wonders whether there is any similarity between a published bone report and the animals exploited by ancient humans. In an ideal situation the data and conclusions contained in the final faunal

3. Elizabeth J. Reitz and Elizabeth S. Wing, *Zooarchaeology*, 2nd ed. (Cambridge: Cambridge University Press, 2008), 118.

> report would reveal something about the original population of animals exploited by man. Sadly, this is rare.[4]

Ideally, scientists would like to obtain a bone with enough collagen in it to allow testing that will yield a date for the specimen. Unfortunately, in most cases in which bones are found, this is not possible. As Terry O'Conner states, "collogen is most vulnerable in well oxygenated, moist, slightly alkaline burial environments, and bones from chalk or limestone soils commonly show good survival of the mineral phase, but poor preservation of collagen." An additional problem is the destruction of collagen from biotic causes such as fungus, bacteria, and microorganisms in the environment where the bone was deposited.[5] Years ago, in a project partially funded by the Foundation for Ancient Research and Mormon Studies, my friend, the late Wade Miller, a paleontologist, was able to track down 49 specimens of horse that were known to archaeologists or reported in published literature in an effort to get them tested for dating. Carbon dates were obtained for 18 of these, while the remaining 31 samples did not have sufficient collagen. When collagen is not available, the researcher tries to obtain dates from charcoal or organic material found in close association with the bone specimen, if the layers are well established and were undisturbed prior to the recovery of the specimen.

Perspective: Carbon Dates vs. Final Extinction Dates

Scientific literature can provide carbon dates which help scholars to develop rough chronologies of life and extinction for different animal species. These are important. When combined with other data, carbon dates help to clarify the vast history of animal life, but they do not tell us when the last animal of any species died. A team of scientists doing work on the DNA of horse and mammoth remains stated in a recent article:

> The youngest reliably dated macro-fossil (usually a bone or tooth) of an extinct species is commonly taken to represent the approximate time of its disappearance. In practice, however, there is a very low probability of discovering fossil remains of the last members of any species, so ages for extinction based on dated macrofossil finds will likely be older than the true ages (raising the possibility of 'ghost ranges' of unknown duration)

---

4. Simon J. M. Davis, *The Archaeology of Animals* (New Haven: Yale University Press, 1987), 23.
5. Terry O' Conner, *The Archaeology of Animal Bones* (Sutton, 2000), 23-24.

> ...Estimating extinction times is a common problem in paleontology.[6]

As another scientist notes in a study of the Pleistocene Mammoth in America:

> LADs [last available dates] are just a Last Date, not a Last Appearance. Given the vagaries of preservation and sampling, and the proposition that rare animals disappear from the fossil record before they go extinct (the Signor-Lipps Effect), the last mammoth dated was almost certainly not the last mammoth standing .... Some genera survived well after their last dated appearance as macrofossils.[7]

In other words, a horse or mammoth bone carbon dated to 4,000 BC., while indicating the death of an animal by that time, does not prove that other horses or mammoths survived hundreds or even thousands of years longer.

Challenge #2: Book of Mormon War Dead

Some writers have suggested that if the Book of Mormon account was true, then we should have recovered the remains of the dead from battles described in text. As one critic states "If the Book of Mormon were true, either the hill in New York or the hill in Mexico should be one enormous pile of ...phosphate (from the bones of all the people slain)."[8] Why, wonders another recent critic, have no remains of "bones" or "hair" from such bodies been found?[9]

Perspective: Parley P. Pratt

The challenge of recovering and identifying ancient human remains is one which also confronts archaeologists. Latter-day Saint apostle Parley P. Pratt a was murdered near Van Buren, Arkansas in 1857, and was buried by local residents at the time. The location of Pratt's grave was subsequently located and, in 2008, descendants excavated the grave in the

---

6. James Haile, Duane G. Froese, Ross D. E. MacPhee, et al., "Ancient DNA Reveals Late Survival of Mammoth and Horse in Interior Alaska," *Proceedings of the National Academy of Sciences* 106/52 (2009): 352.
7. David Meltzer, "Pleistocene Overkill and North American Mammalian Extinctions," *American Review of Anthropology* 44 (2015): 46.
8. Frank Zindler, "How Do You Lose a Steel Mill?" last accessed May 23, 2025, http://nowscape.com/mormon/zindler1.htm.
9. Runnells, *CES Letter* (2017), 12.

hope of retrieving his remains and bringing them to Utah for reburial. "Following strict archaeological protocols, the grave site was excavated. The condition and nature of the grave itself confirmed that previous scientific investigations had correctly identified the location of and existence of the grave." The team of excavators and the Pratt family were disappointed, however, when "no specific identifiable human remains were found that had survived the passage of time."[10]

As one member of the team explained, "We were digging in his grave, but Parley's remains are now part of the soil of Arkansas."[11] "The passage of time and the shallowness of the grave have left no specific identifiable human remains."[12] So, Pratt was murdered and buried in 1857, and after 150 years there was nothing left of his body which could be identified. What can reasonably be expected from the dead of Book of Mormon battles that took place over 1,600 or 2,600 years ago?

Perspective: War Dead and Archaeology

While the dead from ancient conflicts are sometimes found, instances of this tend to be rare, and the results frequently fail to satisfy expectations of identification. According to Slavomil Vencl, "archaeological sources fail to provide evidence of the large number of men lost in battle, and of other war casualties that could not be buried."[13] Mesoamerican archaeologist David Webster note "Skeletal remains [even when they are found] are often in poor condition because of the humid tropical climate."[14] According to the late Michael Coe, who worked at the massive Olmec site of San Lorenzo (1200-900 BC.), a site that was once occupied by tens of thousands, "We never did find an Olmec [human] burial at San Lorenzo. Given the terrible conditions of bone preservation in the acid soils of the Olmec heartland, it is likely that surviving skeletons would have been few or far between."[15]

---

10. "Update Concerning Parley P. Pratt," *Church News*, 26 April, 2002.
11. "No Remains Found in Dig for Parley P. Pratt," *Daily Herald*, Provo, Utah, 23 April 2008.
12. "Archaeologists Unable to Found Pratt's Remains," *Deseret News*, 23 April 2008.
13. Slavomil Vencl, "War and Warfare in Archaeology," *Journal of Anthropological Archaeology* 3 (1984): 57-58.
14. David Webster, "Ancient Maya Warfare," in Raaflaub and Rosenstein, *War and Society in the Ancient and Medieval Worlds*, 1999, 356, note 26.
15. Michael D. Coe and Richard A. Diehl, *In the Land of the Olmec: Volume 1, The Archaeology of San Lorenzo Tenochtitlan* (Austin: University of Texas Press,

In a study of medieval warfare published in 2016, one team of researchers stated:

> Modern archaeologists have so far drawn a blank in finding human remains at virtually all English and French battlefields of the fourteenth and fifteenth centuries … Despite recent archaeological investigation, none have been found at Bosworth (1485), the battle on which we have worked recently, at Shrewsbury (1403), where work was carried out by Pollard or, despite an intensive search, in recent investigation at Bannockburn.[16]

Very often the remains of the dead were not even buried. "Texts from all times since antiquity abound in reports of dead bodies left lying without burial."[17] "The Vanquished might have been left out in the open, their remains being scattered by animals, their organic clothing and equipment swiftly lost."[18]

Following the tremendous battle at Cumorah, the Lamanites did not bother to bury the Nephite dead. Mormon described the remains of the slain Nephites at Cumorah who had been "hewn down" (Mormon 6:11) by their enemies "their flesh, and bones, and blood lay upon the face of the earth being left by the hands of those who slew them to molder upon the land, and crumble and return to their mother earth" (Mormon 6:15).

An additional challenge involves the identification of battlefields and where their dead were interred, if they were buried at all. It would be useful to do an analysis of the Book of Mormon text in order to gather as much potential information as possible for each battle within its pages, and where they may have taken place. I do not know that anyone has done so yet.

Many of the battles described in the Book of Mormon did not take place within cities but were fought outside settlements or within the wilderness. If one wanted to find the remains of those killed in the battle between the Lamanites and the Nephite forces of Antipas and Helaman

---

1980), 392.

16. Anne Curry and Glenn Foard, "Where are the dead of Medieval battles? A Preliminary Survey" *Journal of Conflict Archaeology* 11/2-3 (2016): 62-63.
17. Vencl, "War and Warfare in Archaeology," 127.
18. Jon Coulston, "The Archaeology of Roman Conflict," in P. W. M. Freeman and A. Pollard, eds., *Fields of Conflict: Progress and Prospect in Battlefield Archaeology: Proceedings of a conference held in the Department of Archaeology University of Glasgow, April 2000* (Oxford: Archaeopress, 2001), 26.

(Alma 56:49-57), where should one look? Alma the Younger mentions a significant and unprecedented battle between the Nephites and the Lamanites after the settlement of the people of Ammon in Jershon. The war dead numbered in the tens of thousands and such a battle up to that point in Nephite history "never had been known among all the people in the land from the time Lehi left Jerusalem" (Alma 28:2), but while we know that this battle was fought somewhere in the borders of the land of Zarahemla, we are not told where the deadly encounter occurred or where the dead were buried (Alma 28:1-6, 11-12). If one wanted to find and identify the dead from the battle at Cumorah (Mormon 6:7-15), should one look in New York, or some other location in the Americas such as Mesoamerica? Until one can determine where such battles took place, the search for remains from such battles would be fruitless.

Challenge #3: Book of Mormon Swords and Other Weapons

Another set of challenges have to do with the weaponry mentioned in the Book of Mormon. Some have argued that if the Book of Mormon were in fact what it purports to be, then archaeological evidence of Jaredite and Lehite weaponry ought to be plentiful. As one prominent critic asked, "Where are the Nephite or Lamanite ... swords?"[19]

Critics frequently assume that because some weapons mentioned in the text were metallic, that all or most other weapons must have been as well. This assumption often leads to exaggerated and unjustified characterizations of the text. According to Gordon Fraser, "The Book of Mormon has the Americans in possession of all the metallic paraphernalia of war making. Scimitars, swords, metal shields."[20] Does the Book of Mormon say that scimitars and shields were made of metal? He says, "Swords of steel are mentioned *constantly*."[21]

No, they are not.

He assumes that all swords must have been made of steel, but steel is rarely mentioned in the text either. According to Frank Zindler, "If the Book of Mormon were true, either the hill in New York or the hill in Mexico should be one enormous pile of rusted iron (from the swords

---

19. Jeremy Runnells, *CES Letter*, 12.
20. Gordon H. Fraser, *Is Mormonism Christian?* (Chicago: Moody Press, 1977), 142
21. Gordon H. Fraser, *Joseph Smith and the Golden Plates: A Close Look at the Book of Mormon* (Eugene, OR: Industrial Litho, 1964; rev. ed. 1978), 58, emphasis added.

and other steel objects)" and "If millions and millions of people made and used weapons and tools of steel for a period spanning three millennia, not only should archaeologists find plentiful remains of swords … they should be finding the remains of steel mills all over."[22]

If that were the case, perhaps or perhaps not. There is no reason to read the text in such a way, and no reader needs to be bound to such an interpretation.

Perspective: Metal Weaponry in the Bible

The biblical account says that the Philistine Goliath had a helmet, greaves, and a target of brass (1 Samuel 17:5-6). The word brass should more accurately be translated as "bronze." T. R. Hobbs notes that at this time in the ancient Near East "there is little evidence that helmets of metal were widely used."[23] He additionally states that "the fact that on occasion the Biblical writer deems it necessary to add the word 'bronze' to the use of the term 'helmet', would suggest that the headgear was not normally made of metal."[24]

Perspective: Metal Weaponry and the Book of Mormon Text

The Book of Mormon contains only three references to steel objects being produced in the land of promise.

The early Jaredite prince Shule "came to the hill Ephraim, and he did molten out of the hill, and made swords out of steel for those whom he had drawn away with him; and after he had armed them with swords he returned to the city Nehor, and gave battle unto his brother Corihor, by which means he obtained the kingdom" (Ether 7:8-9). Shule's achievement was considered noteworthy, but the text does not say that he taught this skill to the people. It is interesting, however, that the next generation of Jared's people were nearly wiped out (Ether 9:12). In periods of social anarchy, rare and valuable possessions and even valuable skills would tend to be stolen and lost or destroyed (Ether 14:1; see also Helaman 13:34). That could be an indication that steel technology among the Jaredites was not widespread or that the skill was subsequently lost. It is also worth noting that several generations after the death of Shule,

---

22. Frank Zindler, "How Do You Lose a Steel Mill."
23. T.R. Hobbs, *A Time For War: A Study of Warfare in the Old Testament* (Wilmington, DE.: Michael Glazier, 1989), 128.
24. Hobbs, *A Time For War: A Study of Warfare in the Old Testament*, 130.

when Moroni mentions Jaredite metallurgical skills, he mentions gold, silver, copper, brass, and iron, but significantly, *not steel* (Ether 10:23). That suggests that Shule's notable skill may not have been passed on to later generations.

There is another passage that may indirectly refer to potential Jaredite steel swords, although steel is not actually mentioned specifically. King Limhi's search party found ruins of buildings and bones of the Jaredites, which they mistakenly believed were the ruins of Zarahemla.

> And *for a testimony that the things they had said are true* they have brought twenty-four plates which are filled with engravings, and they are of pure gold. And behold, also, they have brought *breastplates*, which are large, and they are of *brass and of copper*, and are perfectly sound. And again, they have brought swords, the hilts thereof have perished, and the *blades* thereof were *cankered with rust* (Mosiah 8:10-11, emphasis mine).

In addition to the plates recovered by the search party, they found breastplates of copper and brass, and rusted blades from what had once been Jaredite swords. We do not know if those blades were of rusted steel or some other metal, such as bronze, which can also corrode.[25] As I noted, the absence of references to steel after the time of Shule suggests to me that these swords had been rare items of the Jaredite elite. In any case, these things were brought back to King Limhi and his people "for a testimony that the things that they had said are true" (Mosiah 8:9). The need to bring back these rusted blades and breastplates suggests to me that for the Nephites swords with metal blades or breastplates of copper and brass were unusual or rare.

Nephi obtained a sword of "most precious steel" from Laban in Jerusalem, which he brought with him to the land of promise. After his separation from the Lamanites, Nephi states that he "did take the sword of Laban and *after the manner of* it did make swords, lest by any means the people who were now called Lamanites should come upon us to destroy us" (2 Nephi 5:15). What did Nephi mean, when he said that he made swords "*after the manner* of the sword of Laban"? Since Laban had a steel sword, this could mean that Nephi made steel swords like Laban's. Although it is not explicitly stated in the text, that is how it is often read. An alternative reading that is that Nephi made some swords

25. The word "steel" once had a broader range of meaning which included both carburized iron as well as some copper alloys.

after the general pattern of Laban's sword, that is, perhaps a long straight shaft with sharp blades along the edges, rather than a curved sickle sword or one that was bladed only on one side.[26]

In any case, if Nephi did make some steel swords – which the text does not require – how many did he produce? At this early time, Nephi's people could not have been numerous. And after Nephi's death, how many people possessed his steel technology? Did all Nephites know how to work steel or just some? If we take other ancient cultures as a comparative example, relevant metallurgical knowledge was restricted to a few individuals or artisans and could have been lost in just ***one*** Lamanite raid.[27]

The last reference to steel among the Nephites (and not steel swords) is during the time of Jacob's grandson Jarom (Jarom 1:8, emphasis mine). "And we multiplied exceedingly, and spread upon the face of the land, and became exceedingly rich in gold, and in silver, and in precious things, and in fine workmanship of wood, in buildings, and in machinery, and *also in iron and copper, and brass and steel*, making all manner of tools of every kind to till the ground, and weapons of war—yea, the sharp pointed arrow, and the quiver, and the dart, and the javelin, and all preparations for war."

Steel is never mentioned again in the Book of Mormon. It was apparently an exceptional thing for Nephi or King Benjamin to wield the sword of Laban in the defense of their people (Jacob 1:10; Words of Mormon 1:14).[28] That again, suggests to me that steel swords, even if

26. Writing years later, Nephi described Laban's blade as made of "most precious steel" (1 Nephi 4:9), suggesting that there was more than one kind and that some with which he was familiar was considered less "precious." There are early Nephite references to "steel." Nephi broke his bow of "fine steel," and Laban steel blade was of "most precious steel." Do these terms reflect different grades of technological skill? It's possible that Nephi and some early Nephites were able to make other steel swords, but it is also possible that while they were able to work carburized iron (steel) for ornamentation purposes, they were unable to master other steeling techniques, such as tempering, needed to make long effective steel blades.
27. Note Omni 1:5-7.
28. Vencl states, "Specialized weapons often represented objects of such social significance that they are only rarely found in original archaeological context (only disposable weapons were buried in graves; specialized weapons were left only exceptionally in settlements or on battlefields." Slavomil Vencl, "War and Warfare in Archaeology," 126. The sword of Laban made of "most precious

Nephi made a few, were the exception rather than the norm and that among the people of the Book of Mormon metal sword blades were rare elite items, the exception rather than the norm. When the Zeniffites return to the land of Nephi a few generations later, they know about iron and other metals, but *not steel*. This incidentally is also the last reference to Nephite "iron" (Mosiah 11:3, 8). So, references to some metals drop out of the text over time, which could point to a loss of certain technologies that were known earlier.

Perspective: Aztec Swords and Archaeology

How does one find an ancient Pre-Columbian sword? In his important work on Aztec warfare, Ross Hassig observed, "There are no known surviving examples of the macuahuitl."[29] The late Mesoamericanist Michael Coe also noted "No known examples [of Aztec Swords] survive."[30] More recently another specialist in Aztec warfare stated that today, "macuahuitl are practically non-existent."[31] In fact, he noted significantly, "If it were just from Mexica archaeological evidence alone, we might think that this weapon [the *macuahuitl*] was hardly used by this people. Very few archaeological objects have been recovered."[32] Spanish accounts of the war with the Aztecs states that large caches of Aztec weapons, including swords were deliberately gathered up and burned by the conquistadors.[33]

Based upon the activities of the Aztec empire and the size of their armies mentioned in historical texts, it would not be unreasonable to suggests that at the time of the Spanish entrada there, the number of

---

steel" certainly would qualify as a specialized weapon. It was of course, carefully preserved and protected by the Nephite record keepers.

29. Ross Hassig, *Aztec Warfare*, 1988, 85.
30. Michael D. Coe, "Pre-Conquest America," in Michael Coe, Peter Connolly, Anthony Harding, Victor Harris, Donald Larocca, Thomas Richardson, Anthony North, Christipher Spring and Federick Wilkinson, *Swords and Hilt Weapons* (New York: Weidenfeld & Nicolson, 1989), 221.
31. Marco Antonio Cervera Obregon, *Guerreros Aztecas* (Madrid: Nowtilus, 2011), 40.
32. Marco Antonio Cervera Obregon "The Macuahuitl: An Innovative Weapon of the Late Post-classic in Mesoamerica," *Arms and Armour* 3/2 (2006): 137.
33. "The marques ordered all the arms taken out of the arsenal we have mentioned, which were bows and arrows, spears and slings, and wooden swords with flint blades. There were about five-hundred cartloads, and he had them burned." Andres de Tapia, in *The Conquistadors: First Person Accounts of the Conquest of Mexico*, ed. Patricia Fuentes (Norman: University of Oklahoma Press, 1993, 42.

Aztec swords likely numbered in the tens of thousands, yet five hundred years later, according to specialists on Mesoamerican warfare, no archaeological examples of this important weapon survive or have as yet been identified.[34]

Perspective: Ancient Steel in the Mediterranean World

Leonore O. Keene Congdon observes that despite its widespread existence in earlier times, archaeological discoveries of steel are uncommon in the ancient Mediterranean, although rare examples have sometimes been found. "One should recognize that very few items of ancient steel or semi-steel are known, though doubtless many are in archaeological dumps, rusted beyond visual and chemical recognition."[35] If this is so in the Old World anciently, how much more unreasonable it is to insist that steel should be abundant, given its apparent rarity, as indicated by the Book of Mormon text.

Challenge #4: Chariots

Some readers are challenged by references to chariots in the Book of Mormon.[36] No evidence for "horse drawn war chariots" has been found by archaeologists.[37]

Perspective: Chariots and Bible Archaeology

War Chariots are mentioned in the Bible and frequently so during the reign of the kings of Israel and Judah (1 Kings 18:44; 1 Kings 22:31-35, 38; 2 Kings 9:16; 2 Kings 10:15; 2 Kings 13:7). In spite of the frequency of such references, there is little archaeological evidence of chariots in the land of Israel during this time. Mary Littauer and J.H. Crouwel state,

> Unfortunately, despite all the references to chariots in the OT, there are not even fragmentary remains from Palestine. And the

---

34. An example of this Aztec weapon has only recently been discovered. Marco Antonio Cervera Obregon, "Mexica War: New Research Perspectives," in *Oxford Handbook of the Aztecs*, ed. Deborah L. Nichols and Enrique Rodriguez-Alegria (Austin: University of Texas at Austin, 2017), 459.
35. Leonore O. Keene Congdon, "Steel in Antiquity: A Problem of Terminology," in *Studies Presented to George M. A. Hanfmann*, ed. David G. Mitten, et al. (Mainz: Von Zabern, 1971), 26-27.
36. "Chariots … Why are these things mentioned?" Runnells, *CES Letter*, 11.
37. John A. Price, "The Book of Mormon vs. Anthropological Prehistory," *The Indian Historian* 7, no. 3 (Summer 1974): 38.

> only representation of a Palestinian chariot is on an Assyrian relief of the conquest of Lachish by Sennacherib.[38]

So, although the texts mention chariots in biblical times over a period of several hundred years, no archaeological evidence of chariots has (as of 1992) been found in Palestine and the only archaeological evidence of chariots in Palestine is found, *not in Israel*, but in Assyria, at Nineveh. In the Book of Mormon, the only references to chariots are found during the period of about a century during the Reign of the Judges.

Perspective: What Kinds of "Chariots"?

Sometimes we may read too many assumptions into the text of the Book of Mormon. For example, there is no reason to conclude that these were war chariots used for battle. At least, the text never says so. They are mentioned at one point in the land of Nephi, where two Lamanite kings have chariots in connection with a great feast (Alma 18:9-10; Alma 20:6-12). The other reference appears in a description of the Nephites gathering provisions for an extended siege by their enemies (3 Nephi 3:22). When actual battles take place, chariots are never mentioned. So, what *kind* of chariots is the Book of Mormon referring to? Several different possibilities have been suggested, including the possibility that they may have been a kind of palanquin. My own view is that these need not have been anything more elaborate than a remedial cart used for local purposes. There is no reason to see these as war chariots or, given the infrequency of references, that they had any lasting impact on Pre-Columbian civilization.

Now, there is evidence, first discovered decades after the Book of Mormon was published, that at least a remedial knowledge of the wheel was known in certain places at certain times in ancient Mesoamerica, as shown by the recovery of small wheeled figurines. The earliest discovered ones date to the Classic period at Teotihuacan, Veracruz, and El Salvador. Scholars are not sure what to make of these things. Some see them as evidence of transoceanic influences from the Old World, where similar little carts are known. Whatever they were, most have assumed that this knowledge of the wheel had no significant or lasting impact on Mesoamerican civilization.

---

38 Mary Aiken Littauer and J.H. Crouwel, "Chariots." David Noel Freedman, ed., *Anchor Bible Dictionary* (New York: Doubleday, 1992), 891.

Example from Veracruz of an animal on a wheeled platform, likely from ca. 600-800 A.D.

Perspective: Anomalous Cultural Features

During a battle when the Spanish under Alvarado fought against the Maya in highland Guatemala, the Spanish reported that the Quiche warriors had what could be described as ammunition carts on rollers which could be moved from place to place as needed during the battle.[39] Now as far as I know, no archaeologist has ever recovered one of these. Should we conclude from that that the Spanish reports were fabricated? Rather, I think, we have an example of a cultural item of local use and significance that had no lasting impact on the subsequent development of Mayan civilization as far as we can tell.

Wheeled figurines found from Pre-Columbian times suggests a knowledge of and perhaps even a limited use of wheeled carts – such as the Book of Mormon text could suggest – may have at one time been known, but not have been widespread. They could easily be lost, forgotten, or undetected in the archaeological record.

Challenge #5: Reformed Egyptian

The lack of archaeological evidence for reformed Egyptian script in ancient America has been a common challenge from critics since the Book of Mormon was published. Writing in 1886, M. T. Lamb asserted, "We should ... certainly expect to find, in every portion of both continents ... in thousands of places, these reformed Egyptian characters

39. Carmelo Saenz de Santa Maria, *Obras Historical de Don Francisco Antonio de Fuentes y Guzman*. 3 vols. (Madrid: 1972), 2:292.

engraved upon marble blocks and granite pillars, brass plates by the thousand ... Just the contrary of all this is found to be true."[40] Many others have taken Lamb's position, but is that a realistic expectation?

Perspective: Destruction of Records in Pre-Columbian Times

The Book of Mormon indicates that there was a deliberate attempt on the part of the Nephites' enemies to destroy Nephites records and traditions (Enos 1:14; Alma 14:8; Mormon 6:6). Michael Coe, speaking of the destruction at the end of the Classic Maya period, provides perspective on a centuries-later event similar to what may have happened during Book of Mormon times.

> It was not just the 'stela cult'–the inscribed glorification of royal lineages and their achievements - that disappeared with the collapse, but an entire world of esoteric knowledge, mythology, and ritual. Much of the elite cultural behavior ... such as the complex Underworld mythology and iconography found on Classic Maya funerary ceramics, failed to re-emerge with the advent of the Post-Classic era, and one can only conclude that the royalty and nobility, including the scribes who were the repository of so much sacred knowledge, had 'gone with the wind.' They may well have been massacred by an enraged populace, and their screen-fold books consumed in a holocaust similar to that carried out centuries later by Bishop Landa.[41]

Diego de Landa was not the first to oversee the destruction of records. A century or so earlier, Aztec rulers, having risen above their humble origins, oversaw the destruction of many records of rival groups as well as many of their own records, which conflicted with the image of power they worked to project.[42]

Perspective: Lost Pre-Columbian Scripts

While admittedly, no examples of Egyptian script of any kind have been identified by New World archaeologists, is it possible that a Pre-Columbian script that was once known and used could disappear?

---

40. M. T. Lamb. *The Golden Bible; or, The Book of Mormon: Is It From God?* (New York: Ward and Drummond, 1886), 268–269.
41. Michael D. Coe, *The Maya*, Fifth edition (London: Thames and Hudson, 1993), 128.
42. Joyce Marcus, *Mesoamerican Writing Systems: Propaganda, Myth, and History in Four Ancient Civilizations* (Princeton, NJ: Princeton University Press, 1992), 146-51.

In recent decades, several previously unknown Mesoamerican scripts have been identified by epigraphers. The late Mayanist Linda Schele thought it certainly possible that there may have been other writing systems in Mexico and Guatemala that have never been discovered, stating, "There may in fact have been many such writing systems that for one reason or another, did not survive."[43]

One rediscovered Pre-Classic script from southern Mexico, possibly related to the Olmec, has been of interest to scholars. One report states: "The inscription–which can't yet be read and seems unrelated to later Mesoamerican scripts–is unlikely to resolve the heated debate over whether the Olmec were the dominant culture of their time or one of many societies that shaped Mesoamerica." While "the script's influence on later systems is unclear …. the authors conclude that 'the clear linkage of the script to the widely diffused signs of Olmec iconography,' argues in favor of a widespread system that died out before others appeared in succeeding centuries–perhaps as happened to one of the world's first writing systems, the Indus script, which vanished shortly after 2000 B.C.E."[44]

In another report:

> An Olmec serpentine block, incised with a previously unknown script, the earliest known thus far in Mesoamerica and, by extension, the Western Hemisphere. The Cascajal block and the script on it link the Olmec to literacy, document an unsuspected writing system, and reveal a new complexity to this civilization, including the possibility of information tools not hitherto known in this early period …. The discovery of a rich inventory of wooden sculptures, at El Manati, of slightly earlier date, suggests that a dearth of texts today may be misleading. A tradition of co-eval wood-working suggests an ancient reality of abundant wooden inscriptions, of which few would survive in tropical conditions. The small number of texts in Isthmian writing, found also in Veracruz as well as into Chiapas, Mexico, proves that a robust, widely spread script could exist without leaving many examples that last to the present.[45]

---

43. "Stone Slab in Mexico reveals Ancient Writing System," *New York Times*, March 8, 1988.
44. Andrew Lawler, "Claim of Oldest New World Writing Excites Archaeologists," *Science* 313/5793 (15 September, 2006): 1551.
45. Ma. Del Carmen Rodriquez Martinez, Ponciono Ortiz Ceballos, Michael D. Coe, Richard A. Diehl, Stephen D. Housten, Karl A. Taube, Alfred Delgado Calderon, "Oldest Writing in the New World," *Science* 313/5600 (15 September,

Thus, while it is true that no examples of Egyptian or a reformed Egyptian script have been discovered by archaeologists in Mesoamerica or the Western Hemisphere, it is not difficult to understand how a script, once important to a small group of Pre-Columbian elite, such as the record keepers of the Book of Mormon, could disappear.

Conclusion

Questions about archaeology and the Book of Mormon require the same kinds of tools, information, and considerations that archaeologists require for other aspects of their work. While these may help to inform our understanding of the Book of Mormon to some degree, we also need to better understand some of the limitations of archaeology. This helps us to develop patience as we seek answers to questions about the Nephite record, some of which may require time and careful persistent study.

2006): 1611, 1613.

3

The Cross of Christ and Golden Plates

Using an Established Historical Method to Authenticate Ancient Artifacts

Joshua Gehly

The cross of Calvary is accepted as a real artifact based on early source manuscripts, not archaeological proof. This same approach yields compelling results for another undiscovered relic: the golden plates. Cross-examining source evidence for the plates under the same historical method—a minimal facts approach to infer the best explanation—shows that Joseph Smith, Jr. did obtain and possess an ancient record. A historian might not conclude the plates were translated by the gift and power of God, just as a real cross doesn't guarantee a resurrection, but the method points to a core truth. The golden plates are a genuine artifact, as real as the cross of Calvary, illuminating a new pathway for investigating the historicity of the restoration using established resurrection research techniques.

Jesus Christ was a real person who lived in the 1st century CE, that died by crucifixion under the hands of the Romans. That crucifixion rises to the level of historical fact, with secular experts delivering a decisive voice on the topic. Historian John Dominic Crossan reports, "That he was crucified is as sure as anything historical can ever be…".[1] New Testament critic Bart Ehrman concludes, "One of the most certain facts of history is that Jesus was crucified on orders of the Roman prefect of Judea, Pontius Pilate."[2] Atheist scholar Gerd Lüdemann slams the

1. John Dominic Crossan, *Jesus: A Revolutionary Biography* (New York: Harper Collins, 2009), 187.
2. Bart Ehrman, *The New Testament: An Historical Introduction to the Early Christian Writings* (New York: Oxford University Press, 2011), 261-262.

door shut proclaiming, "Jesus' death as a consequence of crucifixion is indisputable."[3] "Sure", "certain", "indisputable"—concrete words from unsympathetic authorities. These specialists all substantiate the physical reality of an ancient artifact without its actual discovery.

The crucifixion of Jesus Christ requires a wooden cross for the execution, but a problem confronts serious inquiry into the matter: there is no archaeological evidence for the cross of Jesus Christ or any other cross from the time period.[4] Despite Romans adopting crucifixion as means of capital punishment in the 1st century BCE—and thereafter executing tens of thousands across the empire and in the Levant—no trace of any abused body leaving behind marks from such a torture were discovered there prior to 1968. The archaeologist who uncovered the first skeletal remains of any crucifixion in Palestine reflected that when, "...I excavated the bones of this crucified man, I did not know how he had died."[5] Only after the bones were sent for osteological analysis, did a nail penetrating the executed man's heel bone unravel his cause of death. This random person died a few decades before Jesus, on yet another unrecovered cross.

The cross of Jesus Christ is not confirmed by extant blocks of wood or rusted nails, but through source manuscripts which document the event. The crucifixion is recorded in all four Gospels, and several additional, independent documents survive from the ancient world. Roman historian Tacitus wrote of "Christ, who, during the reign of Tiberius, had been executed by the procurator Pontius Pilate."[6] Greek novelist Lucian,

3. Gerd Ludemann, *The Resurrection of Christ: A Historical Inquiry* (Amherst, NY: Prometheus Books, 2004), 50.
4. Legends and lore do exist for the cross and golden plates. Emperor Constantine's mother Helena is attributed in several church traditions as having discovered the cross. These loose attribution accounts date to hundreds of years after the activating event and cannot meet any historical standard for evidence. The legends go as far as having the wood come from a tree linked to the Tree of Knowledge in Genesis and planted by Seth in the mouth of Adam's corpse. Thus, a piece of wood without provenance becomes legendary. The same can be said for modern claims of having the golden plates. Several current publications widely available online claim to have translated from additional portions of the golden plates. One such claim of plates copied characters from a known forgery of the Anthon Transcript. It seems false and fake claims follow many faith traditions, making this serious inquiry all the more necessary.
5. Vassilios Tzaferis, "Crucifixion—The Archaeological Evidence," *Biblical Archaeology Review* 11:1, January/February 1985.
6. Tacitus, *Ann.* 15.44 English translation as quoted in J.P. Meier *A Marginal Jew:*

critical of both Jews and Christians alike, recounted, "The Christians, you know, worship a man to this day—the distinguished personage who introduced their novel rites, and was crucified on that account..."[7] Over 30 independent sources speak on the life and death of Jesus Christ relatively close—for the ancient world—to His death.[8] Rejecting how Jesus died undermines the building blocks of history and leaves all known facts from the distant past in a fog of mystery. A missing cross cannot evaporate it from reality.

The cross represents a critical building block upon which Christianity is constructed. Without Jesus dying on the cross, there is no sacrificial atonement or resurrection to be witnessed (see 1 Nephi 11:33). It is the same with the golden plates. Joseph Smith, Jr. claimed to uncover the ancient record with engravings from a hill in New York. Within a few years, he dictated or translated about 608 pages of an original manuscript later copied for printing.[9] A heavenly voice spoke to multiple witnesses of the golden plates declaring the translation to be correct—sealing the artifact of the golden plates to the words inside the Book of Mormon by divine approval. In the early spring of 1830, books were for sale at the printer's bookshop, and missionaries began preaching a restoration of primitive Christianity from new scripture. If the cross represents a quintessential artifact for the crucifixion, resurrection, and subsequent New Testament church—the golden plates represent the same for the Restoration Movement. Even if the golden plates are never revealed, can they be verified on the same historical grounds—early source documents—as the cross? Five foundational principles help lay the cornerstones of facts into history.[10]

Rethinking the Historical Jesus. Vol 1, *The Roots of the Problem and the Person.* (New York: Doubleday, 1991), 89-90.

7. Lucian, *The Death of Peregrine* 11–13, translated by H.W. Fowler and F.G. Fowler in *The Works of Lucian of Samosata* (Oxford: Clarendon Press, 1949), vol. 4, as quoted by Gary R. Habermas, *The Historical Jesus: Ancient Evidence for the Life of Christ* (Joplin, MO: College Press, 1996, 2008), 69-75.
8. Bart Ehrman, "Gospel Evidence that Jesus Existed," accessed September 12, 2023, https://ehrmanblog.org/gospel-evidence-that-jesus-existed/.
9. Royal Skousen, *The Original Manuscript of the Book of Mormon* (Provo, Utah: Foundation for Ancient Research and Mormon Studies, 2001), 35–36.
10. Gary Habermas and Michael Licona, *The Case for the Resurrection of Jesus* (Grand Rapids, MI: Kregel Publications), 37.

1. **Eyewitness Testimony:** When someone witnesses an event for themselves, they can provide extremely valuable information about what they saw.
2. **Multiple, Independent Sources:** Several eyewitnesses reporting separately from one another helps to build consensus about the event in question.
3. **Unsympathetic Sources:** If an unbelieving or antagonistic source provides affirming information about a person or event, the data is likely accurate.
4. **Embarrassing Admission:** People rarely self-incriminate themselves, unless they are telling the truth.
5. **Early Testimony:** People tend to relay information most accurately the closer they are in time to the activating event.

Historians evaluate their sources based upon the criteria above and strip their data down to the most bare-boned and undisputed truths about what happened. This breaks down controversial topics from various sources into core sets of facts, agreed upon by nearly all the spectrum of scholars focused on the topic. This builds a foundational consensus for topics as religiously charged as the crucifixion of Jesus Christ or the coming forth of the Book of Mormon. A minimal set of facts approach organizes the edges of the puzzle in place from which researchers can piece together their conclusions on what actually happened. Historians then infer their best explanation of those facts. "Inference to the best explanation of the facts attempts to finally solve the jigsaw puzzle of history with the least tampering, jamming or ignoring pieces of evidence. It provides a benchmark upon which historians judge their conclusions. Anybody can write about history, just like anybody can have an opinion. The best explanation outcompetes all rivals."[11]

The best explanation of the facts provides the greatest explanatory scope and power, is the most plausible, is the least ad hoc, and contains the fewest contradictions. In other words, the best explanation of the facts fits most pieces of evidence together well, without making things up or contradicting other pieces of evidence. Philosopher of history Behan McCullagh surmised, "Each plausible hypothesis is judged according to these five criteria, and if one exceeds the others by a considerable

11. Joshua Gehly, *Witnessing Miracles: Historical Evidence for the Resurrection and the Book of Mormon* (Monongahela, PA: The Church of Jesus Christ, 2022), 108.

degree…then it is judged to be credible."[12] This evaluation positions the best explanation at the top through a process to eliminate lesser conclusions which account for less data, fill their own gaps, and ignore key sources.[13]

Regarding the golden plates and the Book of Mormon, a series of undisputed facts must be established from investigation of manuscript evidence. After excavation of core facts from the historical record, a hypothesis must be formed to best explain those facts. Competing views and critiques are welcomed but must conform to the same methodology as a baseline.

Minimal Fact #1: The Book of Mormon Exists

One minimal fact unites all those interested in the origins of the Book of Mormon. It exists.

How? Debatable. From whom? Hotly contested. Its presence is self-evident, and its distribution exceeds any book besides the Bible printed in the Western Hemisphere.[14] The Book of Mormon's existence is relevant as a fundamental fact regarding the reality of the golden plates. In the eyes of Joseph Smith and other eyewitnesses, without the plates there would be no new, controversial scripture available for deliberation.

Minimal Fact #2: Multiple People Sincerely Believed They Saw and/or Held the Golden Plates

Extant documents corroborate the Three and the Eight Witnesses testifying to seeing golden plates, but the manuscript evidence expands beyond these most famous testators. Firsthand letters, interviews, newspaper articles, and testimonies abound. The manuscript evidence from first and secondhand sources dating to the lifetime of the eyewitnesses numbers in the hundreds. They include original signatures and unsympathetic sources. Several sources date extremely close in proximity to the day that eyewitnesses saw the plates for themselves.

---

12. C. Behan McCullagh, *The Logic of History: Putting Postmodernism in Perspective* (New York: Routledge, 2004), 52.
13. C. Behan McCullagh, *Justifying Historical Descriptions* (United Kingdom: Cambridge University Press, 1984), 23-24.
14. Terryl Givens, *The Book of Mormon: A Very Short Introduction* (New York: Oxford University Press, 2009), 4.

The strength of this plethora of extant evidence cannot be overstated. Disciples abandoned Christ at the crucifixion, making eyewitness reports scant. The Gospel of John purportedly includes eyewitness testimony but was not written until decades after the Lord's death. In sharp contrast, the Book of Mormon printings contain official witness statements from the Three and Eight Witnesses. Due to careful preservation by Oliver Cowdery, David Whitmer, and others who revered the printer's manuscript, an early copy of their original testimony survives to this day. It represents a collaborative statement from eyewitnesses to the golden plates. If nearly a dozen people signed a document asserting their eyewitness of the cross or resurrected Jesus and a close copy of their signatures still existed—it would be the most revered manuscript promoted as evidence for the Lord in all of Christendom.

The Three Witnesses—Oliver Cowdery, David Whitmer, and Martin Harris—published that, "...we, …have seen the plates which contain this record...wherefore we know of a surety that the work is true. And we also testify that we have seen the engravings which are upon the plates; and they have been shown unto us by the power of God, and not of man. And we declare with words of soberness, that an angel of God came down from heaven, and he brought and laid before our eyes, that we beheld and saw the plates, and the engravings thereon…we beheld and bear record that these things are true."[15]

Eight Witnesses of the golden plates were presented with the plates by Joseph in a much more physical manner. According to one of the eight, John Whitmer, Joseph presented the plates before two groups of four, not including Joseph himself. They signed the following statement, "Joseph Smith, Jun., the translator of this work, has shown unto us the plates of which hath been spoken, which have the appearance of gold; and as many of the leaves as the said Smith has translated we did handle with our hands; and we also saw the engravings thereon…we have seen and hefted, and know of a surety that the said Smith has got the plates of which we have spoken."[16]

Eyewitness Testimony

Book of Mormon witnesses took pride in sharing something they knew to be true. Out of hundreds of available sources, a few examples

---

15. Book of Mormon, 1830, p. 589, online at josephsmithpapers.org.
16. Book of Mormon, 1830, p. 590, online at josephsmithpapers.org.

give justice to their unwavering testimony and confident declarations. Martin Harris once affirmed the plates while several men tried to get him drunk to reveal the truth. Whether inebriated or sober, Martin revealed:

> Gentlemen, what I have said is true, from the fact that my belief is swallowed up in knowledge; for I want to say to you that as the Lord lives I do know that I stood with the Prophet Joseph Smith in the presence of the angel....[17]

On a different occasion, Martin told a group:

> No, I don't believe anything about it. Knowledge supersedes belief. I know it is true. I saw the angel and saw the plates from which the Book of Mormon was translated and heard the voice of God declare it was translated correctly.[18]

On multiple occasions, David Whitmer rebuked those who questioned his official testimony and firsthand eyewitness. He once rebuffed any deception in the matter stating, "No, sir! I was not...deceived! I saw with these eyes and I heard with these ears! I know whereof I speak!"[19]

John Whitmer, one of the most interviewed of the Eight Witnesses, wrote in his own words:

> Therefore I desire to testify to all that...I have most assuredly seen the plates from whence the book of Mormon is translated, and that I have handled these plates, and know of a surety that Joseph Smith, jr. has translated the book of Mormon by the gift and power of God...[20]

The witnesses testified about seeing, feeling, and handling. They manifested the plainness of having these natural senses utilized when

---

17. Letter of Elder Edward Stevenson to the *Millennial Star* Vol. 48, 367-389. (1886) quoted in William Edwin Berrett, *The Restored Church* (Salt Lake City: Deseret Book Company, 1974), 57–58, in Vogel ed., *Early Mormon Documents*, Volume II, 323-324.
18. Thomas Godfrey, Affidavit, 2 July 1933, LDS Church Archives, Salt Lake City, Utah. Published in Deseret News (church section), 15 July 1933, 3, in Vogel ed., *Early Mormon Documents*, Volume II, 369.
19. Interview with Joseph Smith III et al. (Richmond, Missouri, July 1884), originally published in *The Saints' Herald* (28 January 1936) as quoted in Anderson, *Investigating the Book of Mormon Witnesses*, 53.
20. John Whitmer, "Address to the Patrons of the Latter Day Saints' Messenger and Advocate," *Latter-day Saints Messenger and Advocate* Vol. 2, no. 6, March 1836, in Larry E. Morris, ed., *A Documentary History of the Book of Mormon* (New York, NY: Oxford University Press, 2019), 426.

observing the golden plates for themselves. Oliver Cowdery wrote in one of his last public declarations in 1848, "I beheld with my eyes, and handled with my hands, the gold plates from which it was transcribed."[21] Martin Harris' eyewitness includes three physical senses. He saw, felt, and heard. In an interview with William Waddoups, Martin shared:

> 'I had the privilege of being with the Prophet Joseph Smith, and with these eyes of mine,' pointing to his eyes, 'I saw the angel of the Lord and I saw the plates...and with these ears,' pointing to his ears, 'I heard the voice of the angel, and with these hands,' Holding out his hands, 'I handled the plates containing the record of the Book of Mormon, and I assisted the Prophet in the translation thereof.'[22]

Early Sources

The Book of Mormon was printed and first went on sale in E.B. Grandin's store on March 26, 1830. Joseph Smith claimed to procure the golden plates in 1827, and rapid translation efforts occurred in 1829. Oliver Cowdery directly provides the earliest eyewitness source on record. In November 1829—mere months after seeing the plates for himself and before any printing endeavors—he penned a letter to a doubting Cornelius Blatchly sharing:

> It was a clear, open beautiful day, far from any inhabitants, in a remote field, at the time we saw the record, of which it has been spoken, brought and laid before us, by an angel, arrayed in glorious light...[23]

A critical newspaper in Ohio, the Painesville Telegraph, reported about a missionary visit from Oliver in 1830:

> About two weeks since some persons came along here with the book, one of whom pretends to have seen Angels, and assisted in translating the plates....The name of the person here,

---

21. Reuben Miller, "Last Days of Oliver Cowdery," *Deseret News*, April 13, 1859. Reprinted in *Millennial Star* 21 (1859): 544-546, cited in Dan Vogel ed, *Early Mormon Documents*, Volume II (Salt Lake City: Signature Books, 1998), 495.
22. Martin Harris, interview with William Waddoups, September 1870, "Martin Harris and the Book of Mormon," *Improvement Era* 26 (September 1923): 980; in Vogel ed., *Early Mormon Documents*, Volume II, 335.
23. Oliver Cowdery and Martin Harris, in a letter dated 29 November 1829, quoted in Cornelius C. Blatchly, "THE NEW BIBLE, written on plates of Gold or Brass," *Gospel Luminary* 2/49 (10 Dec. 1829): 194.

> who pretends to have a divine mission, and to have seen and conversed with Angels, is Cowdray [sic].[24]

In a church meeting in 1832, eyewitness Samuel Smith spoke on the "...circumstances of the coming forth of the Book of Mormon, of which he said he was a witness...his brother Joseph had the plates, for the prophet had shown them to him, and he had handled them and seen the engravings theron."[25] The abundant eyewitness testimony is prolific and many examples date within months of the activating events of procurement and translation from the golden plates.

Unsympathetic Sources

Unbelievers and critical newspapers, like the Painesville Telegraph, left a trail of sources about the witnesses to the golden plates. They might not have been convinced of their reality, but their reporting demonstrably supports the beliefs of the witnesses themselves. Consider the very early report from an unsympathetic Baptist minister named David Marks who stayed at Peter Whitmer's household in March 1830. He summarized his conversations with multiple witnesses to the golden plates as follows:

> ...two or three of his [Peter Whitmer, Sr.'s] sons, and others to the number of eight, who said they were witnesses of a certain book just published, called the 'Golden Bible,' or 'Book of Mormon.' They affirmed...certain plates of metal, having the appearance of gold, that were dug out of the ground by one Joseph Smith...and, that the Lord had inspired him to translate and publish the book, -- that none, but twelve chosen witnesses, had been allowed to see these plates....'[26]

During Oliver's 1830 missionary trip which eventually reached the western frontier of modern-day Kansas, he unsuccessfully attempted to convert a Shaker named Richard McNemar. Richard wrote a journal entry about the encounter. He reported Oliver as describing:

> The engraving being unintelligible to learned & unlearned. there is said to have been in the box with the plates two transparent

24. "The Golden Bible," *Painesville Telegraph* (Ohio) (16 Nov. 1830).
25. Daniel Tyler, "Incidents of Experience," *Scraps of Biography, Faith Promoting Series* (Salt Lake City, UT: 1883), 10:23; cited in Anderson, *Investigating the Book of Mormon Witnesses*, 140.
26. David Marks, *The Life of David Marks: To the 26th Year of His Age, Including the Particulars of His Conversion, Call to the Ministry, and Labours in Itinerant Preaching for Nearly Eleven Years* (Limerick, ME: The Morning Star, 1831), 340.

> stones in the form of spectacles thro which the translator looked on the engraving & afterwards put his face into a hat & the interpretation then flowed into his mind. which he uttered to the amanuensis who wrote it down, The said amanuensis by name Oliver Cowdery...gave this account...[27]

Josiah Stowell financed Joseph Smith as a treasure digger. He was never compensated for his investments, and multiple members of his family felt that Joseph had swindled the man. Instead of jumping on the bandwagon of persecution against the Smiths, Josiah testified the following under oath:

> ...witness saw a corner of it; it resembled a stone of a greenish caste; should judge it to have been about one foot square and six inches thick...it was unknown to Smith that witness saw a corner of the bible...the leaves were gold; there were written characters on the leaves.[28]

A local newspaper, the *Richmond Conservator*, published a statement from David Whitmer testifying to the truth of the Book of Mormon on his deathbed. The *Richmond Democrat* further observed:

> ...no man can listen to Mr. Whitmer as he talks of his interview with the Angel of the Lord, without being most forcibly convinced that he has heard an honest man tell what he honestly believes to be true.[29]

Embarrassing Admissions

Like the cross of Christ, the golden plates represent an artifact intimately connected to the establishment of a church. In April 1830, the Church of Christ was organized by Joseph Smith, Jr. alongside a small group of believers including the official witnesses. Regretfully, by July 1844, all witnesses to the Book of Mormon would be dead or disfellowshipped from the church they founded. Those without the last name of Smith were formally excommunicated, besides Hiram Page, who simply left the church. The divorce between Joseph and many of the

27. Richard McNemar, Diary entry for January 29, 1831, 45-46, Library of Congress, Manuscript Division, Shaker Collection, Item 253. Available online at mormonr.org.
28. "Trial Report, 28 August 1832 [State of New York v. JS–C]," p. [2], online at www.josephsmithpapers.org.
29. *Richmond Democrat* 16/6 (2 February 1888), in Eldin Ricks, *The Case of the Book of Mormon Witnesses* (Salt Lake City: Deseret News Press, 1971), 16.

eyewitnesses to the golden plates glares like a stain on the garment of the Book of Mormon and a black eye to its translator, but a minimalist facts approach sifts out truth from the ashes of broken relationships and estrangement.

In isolation from the church they helped found, the witnesses do not shrivel into obscurity or famously expose a fraud. They doubled down on their belief in the truthfulness of what they saw and heard. George A. Smith recalled a meeting with the splintered group in Kirtland in which:

> ...a division arose among the Parrish party about the Book of Mormon; John F. Boynton, Warren Parrish, Luke Johnson and others said it was nonsense. Martin Harris then bore testimony of its truth and said all would be damned if they rejected it.[30]

During a period of persecution and strife both inside and outside the church, David Whitmer and Oliver Cowdery were confronted by an excommunicated apostle named Thomas B. Marsh. According to Marsh:

> I enquired seriously at David if it was true that he had seen the angel, according to his testimony as one of the witnesses of the Book of Mormon. He replied, as sure as there is a God in heaven, he saw the angel, according to his testimony in that book. I asked him, if so, how did he not stand by Joseph? He answered, in the days when Joseph received the Book of Mormon, and brought it forth, he was a good man filled with the Holy Ghost, but he considered he had now fallen. I interrogated Oliver Cowdery in the same manner, who answered me similarly.[31]

Disfellowshipped Apostle William McLellin regarded the Book of Mormon as inspired even when disenfranchised with organized religion. He did so due to interactions with Hyrum Smith, Oliver Cowdery and David Whitmer—all witnesses to the golden plates. He recorded Oliver and David defending their eyewitness, even after leaving the church.[32]

The majority of the extant eyewitness testimonies date after being separated from the church they helped to found, organize, and lead for several years. Storms of opposition came into their lives including financial ruin, imprisonment, threats, verbal, and physical abuse. Being

---

30. George A. Smith to Josiah Fleming, 30 March 1838, Kirtland, Ohio.
31. "History of Thomas Baldwin Marsh," November 1857; printed in *Deseret News* (24 March 1858) and *Millennial Star* 26 (1864): 406, in Anderson, *Investigating the Book of Mormon Witnesses*, 56-57.
32. Mitchell K. Schaefer, ed., *William E. McLellin's Lost Manuscript* (Salt Lake City: Eborn Books, 2012), 166-167.

rejected from their own church might have been a pinnacle of embarrassment, but that truth never defrauded their foundational testimony. They unabashedly believed they saw the plates. If this is not true, every single accepted fact from any historical textbook should be called into question.

Minimal Fact #3: Multiple People Sincerely Believed There Was An Empty Stone Box on a Hill near Palmyra, New York

Joseph Smith, Jr. procured the plates on September 22, 1827, from a well-known hill located in Ontario County, New York. Joseph Smith, Jr. and Oliver Cowdery described the hill and stone box which contained the plates. Joseph shared:

> ...on the west side of this hill, not far from the top, under a stone of considerable size, lay the plates, deposited in a stone box: this stone was thick and rounding in the middle on the upper side, and thinner towards the edges, so that the middle part of it was visible above the ground, but the edge all around was covered with earth. ...The box in which they lay was formed by laying stones together in some kind of cement; in the bottom of the box were laid two stones crossways of the box, and on these stones lay the plates and the other things with them.[33]

A random hole in the ground held a coffin of stone and cement large enough to fit the plates. Joseph's retelling of the place and location came through a periodical after already moving multiple states west from New York. Nearly a half-century later, an unbelieving local still knew exactly where the plates originated. The elderly gentleman directed a group of curious inquirers to, "...the spot of ground where the stone box was placed, near the summit, and on the west side of the point of the hill."[34]

At this point, we have a direct testimony relatively early by historical standards and a corroborating, independent attestation from a non-believer, but an enemy to the Smiths gives the third confirmation. An extremely cynical Lorenzo Saunders still alluded in an interview to, "... where he [Joseph Smith, Jr.] took them [the golden plates] out, that is

33. Joseph Smith, "History of Joseph Smith. Continued.," *Times and Seasons*, vol. 3, no. 13, (May 1842), 772.
34. Edward Stevenson, *Reminiscences of Joseph the Prophet, and the Coming Forth of The Book of Mormon* (Salt Lake City: Self-pub., 1893), 13.

on the west [side of the] hill..."[35] There was a hole in the ground with a stone box located on the west side of the hill Joseph identified. Lorenzo originally meant to marginalize Joseph and discredit his claims about the plates, but his testimony even revealed timing of breaking ground precisely matching Joseph Smith's original claims.[36]

Minimal Fact #4: Joseph Smith, Jr. Had Something of Comparable Weight and Size as the Purported Golden Plates During the Time He Claimed to Have Them

People describing the golden plates did so with astonishing consistency. Seven identified the color as pure gold, golden, yellow, or having the appearance of gold. Eight commented that the leaves contained engravings and two elaborated a black patina on the script. Nearly a dozen recalled the size of the artifact ranging from 7-8 inches long by 6-7 inches wide by 6-8 inches thick. Five different individuals spoke about the plates having a sealed portion, and seven acutely described the binding via three rings shaped in a reverse 'D'.[37] 21 people had physical interactions with the plates.[38] This is the definition of independent attestation.

These four core facts should be uncontested by believers and skeptics alike. First, the Book of Mormon exists. Second, multiple people sincerely believed they saw and/or held the golden plates. Third, multiple people sincerely believed there was a man-made hole and empty stone box on a hill near Palmyra, New York, and finally Joseph Smith, Jr. had something of comparable weight and size as the purported golden plates during the time he claimed to have them.

35. Lorenzo Saunders, Interviewed by E. L. Kelley, 12 November 1884, 1-22, E. L. Kelley Papers, "Miscellany," RLDS Church Library-Archives, Independence, Missouri, in Vogel ed., *Early Mormon Documents*, Volume II, 160.
36. See Gehly, *Witnessing Miracles: Historical Evidence for the Resurrection and the Book of Mormon*, 93-101.
37. Jerry Grover, *Ziff, Magic Goggles, and Golden Plates: Etymology of Zyf and a Metallurgical Analysis of the Book of Mormon Plates* (Provo, UT: Grover Publishing, 2015), 67-95.
38. Joseph Smith, Jr. & Sr. Samuel and Hyrum Smith; Peter, David, Jacob, John and Christian Whitmer; Oliver Cowdery, Martin Harris, Hiram Page, Katharine Salisbury, Emma Smith, Lucy Smith, William Smith, Josiah Stowell, Mary Whitmer, and possibly Alvah Beman, Lucy Harris and Isaac Hale.

Inference to the Best Explanation Hypothesis

Joseph Smith, Jr. had in his possession authentic golden plates.

Physical golden plates obtained by Joseph Smith demonstrate—by far—the greatest explanatory scope and power to the facts on hand. The hundreds of sources relating to the golden plates and empty stone box in the hill fit reasonably into place. This is the best fit narrative with hundreds of supporting documents.

The plethora of independent narratives from eyewitnesses and enemies alike converge together in support of this truthful conclusion. The witnesses provide ample and vivid details asserting the reality of an artifact and means and mode of book production even when those providing the details are separated widely in time and place from one another. This explanation not only accounts for the existence of an artifact, but why so many would willingly suffer financial and physical hardships, threats, and excommunication without wavering from their first published testimony.

Contrary explanations must not only address the abundance of eyewitness testimony, but the enduring actions of those who stood by those testimonies to their deaths. Why did Martin Harris mortgage his farm to print the translation of the golden plates? Why did David Whitmer bear his testimony in the face of rifles and murderous threats? Why did witnesses not expose the golden plates as fraudulent after being excommunicated from the church founded upon their original testimony? Without real golden plates, where did Joseph originate the idea for them in the first place? Why does a treasure digger start a church? How does a youth produce a text of size, volume, complexity, and believability for Joseph's contemporaries and current readers alike? Any other explanation will struggle to reconcile the actions of the witnesses with their abundant dialog. Real golden plates harmonize their actions and words perfectly together. Genuine golden plates make perfect sense as to why the Book of Mormon text further makes extraordinary claims about itself as divinely inspired scripture and Jesus Christ as the risen Son of God.

The leading naturalistic explanation for the golden plates is posited by Dan Vogel and endorsed by others.[39] Vogel appears to accept three

---

39. See the following pages and associated endnotes to Dan Vogel, *Joseph Smith: The Making of a Prophet* (Salt Lake City, UT: Signature Books, 2004), 43-98. See also Robert Bowman, Jr. *Jesus' Resurrection and Joseph's Visions: Examining*

out of four minimal facts above. He knows the Book of Mormon exists, and readily confirms multiple witnesses sincerely believed in the reality of the golden plates. Vogel concedes the many physical reports of "hefting" and "handling" the plates, concluding that Joseph Smith must have manufactured a fake set of tin plates. His inference cannot be the best explanation of the facts on historical grounds, however. All reports are of gold or golden colored plates, not tin. Faked, tin plates are the very definition of ad hoc as no extant early source leaves any hints towards a tin artifact. Besides rough weight, nothing else fits. Accepting weight, while ignoring color, engraving, and patina descriptions is cherry-picking. How did Joseph dupe a dozen people, especially Josiah Stowell, into sincerely believing they saw the real thing? Vogel's proposal of forgery further fails to provide any reasoning beyond musing for the origin of the idea of golden plates in the first place.[40] Nobody tried to convince the Smiths or their neighbors that they were being duped by a fake artifact. Nearby enemies believed in the plates and tried to steal them. Others rejected the whole enterprise. Surprisingly, several converted. Real plates provide an explanation for why no plates are available today. The angel took them back. Vogel's account leaves the lack of discovery of forged plates as an unsolved mystery. By not being open to heavenly intervention, this naturalistic explanation falls far short in explanatory scope and power and checks off the boxes as being both ad hoc and contrived. Tin plates are a forced fit originating from within Vogel's agnostic and skeptical mind.

Crosses might have been common while the golden plates are one-of-a-kind, but plausibility to infer the best explanation is not based upon an artifact or event in question being unique or rare. Rare, unique, and exceptional artifacts are routinely discovered worldwide. The golden plates are plausible given the background data through the historical sources presented above. Respected scholars like William Lane Craig, Michael Licona, and Gary Habermas argue—with substantially less documented sources—for a much more extreme plausibility of the res-

---

the Foundations of Christianity and Mormonism (Tampa, FL: DeWard Publishing, 2020).

40. Consider the commentary on this topic from Richard Bushman, *Joseph Smith's Golden Plates: A Cultural History* (New York, NY: Oxford University Press, 2023), 144-146.

urrection of Jesus Christ, even though the dead do not naturally rise.[41] The golden plates coupled with the religious movement that followed and angelic reporting from the Three Witnesses require only two assumptions: God exists, and Jesus Christ was raised from the dead. Nothing ad hoc exists or is contrived with those two prerequisites assumed.

Jesus Christ died on a cross. Joseph Smith, Jr. obtained golden plates from a hill in New York. Both these statements are inferred on historical grounds as the best explanation of the facts. For someone to refute the method and mode of Jesus' death, they must first present an alternate hypothesis which better accounts for the sources on hand. The cross stands undisputed because of the background evidence applied to a historical method. Jesus Christ's death by crucifixion is the best explanation of the facts. The demonstrable available evidence for the golden plates must dictate an equally resounding conclusion. The reality of the golden plates has been confirmed as certain, sure, and indisputable on the same historical grounds previously set for the cross of Jesus Christ. Joseph Smith, Jr. truly had golden plates in his possession.

41. See William Lane Craig, *Reasonable Faith: Christian Faith and Apologetics* (Wheaton, IL: Crossway Books, 2008), 359-399 and Michael R. Licona, *The Resurrection of Jesus: A New Historiographical Approach* (Downers Grove, IL: InterVarsity Press, 2010).

4

"Written Upon Gold Plates"

Comparing Witness Descriptions with Artifacts from the Pre-Modern World

Neal Rappleye

The eyewitness testimony makes it virtually indisputable that Joseph Smith had a real set of metal plates, a fact that even skeptical scholars have accepted. Likewise, the practice of writing on metal plates in antiquity is well-known, as thousands of ancient metal documents have been discovered. But some still raise questions about whether the Book of Mormon plates are consistent with known ancient examples, and hypothesize that Joseph made a fake set of plates to fool his followers. To address this issue, I compare the descriptions of the plates given by the witnesses who saw and/or handled the plates for themselves with authentic metal plates and other artifacts from the pre-modern world. Features such as their appearance, how they were bound and sealed, the size individual plates and the bound set, and the characters said to be on the plates can be directly compared with real-world examples of pre-modern inscriptions, metal plates, and other metallic artifacts. Every detail has precedent and is within the scope of practices and capabilities of pre-modern peoples. In contrast, it would have been difficult for someone unskilled in metallurgy (such as Joseph Smith) to create a fake set of plates consistent with the specifications provided by the witnesses.

Approximately two-hundred years ago, in the early morning hours of September 22, 1823, an angel appeared to Joseph Smith and informed him of "a book deposited" in a nearby hill, "written upon gold plates, giving an account of the former inhabitants of this continent" (Joseph Smith—History 1:34). According to Joseph's own account, this record kept on gold plates contained the original language source of the Book of Mormon, which he translated and published in 1830. Many of Joseph's contemporaries doubted the existence of these plates, which they derisively referred to as the "Golden Bible."[1] There were several others besides Joseph Smith, however, who had first-hand interactions with these plates—either seeing and handling the uncovered plates as official witnesses, or physically interacting with the plates while under a cover or in a box.[2] The testimony of these witnesses, as left behind in the historical record, is persuasive.[3] Even historians and scholars skeptical of Joseph Smith's religious claims agree that he must have had a real, tangible set of metal plates—although they argue that the plates were of modern, rather than ancient, origin.[4]

---

1. For a convenient collection of several examples, see Larry E. Morris, ed., *A Documentary History of the Book of Mormon* (New York, NY: Oxford University Press, 2019), 64, 66, 73, 84, 89–94, 121, 128–129, 168, 173–174, 195, 199, 203, 218, 222–223, 235, 238, 247, 263, 266, 384–385, 395–396, 430, 440, 466, 485, 489, 491, 500–502. Further reference to Morris's collection will use the abbreviation *DHBM*.
2. Most of the relevant individuals are identified and discussed in Larry E. Morris, "Empirical Witnesses of the Gold Plates," *Dialogue: A Journal of Mormon Thought* 52, no. 3 (2019): 59–84.
3. The classic treatment on the witnesses remains Richard Lloyd Anderson, *Investigating the Book of Mormon Witnesses* (Salt Lake City, UT: Deseret Book, 1981). See also Morris, "Empirical Witnesses," 59–84; Alexander L. Baugh, "The Testimonies of the Book of Mormon Witnesses," in *A Reason for Faith: Navigating LDS Doctrine and Church History*, ed. Laura Harris Hales (Provo, UT: Religious Studies Center, Brigham Young University; Salt Lake City, UT: Deseret Book, 2016), 45–58; Steven C. Harper, "The Eleven Witnesses," in *The Coming Forth of the Book of Mormon: A Marvelous Work and a Wonder*, ed. Dennis L. Largey, Andrew H. Hedges, John Hilton III, and Kerry Hull (Provo, UT: Religious Studies Center; Salt Lake City, UT: Deseret Book, 2015), 117–132; Michael R. Ash, *Shaken Faith Syndrome*, 2nd ed. (Redding, CA: FairMormon, 2013), 127–133.
4. See Fawn Brodie, *No Man Knows My History: The Life of Joseph Smith, The Mormon Prophet*, 2nd rev. ed. (New York, NY: Vintage Books, 1971), 79–80; Ann Taves, "History and the Claims of Revelation: Joseph Smith and the Materialization of the Golden Plates," *Numen* 61 (2014): 182–207; Sonia Hazard, "How Joseph Smith Encountered Printing Plates and Founded Mormonism," *Religion and American Culture* 31, no. 2 (2021): 137–192; Dan Vogel, *Joseph Smith: The Making of a Prophet* (Salt Lake City, UT: Signature Books, 2004), xi, 98–99; Dan Vogel, *Charisma Under Pressure: Joseph Smith, American Prophet, 1831–1839* (Salt Lake City, UT: Signature Books, 2023), ix.

Defenders of the Book of Mormon have eagerly pointed out that in the 200 years since the angel first appeared to Joseph, thousands of examples of ancient and medieval writings on a variety of metals have been discovered and documented.[5] Skeptics have responded by arguing that the golden plates are not consistent with these ancient precedents, but rather fit with 19th-century notions of writing on metal.[6] Without the original plates available to directly examine, it is impossible to settle this issue once and for all. Nonetheless, one way to test these theories is to systematically compare the descriptions of the Book of Mormon plates provided by Joseph Smith and other witnesses to known inscriptions and metallic artifacts from the pre-modern world. These provide a control against which we can evaluate whether the witnesses are realistically describing an ancient artifact or a modern forgery.

Eyewitness Accounts of the Golden Plates

There are three different groups of witnesses to the Book of Mormon plates: (1) The Three Witnesses—Oliver Cowdery, David Whitmer, and Martin Harris—who were shown the plates by an angel. (2) The

5. See Hugh Nibley, *An Approach to the Book of Mormon*, 3rd ed. (Salt Lake City, UT: Deseret Book; Provo, UT: FARMS, 1988), 21–28; H. Curtis Wright, "Metallic Documents of Antiquity," *BYU Studies* 10, no. 4 (1970): 457–477; Paul R. Cheesman, *Ancient Writing on Metal Plates: Archaeological Findings Support Mormon Claims* (Bountiful, UT: Horizon Publishers, 1985); H. Curtis Wright, "Ancient Burials of Metal Documents in Stone Boxes," in *By Study and Also by Faith*, 2 vols., ed. John M. Lundquist and Stephen D. Ricks (Salt Lake City, UT: Deseret Book; Provo, UT: FARMS, 1990), 2:273–334; John A. Tvedtnes, *The Book of Mormon and Other Hidden Books: "Out of Darkness Unto Light"* (Provo, UT: FARMS, 2000), 145–154; William J. Hamblin, "Sacred Writing on Metal Plates in the Ancient Mediterranean," *FARMS Review* 19, no. 1 (2007): 37–54; Michael R. Ash, *Of Faith and Reason: 80 Evidences Supporting the Prophet Joseph Smith* (Springville, UT: Cedar Fort, 2008), 86–89; Noel B. Reynolds, "An Everlasting Witness: Ancient Writings on Metal," in *Steadfast in Defense of Faith: Essays in Honor of Daniel C. Peterson*, ed. Shirley S. Ricks, Stephen D. Ricks, and Louis C. Midgley (Orem, UT: The Interpreter Foundation; Salt Lake City, UT: Eborn Books, 2023), 143–158; Matthew Roper, "'Records of Every Kind': The Content of Metal Plates in Antiquity and the Book of Mormon" (forthcoming).
6. See Ryan Thomas, "The Gold Plates and Ancient Metal Epigraphy," *Dialogue: A Journal of Mormon Thought* 52, no. 2 (2019): 37–58; Michael G. Reed, "The Notion of Metal Records in Joseph Smith's Day," Neal A. Maxwell Institute Summer Seminar on Mormon Culture, Working Paper (2011).

TABLE 1: Specifications of the Gold Plates Based on Eyewitness Descriptions
DESIGN
Material and Appearance: gold/golden; greenish (on a corner); mixture of gold and copper Binding: three D-shaped rings Sealed: between 1/3 and 2/3 of the plates sealed shut; a circular seal on the last plate
DIMENSIONS
Individual Plates: about 6 x 8 inches, very thin; pliable, compared to common tin, window glass, thick paper, or paste board Height: between 4–6 inches Weight: between 30–60 pounds
CHARACTERS
Script: Egyptian (reformed/short-hand), corrupted Hebrew mixed w/Egyptian Size and Density: small/fine, each plate filled/covered front and back Color: a black stain or cement filled each character

Eight Witnesses—Christian Whitmer, Jacob Whitmer, Peter Whitmer Jr., John Whitmer, Hiram Page, Joseph Smith Sr., Hyrum Smith, and Samuel H. Smith—who were permitted to see and handle the plates by Joseph Smith. (3) Others who had occasion to lift, handle, move, or otherwise interact with the plates while they were covered, such as members of Joseph's family (e.g., Emma Hale Smith, Lucy Mack Smith, William Smith) and close supporters (e.g., Josiah Stowell, Martin Harris); or were shown the plates by divine means independently of Joseph Smith (e.g., Mary Whitmer). Some of these witnesses left behind accounts that provide details about the plates' appearance, size and dimensions, how they were bound, how much they weighed, what the characters looked like, etc.[7] When all this information is brought together, a general picture of the plates emerges (see table 1).

Each of these details will be examined more fully below and compared against known metal documents and artifacts from the pre-modern world to determine if they are realistic for an ancient artifact. Although examples will be drawn from all around the world, special attention will

7. Kirk B. Heinrichsen, "How Witnesses Described the 'Gold Plates'," *Journal of Book of Mormon Studies* 10, no. 1 (2001): 16–21, 78; Matthew B. Brown, *Plates of Gold: The Book of Mormon Comes Forth* (American Fork, UT: Covenant Communications, 2003), 148–151; Jerry D. Grover Jr., *Ziff, Magic Goggles, and Golden Plates: Etymology of Zyf and a Metallurgical Analysis of the Book of Mormon Plates* (Provo, UT: Grover Publishing, 2015), 67–70; Josh Coates, "A Combinatorial Approach to Modeling All Possible Golden Plates," *Interpreter: A Journal of Latter-day Saint Faith and Scholarship* 66 (2025): 39–68.

be given to artifacts demonstrating that the requisite metallurgical technology existed in pre-Columbian America around the middle of the first millennium AD (ca. AD 200–800)—the general time-period in which the Book of Mormon plates were made—or earlier.

Design

Witnesses provided details about the general appearance of the plates, the materials they seemed to be made out of, and how they were bound together. They also mentioned that some of the plates could be opened and thumbed through like a book while another portion seemed to be sealed shut in some way. I refer to these features as the overall *design* of the plates. Each of the attributes of this design can be compared and contrasted with parallels from the ancient world.

Material and Appearance

The very day he first recovered the plates, Joseph Smith told Joseph Knight "they appear to be Gold."[8] Later in life, Joseph continued to describe the plates as having "the *appearance* of gold," which is how the Eight Witnesses also described the plates.[9] On one occasion while preaching in July 1831, Samuel H. Smith similarly said they had "the appearance of fine Gold."[10] In a letter written in November 1829, Oliver Cowdery also described them as "plates, which have the appearance of gold; and they are of very curious workmanship."[11] An early newspaper account reported Oliver Cowdery describing them as "something *resembling* golden plates."[12] But were they made of *pure* gold? According to

8. Joseph Knight, Recollection of Early Mormon History, 1833–1847, in Dean C. Jessee, "Joseph Knight's Recollection of Early Mormon History," *BYU Studies* 17, no. 1 (1977): 33.
9. Joseph Smith, "Church History," in *Times and Seasons* 3, no. 9 (1 March 1842): 707; Testimony of Eight Witnesses, ca. June 1829, emphasis added. David Whitmer also once said that they "*appeared* to be of gold" (emphasis added). See "David Whitmer: The Only Living Witness," *Kansas City Journal*, 5 June 1881, in Lyndon W. Cook, ed., *David Whitmer Interviews: A Restoration Witness* (Orem, UT: Grandin Book Company, 1991), 64.
10. William E. McLellin to Samuel McLellin, 4 August 1832, CHL MS 617, online at bhroberts.org (accessed 17 April 2024). I appreciate Jerry Grover bringing this source to my attention.
11. Oliver H. P. Cowdery to Cornelius C. Blatchly, 9 November 1829, in *Gospel Luminary* 2, no. 49 (10 December 1829): 194, in Morris, *DHBM*, 375.
12. "The Golden Bible, or Campbellism Improved," *Observer and Telegraph* (18

Joseph Smith's brother William, while the plates "were in a good state of preservation, [and] had the appearance of gold,"[13] they were in fact "a mixture of gold and copper."[14] Josiah Stowell provides an interesting account that may corroborate that conclusion. He was present the day Joseph brought the plates home, and said he caught a glimpse of an exposed corner as the covering briefly slipped off, and it "resembled a stone of a greenish caste."[15] This is an odd way to describe "gold plates," but makes sense if there was a copper component that had been exposed to the elements and oxidized. The Statue of Liberty, for instance, looks like it is made of bluish-greenish stone, but is in fact made of copper that has oxidized.

Based on these details, there are two possibilities for the material the plates were made of. One is that they were made primarily of copper, but were then gilded with gold, giving the appearance of solid gold.[16] Techniques for gilding copper with gold were known in both Central and South America during pre-Columbian times.[17] For example, some Moche-Vicús artifacts roughly contemporary to Mormon and Moroni were made of thin copper sheet metal gilded with gold through an electrochemical process.[18] When initially recovered, several of these items

---

November 1830), in Morris, *DHBM*, 385, emphasis added.

13. James Murdock to *Congregational Observer*, 19 June 1841, "The Mormons and Their Prophet," *Congregational Observer* 2 (3 July 1841), in Dan Vogel, ed., *Early Mormon Documents*, 5 vols. (Salt Lake City, UT: Signature Books, 1996–2003), 1:479. Further reference to Vogel's collection will be abbreviated as *EMD*.
14. William Smith, Sermon, 8 June 1884, "The Old Soldier's Testimony," *Saints' Herald* 31, no. 40 (4 October 1884): 644.
15. "Mormonism," *New England Christian Herald* (Boston, MA) 4, no. 6 (7 November 1832), transcribed online at sidneyrigdon.com (accessed 14 August 2023).
16. See Grover, *Ziff, Magic Goggles, and Golden Plates*, 83–85 for a more technical discussion of gold gilding techniques known in antiquity, including pre-Columbian America.
17. Warwick Bray, "Techniques of Gilding and Surface-Enrichment in Pre-Hispanic American Metallurgy," in *Metal Plating and Patination: Cultural, Technical, and Historical Developments*, ed. Susan La Niece and Paul Craddock (Boston, MA: Butterworth-Heinemann, 1993), 183–187; David A. Scott, "A Review of Gilding Techniques in Ancient South America," in *Gilded Metals: History, Technology and Conservation*, ed. Terry Drayman-Weisser (London: Archetype Publications, 2000), 203–207, 213–218.
18. Heather Lechtman, "A Pre-Columbian Technique for Electrochemical Replacement Plating of Gold and Silver on Copper Objects," *Journal of Metals*

were "entirely covered with green corrosion products of copper,"[19] but removal of the corrosion revealed that "the copper had originally been covered with a thin coating of silver or gold, so that the objects would have appeared to be made entirely out of those precious metals."[20] Others were found with more limited copper corrosion along the edges, while the rest of the object still retained the appearance of gold.[21] For example, the gilded copper headdress of the Lady of Cao, dated to around AD 400, generally maintained a pristine golden luster with only minor indications of green oxidized corrosion.[22] Well preserved copper plates gilded with gold, therefore, could be consistent with descriptions of the Book of Mormon plates as having the appearance of gold, while a corner

---

31 (1979): 154–160; Heather Lechtman, Antonieta Erlij, and Edward J. Barry Jr., "New Perspectives on Moche Metallurgy: Techniques of Gilding Copper at Loma Negra, Northern Peru," *American Antiquity* 47, no. 1 (1982): 3–30; Heather Lechtman, "Pre-Columbian Surface Metallurgy," *Scientific American* 250, no. 6 (1984): 56–59; A. Alviz-Meza, et al., "A Pre-Columbian Galvanic Technique able to Explain the Gilding of Copper in Northern Peru," *Journal of Archaeological Science: Reports* 47 (2023): 103818. See also Bray, "Techniques of Gilding," 185–187.

19. Lechtman, "Pre-Columbian Technique for Electrochemical Replacement Plating," 154. See also Lechtman et al., "New Perspectives on Moche Metallurgy," 10; Lechtman, "Pre-Columbian Surface Metallurgy," 56; Bray, "Techniques of Gilding," 186.
20. Lechtman, "Pre-Columbian Surface Metallurgy," 56 (see also p. 57 for images of a miniature mask before and after the copper corrosion was removed). See also Lechtman, "Pre-Columbian Technique for Electrochemical Replacement Plating," 154; Lechtman et al., "New Perspectives on Moche Metallurgy," 10; Bray, "Techniques of Gilding," 186.
21. See items 66-141-171b, DC-10, and M-3046a/c in table 1 of Alviz-Meza, et al., "A Pre-Columbian Galvanic Technique," 3; Roberto Cesareo et al., "Multilayered Artifacts in the pre-Columbian Metallurgy from the North of Peru," *Applied Physics A: Materials Science and Processing* (2013), fig. 11.
22. A. R. Williams, "Mystery of the Tattooed Mummy," *National Geographic*, June 2006, 82 (see also the other well-preserved gilded copper artifacts on pp. 78–80); Joanne Pillsbury, "Headdress Ornament, ca. AD 400," in *Golden Kingdoms: Luxury Arts in the Ancient Americas*, ed. Joanne Pillsbury, Timonthy Potts, and Kim N. Richter (Los Angeles, CA: The J. Paul Getty Museum and The Getty Research Institute, 2017), 154–155. Since these items were recovered in 2004 and date to about the same time as Mormon's plates, they serve to illustrate that gilded copper plates could very well have remained sufficiently well-preserved so as to still generally have "the appearance of gold" after 1400 years.

looked like greenish stone.

More likely, however, is that the plates were made of *tumbaga*, which is a copper-gold or copper-gold-silver alloy used in pre-Columbian Central and South America.[23] In South America, the use of tumbaga goes back to the early first millennium BC, as attested to by a gold-copper artifact recovered from a site in Ecuador and dated to around 915–780 BC.[24] This metallurgical technology had made its way northward into Central America by the early centuries AD, and a tumbaga pendant from Panama, made in a style dated to AD 400–900, was found in the Yucatan, indicating "the transference of metallurgical objects, knowledge, styles, and iconography" from South America into Mesoamerica by the mid-first millennium AD.[25] Tumbaga does not naturally look like

---

23. See Grover, *Ziff, Magic Goggles, and Golden Plates*, 45–51, 91–95 for the most detailed argument for tumbaga plates. For previous treatments, see Read H. Putnam, "Were the Golden Plates Made of Tumbaga?," *Improvement Era* 69, no. 9 (1966): 788–789, 828–831; Robert F. Smith, "The 'Golden' Plates," in *Reexploring the Book of Mormon*, ed. John W. Welch (Salt Lake City, UT: Deseret Book; Provo, UT: FARMS, 1992), 275–278; "Of What Material Were the Plates?," *Journal of Book of Mormon Studies* 10, no. 1 (2001): 21, 78–79; Ash, *Of Faith and Reason*, 110–112; Ash, *Shaken Faith Syndrome*, 159–160; Caroline Sorenson, "The Metallurgical Plausibility of the Gold Plates," Neal A. Maxwell Institute Summer Seminar on Mormon Culture, Working Paper (2011). According to Nissim Amzallag, "Beyond Prestige and Magnificence: The Theological Significance of Gold in the Israelite Tabernacle," *Harvard Theological Review* 112, no. 3 (2019): 296–318, the distinction between "gold" and "pure gold" in the description of the Israelite Tabernacle is that regular, non-pure "gold" is actually a copper-gold alloy. Thus, "gold plates" (JS–H 1:34) could in fact refer to plates made of something like tumbaga from an ancient Israelite perspective.
24. Francisco Valdez et al., "Evidencia temprana de metalurigia en la Costa Pacífica ecuatorial," *Boletín Museo del Oro* 53 (June 2005): 1–9; Bryan Cockrell, "Headdress Ornament, 600 BC–AD 400," in *Golden Kingdoms*, 180.
25. James A. Doyle, "Pendant, AD 500–900," in *Golden Kingdoms*, 230. See also Ana María Falchetti, "The Darién Gold Pendants of Ancient Colombia and the Isthmus," *Metropolitan Museum Journal* 43 (2008): 59; Samuel Kirkland Lothrop, *Metals from the Cenote of Sacrifice Chichen Itza, Yucatan* (Cambridge, MA: Peabody Museum of Archaeology and Ethnology, Harvard University, 1952), 94–95; Clemency Chase Coggins and Orrin C. Shane III, eds., *Cenote of Sacrifice: Maya Treasures from the Sacred Well at Chichén Itzá* (Austin, TX: University of Texas, 1984), 65; Warwick Bray, "Sitio Conte Metalwork in its Pan-American Context," in *River of Gold: Precolumbian Treasures from Sitio Conte*, ed. Pamela Hearne and Robert J. Sharer (Philadelphia, PA: The University Museum

gold, but ancient American metalsmiths employed a depletion gilding process that gave it the appearance of pure gold on the surface.[26] According to Stuart J. Fleming, "This technology … is thought to have been developed among the cultures of ancient Peru as early as 400 BC and to have been in use throughout Mesoamerica at least a millennium before the conquistadors arrived."[27]

The ratio of copper to gold in tumbaga can vary, and objects with a higher proportion of gold tend to preserve better over time.[28] If the underlying alloy is high in copper, however, it can be more susceptible to corrosion, especially along "a sharp edge produced by hammering or folding during manufacture," where the gold gilding is more stressed and "prone to hair-line cracking."[29] Yet under the right conditions, even a high-copper tumbaga object that is interred in the ground can be well preserved and retain its golden luster after more than 1400 years.[30] Several pre-Columbian tumbaga artifacts recovered from Central America exhibit the combination of a golden-looking surface with portions

---

of Archaeology and Anthropology, University of Pennsylvania, 1992), 34–39.

26. Bray, "Techniques of Gilding," 188–190; Scott, "A Review of Gilding Techniques," 207–213; Lechtman, "Pre-Columbian Surface Metallurgy," 59–63; Stuart Fleming, "Sitio Conte Goldwork: Alloying and the Treatment of Surfaces," in *River of Gold*, 54–58; Mark Grimwade, "The Surface Enrichment of Carat Gold Alloys: Depletion Gilding," *Gold Technology* 26 (1999): 16–23.
27. Stuart J. Fleming, "Confounding the Conquistadors: Tumbaga's Spurious Luster," *Expedition* 41, no. 2 (1999): 6.
28. Fleming, "Confounding the Conquistadors," 6–7.
29. Fleming, "Confounding the Conquistadors," 7. See also David A. Scott, "The Deterioration of Gold Alloys and Some Aspects of their Conservation," *Studies in Conservation* 28, no. 4 (1983): 194–203.
30. On the podcast Scriptural Mormonism, "Episode 44: Jerry Grover Addressing Issues Relating to the Golden Plates and Book of Mormon Chronology," online at youtube.com (accessed 2 September 2023), time stamp 50:00–58:25, Jerry Grover notes that tumbaga objects recovered from a royal tomb in Sipán, Peru, were buried ca. AD 350 and recovered in 1987—a span of more than 1600 years—which were in pristine condition with no signs of corrosion. These items still had the appearance of pure gold, but recent metallurgical testing indicates that the underlying alloy in all of them was high (over 50%) in copper, with the copper-gold-silver ratio in the tooth protector in particular being close to the specifications Grover has hypothesized for the Book of Mormon plates. See Antonio Brunetti et al., "Combining X-ray Fluorescence and Monte Carlo Simulation Methods to Differentiate between Tumbaga and Gold-Alloy or Gildings," *Materials* 15 (2022): 4452.

covered by green corrosion.[31] So plates made of a high-copper tumbaga alloy, if well preserved (and the stone box the plates were stored in was designed for optimal preservation),[32] could have generally retained a golden appearance while the edges or corners could have been susceptible to corrosion and thus had a greenish color, consistent with the descriptions of the Book of Mormon plates.

Binding

Several witnesses explained that the plates were bound by rings, and some specified the number and shape of those rings. Joseph's brother William, for instance, felt the plates through a covering and said, "I could tell they were plates of some kind and that they were fastened together by rings running through the back."[33] David Whitmer said there were "massive rings passing through the back edges" of the plates,[34] and elsewhere specified that these were "three gold rings."[35] According to the editor of the *Palmyra Reflector*, one of the Whitmers had said the plates were "secured with three small rings ... passing through each leaf in succession."[36] Joseph Smith's own description of the plates confirms

31. See Scott Fulton and Sylvia Keochakian, "The Conservation of Tumbaga Metals from Panama at the Peabody Museum, Harvard University," *Objects Specialty Group Postscripts* 12 (2005): 78 fig, 3, 82 fig. 8, 84 fig. 10, 85 fig. 11 for various examples of tumbaga objects in varying states of preservation and with varying degrees of green copper corrosion. See also the images at "Brid-form Pendant, Panama or Costa Rica, AD 700–1500 (Lot #47063)," *Heritage Auctions*, online at fineart.ha.com (accessed August 16, 2023); "Pre-Columbian Costa Rican Tumbaga Gold Bird Pendant," *Hartman Antiques*, online at hartmangalleries.com (accessed August 16, 2023); "Pre-Columbian Gold Tumbaga Avian Pendant," *Auction Life*, online at auctionlifeflorida.com (accessed August 16, 2023).
32. Grover, *Ziff, Magic Goggles, and Golden Plates*, 70–71.
33. J. W. Peterson, "Wm. B. Smith's Last Statement," *Zion's Ensign* 5, no. 3 (13 January 1894): 6, in *EMD* 1:511.
34. "David Whitmer," *Kansas City Journal*, 5 June 1881, in Cook, *David Whitmer Interviews*, 64.
35. *Chicago Tribune*, December 17, 1885; *Chicago Tribune*, 24 January 1888, both in Cook, *David Whitmer Interviews*, 172, 221. Martin Harris, on the other hand, said that they were "three silver rings" in Joel Tiffany, "MORMONISM—No. 2," *Tiffany's Monthly* 5, no. (August 1859): 165, in Morris, *DHBM*, 194.
36. "Golden Bible, no. 6," *Palmyra Reflector*, 19 March 1831, in *EMD* 2:249. The article does not specify *which* Whitmer is reportedly the source of this description, but the beginning of the article mentions "the stories told by the famous three witnesses to the Gold Bible," implying it is David Whitmer, and E. D. Howe,

that they were "bound together in a volume, as the leaves of a book with three rings running through the whole."[37] When Hyrum Smith and William E. McLellin preached together in Jacksonville, Illinois, they described the plates as being "connected with rings in the shape of the letter D, which facilitated the opening and shutting of the book."[38] John Whitmer also reported that the "three rings [were] … in the shape of a D with the straight line toward the center,"[39] a detail that was also described by his mother, Mary Whitmer, after the plates were shown to her by a mysterious messenger.[40]

In the Roman Empire, military diplomas were inscribed on a pair of bronze plates bound together by two rings so that each diploma could be

---

Mormonism Unvailed: Or, a Faithful Account of that Singular Imposition and Delusion (Painesville, OH: E. D. Howe, 1834), 15–16 attributes this account to David. Although the setting described fits with the Three Witnesses' experience (in a field outside the Whitmer farm), all the other details in the account harmonize better with descriptions of the Eight Witnesses' experience. The *Reflector*'s editor appears to be reporting what he heard from an unnamed "informant" who is conflating details that come from David with other details from one of the Whitmer brothers among the Eight Witnesses. In any case, the identification of three rings is consistent with other sources.

37. Joseph Smith, "Church History," 707.
38. "Mormonism," *New Hampshire Miscellany*, 11 October 1831, reprinted from the *Illinois Patriot*, ca. 16 September 1831 (see *EMD* 3:292), in Francis W. Kirkham, *A New Witness for Christ in America*, rev. and enlarged ed., 2 vols. (Salt Lake City, UT: Brigham Young University, 1959), 2: 405–406. The article merely identifies its source as "a preacher" from the "Mormonite" sect, but the timing and events correlate with William E. McLellin's journal entry for 10 September 1831, in which he and Hyrum Smith preached to a congregation of about five hundred. McLellin "gave them a brief history of the book of Mormon, of its coming forth &c.," and then Hyrum "arose and bore testimony to the truths which they had heard and gave them his evidence of the truth of the book," meaning he bore witness to seeing and handling the plates. See William E. McLellin Journal, 10 September 1831, in Jan Shipps and John W. Welch, eds., *The Journals of William E. McLellin 1831–1836*, (Provo, UT: BYU Studies; Urbana and Chicago, IL: University of Illinois Press, 1994), 39. See also Richard Lloyd Anderson, "Attempts to Redefine the Experience of the Eight Witnesses," *Journal of Book of Mormon Studies* 14, no. 1 (2005): 30, 127n73.
39. P. Wilhelm Poulson, Letter, 31 July 1878, rep. "Correspondence. Death of John Whitmer. Testimony to the Book of Mormon," *The Deseret News,* 14 August 1878, in Morris, *DHBM*, 453.
40. Edward Stevenson, Diary, 23 December 1877, in Cook, *David Whitmer Interviews*, 13.

opened and shut like a book.[41] In India, beginning as early as the third century AD, thousands of grants were issued on sets of copper plates bound together by either one or two rings.[42] So binding plates via rings was practiced by some in the ancient world. Interestingly, the ring-binding used for the Book of Mormon plates improves upon those used in India and the Roman Empire. The use of three-rings in a D-shape has proven to be the most optimal form of ring-binding (hence the ubiquity of three-ring binders today), something that was only determined in modern times in the 20th century through a decades-long process of trial and error.[43] This suggests that the Book of Mormon plates were crafted

41. John W. Welch and Kelsey D. Lambert, "Two Ancient Roman Plates," *BYU Studies* 45, no. 2 (2006): 57, 72; John W. Welch, "The Seven Seals in the Apocalypse of John: Possible Cultural, Legal, and Imperial Contexts," in *Steadfast in Defense of Faith*, 408. A well-preserved example, with the rings intact is the diploma of Liccai son of Birs, issued in AD 71, which can be seen on the *Coprus Inscriptionum Latinarum* website, online at cil.bbaw.de (accessed 22 August 2023). See "Military Diploma from Slavonski Šamac (Pannoni Inferior)," online at edh.ub.uni-heidelberg.de (accessed 22 August 2023) for further information on this particular diploma.
42. See Richard Salomon, *Indian Epigraphy: A Guide to the Study of Inscriptions in Sanskrit, Prakrit, and Other Indo-Aryan Languages* (New York, NY: Oxford University Press, 1998), 113–114; Emmanuel Francis, "Indian Copper-Plate Grants: Inscriptions or Documents?" in *Manuscripts and Archives: Comparative Views on Record-Keeping*, ed. Alessandro Bausi, Christian Brockmann, Michael Friedrich, and Sabine Kienitz (De Gruyter, 2018), 398, 400 figs. 3 and 4; Francesco Bianchini, "Legally Binding: The Textual Layout of a Copper-Plate Grant from South Asia," *Manuscript and Text Cultures* 2, no. 1 (2023), figs. 1, 2, 3, 7, 9 online at mtc-journal.org (accessed 22 August 2023). Facsimile images of several such plates, variously showing one or two holes where the rings once were, can be accessed on *The Indian Analyst* website, online at whatisindia.com (accessed 22 August 2023). These were first mentioned in relation to the Book of Mormon in Hugh Nibley, *Lehi in the Desert, The World of the Jaredites, There Were Jaredites* (Salt Lake City, UT: Deseret Book; Provo, UT: FARMS, 1988), 106–107. For more information on these copper plate grants and their similarities to the Book of Mormon plates, see Evidence Central, "Book of Mormon Evidence #246: Indian Copper Plate Grants," online at evidencecentral.org (accessed August 22, 2023).
43. Warren P. Aston, "The Rings that Bound the Gold Plates Together," *Insights: A Window on the Ancient World* 26, no. 3 (2006): 3–4; Jeff Lindsay, "A 'D' for Plausibility of the Gold Plates: The Book of Mormon in an Interesting Bind," *Arise from the Dust* (blog), 29 August 2006, online at arisefromthedust.com (accessed 22 August 2023); Elizabeth Fenton, "The Book of Mormon and Book

by someone who came from a culture with extensive experience in using rings to bind plates together, and had thus learned how to best achieve maximum space and stability.

Sealed

Joseph Smith said that "a part of [the record] was sealed,"[44] and Martin Harris famously informed Charles Anthon "that part of the plates were sealed."[45] The exact proportion that was sealed varies somewhat in the sources. According to an early newspaper report, Orson Pratt, presumably drawing on information he gleaned from either Joseph Smith or one of the witnesses, said that Joseph had "translated about two thirds of what the plates contained," thereby implying that one-third was sealed, an estimate George Q. Cannon also gave.[46] In a later sermon, Orson Pratt inverted that ratio, saying "about two-thirds were sealed,"[47] and on one occasion David Whitmer similarly indicated that "about one-third of [the plates] appeared to be loose" while the remainder (two-thirds) "seemed to be sealed."[48] On another occasion, however, David is reported as estimating "about half of the book was sealed."[49] The *Palmyra Reflector* also reported one of the Whitmers as saying that "the leaves were divided equi-distant" between the sealed and unsealed portions, suggesting the two parts were each about half the volume.[50] All told, these sources suggest that anywhere between one-third and two-thirds of the plates were sealed.

Many legal documents in the ancient Near East were sealed in a way that allowed part of the document to be left open for daily use while the other portion was bound and sealed to ensure there was no tampering

History," *Journal of Book of Mormon Studies* 32 (2023): 94–95.

44. Joseph Smith, "Church History," 707.
45. Joseph Smith, History Draft, ca. June 1839–ca. 1841 [Draft 2], p. 9.
46. B. Stokley, "The Orators of Mormon," *Catholic Telegraph*, 14 April 1832; George Q. Cannon, *The Latter-day Prophet: History of Joseph Smith, written for Young People* (Salt Lake City, UT: Juvenile Instructor Office, 1900), 25. It is possible Stokley misunderstood Pratt and inverted the ratio of sealed to unsealed plates.
47. Orson Pratt, "The Faith and Visions of the Ancient Saints—The Same Great Blessings to Be Enjoyed By the Latter-Day Saints," delivered in the Tabernacle, Salt Lake City, 13 April 1856, *Journal of Discourses* 3:347.
48. *Chicago Times*, 17 October 1881, in Cook, *David Whitmer Interviews*, 75.
49. P. Wilhelm Poulson Interview, *Deseret Evening News*, 16 August 1878, in Cook, *David Whitmer Interviews*, 21.
50. "Golden Bible, no. 6," in *EMD* 2:249.

with the text, a practice attested in Jeremiah 32:6–15. If needed, the sealed portion could be brought before a judge and opened to settle any legal disputes over the details of the document. The sealed portion could be a duplicate copy of the exterior text, thus resulting in equal halves sealed and unsealed, or one of the texts could be abridged so that either the sealed or unsealed portion was longer than the other.[51] Although this practice was most commonly done using softer, more perishable material, such as parchment or papyrus, it could be done using metal plates as well. Roman military diplomas on bronze plates were bound shut by a wire so that the text on the exterior of the plates could be read and used in day-to-day interactions, but the text on the interior of the plates was sealed up so that it could only be accessed by cutting the wire and breaking the seal, an action intended to take place in a legal setting.[52] John W. Welch has noted that the Book of Mormon documents the binding covenants of the Lord, similar to the purposes of partially sealed legal documents of antiquity.[53]

Sealing a document did not merely mean binding all or a portion of it so it could not be read, but also normally included witnesses or authorities impressing their seal on the document to certify that the text was authoritative and legally binding. Many of the doubled and sealed legal documents of antiquity feature three seals, while the Roman bronze diplomas frequently had seven.[54] The copper plates found in India typically include a bronze seal soldered to the ring or welded directly onto an inscribed copper plate, "intended to certify the authenticity of the document and to prevent tampering by the addition or removal of plates."[55] On a small copper amulet found in Galilee and inscribed bilingually in Hebrew and Greek, the opening invocation written in Hebrew concludes

---

51. See John W. Welch, "Doubled, Sealed, Witnessed Documents: From the Ancient World to the Book of Mormon," in *Mormons, Scripture, and the Ancient World: Studies in Honor of John L. Sorenson*, ed. Davis Bitton (Provo, UT: FARMS, 1998), 391–444.
52. Welch, "Doubled, Sealed, Witnessed Documents," 401–404, fig. 5; Welch and Lambert, "Two Ancient Roman Plates," 57–59; Welch, "Seven Seals," 407.
53. Welch, "Doubled, Sealed, Witnessed Documents," 421–437.
54. Welch, "Doubled, Sealed, Witnessed Documents," 401; Welch, "Seven Seals,"406–407.
55. Salomon, *Indian Epigraphy*, 114. See Bianchini, "Legally Binding," fig. 4 for an example of the seal being welded directly to a copper plate.

with the divine name (YHWH) inscribed in a seal-like circular design, likely meant to "seal" the prayer with God's name.[56]

The Book of Mormon was "sealed by the hand of Moroni" (title page), and the last thing he did before he "seal[ed] up these records" was invoke the name of "the great Jehovah [YHWH]" (Moroni 10:2, 34). This "sealing" by Moroni may have included him somehow affixing or engraving his seal onto the final plate.[57] Although none of the witnesses described such a detail, Charles Anthon said that on the transcript brought to him by Martin Harris—which Martin reportedly identified as "the manuscript title page"—there was "a circle divided into various compartments … evidently copied after the Mexican Calendar," or "Mexican Zodiac."[58] Others who apparently saw the document said it resembled a Turkish passport, which would have included a circular seal.[59] Another source close to Martin said that the last plate had "a circle

56. Roy Kotansky, "An Inscribed Copper Amulet from ʿEvron," *ʿAtiqot* 20 (1991): 81–87. On "sealing" with the divine name (and using circular patterns to do so) in late antiquity and the Middle Ages, see Jarl E. Fossum, *The Name of God and the Angel of the Lord: Samaritan and Jewish Concepts of Intermediation and the Origin of Gnosticism* (Tübingen: Morh Siebeck, 1985), 245–253; Marla Segol, *Word and Image in Medieval Kabbalah: The Texts, Commentaries, and Diagrams of Sefer Yetsirah* (New York, NY: Palgrave Macmillan, 2012), 92, 99, 106, 109, 111–112.
57. Joseph Smith, History Draft, ca. June–October 1839 [Draft 1], p. 9 indicates that the title page was translated "from the last leaf of the plates." As noted by William J. Hamblin, "Metal Plates and the Book of Mormon," in *Pressing Forward with the Book of Mormon: The FARMS Updates of the 1990s*, ed. John W. Welch and Melvin J. Thorne (Provo, UT: FARMS, 1999), 20–22, this is consistent with the ancient Near Eastern practice of *subscriptio*.
58. Charles Anthon to E. D. Howe, 17 February 1834, in Morris, *DHBM* 231; Charles Anthon to Rev. T. W. Coit, 3 April 1841, Morris, *DHBM* 232. On Martin identifying this document as a transcript of the untranslated title page, see Orsamus Turner, *History of the Pioneer Settlement of Phelps and Gorham's Purchase, and Morris' Reserve* (Rochester, NY: William Alling, 1852), 215, which also describes the document as having "concentric circles."
59. See Don Bradley, *The Lost 116 Pages: Reconstructing the Book of Mormon's Missing Stories* (Salt Lake City, UT: Greg Kofford Books, 2019), 23–24; Michael Hubbard MacKay, "'Git Them Translated': Translating the Characters on the Gold Plates," in *Approaching Antiquity: Joseph Smith and the Ancient World*, ed. Lincoln H. Blumell, Matthew J. Grey, and Andrew H. Hedges (Provo, UT: Religious Studies Center; Salt Lake City: Deseret Book, 2015), 93; Erin B. Jennings, "Charles Anthon—The Man Behind the Letters," *John Whitmer Historical Association Journal* 32, no. 2 (2012): 171–172.

with rays proceeding from it resembling the sun."[60] This circular design described in these sources may have been Moroni's seal, engraved onto the title page as a witness to the record's purity (see 1 Nephi 14:26).[61]

Dimensions

Moving on from the general design of the plates, witnesses also provided many details regarding the size and dimensions of the record they examined. This includes details about the size of individual plates, and of the record as a whole, specifically providing details about its height (or thickness) and weight. These allow comparisons to both singular metal plates and tablets of similar dimensions, as well as to the total volume or quantity of metal used in longer examples of metallic epigraphy from the pre-modern world.

Individual Plates

Joseph Smith said "each plate was six inches wide and eight inches long."[62] The same dimensions were reported by Palmyra printer Jonathan Hadley in 1829 shortly after he spoke with Joseph Smith and Martin Harris about potentially printing the translation.[63] Lucy Mack Smith, who handled the covered plates, also gave these same dimensions to Henry Caswall when he visited Nauvoo.[64] Others gave estimates that varied by an inch or two. For example, according to Orson Pratt, the Eight Witnesses generally described the plates as "about eight inches in length, and from six to seven in breadth."[65] While preaching roughly a

---

60. Francis Gladden Bishop, *An Address to the Sons and Daughters of Zion, Scattered Abroad, Throughout All the Earth* (Kirtland, OH: F. G. Bishop, 1851), 48, as cited in Bradley, *Lost 116 Pages*, 23. Although Bishop claims to know this due to his own vision of the plates, Bradley suggests he actually gleaned it from conversations with Martin.
61. See Bradley, *Lost 116 Pages*, 20–26.
62. Joseph Smith, "Church History," 707.
63. Jonathan A. Hadley, "Golden Bible," *Palmyra Freeman* (11 August 1829), reprinted in *Rochester Advertiser and Daily Telegraph* (31 August 1829), in Morris, *DHBM*, 238. "Golden Bible," *The Rochester Gem* 1 (5 September 1829), in Morris, *DHBM*, 491 reports the same information, attributing it to Martin Harris.
64. Henry Caswall, *The City of the Mormons* (London: J. G. F. & J. Rivington, 1842), 27. On Lucy handling the plates while covered, see Sally Parker to John Kempton, 26 August 1838, in Janiece L. Johnson, "'The Scripture Is a Fulfilling': Sally Parker's Weave," *BYU Studies* 44, no. 2 (2005): 115–116.
65. Orson Pratt, "Evidences of the Bible and Book of Mormon Compared," delivered

year after seeing the plates, Samuel H. Smith said each plate was "about 8 inches long [and] 5 or 6 wide."[66] On separate occasions, both David Whitmer and Martin Harris estimated that the plates were "about eight inches long, seven inches wide."[67] Oliver Cowdery was reported as estimating their size as slightly smaller, "7 inches in length, 6 inches in breadth."[68] In a later reminiscence Fayette Lapham recalled Joseph Smith Sr. estimating their size as "about six inches wide, and nine or ten inches long."[69] A Palmyra newspaper reported that one of the Whitmers remembered the plates as "being something like 8 inches square," although the newspaper's informant admitted this detail may be imprecise.[70] In a late reminiscence, a childhood friend of Joseph Smith's sister Sophronia recalled frequently seeing Joseph carrying "what he claimed were the plates ... covered with a cloth" and said "they appeared to be six or eight inches square."[71] Each witness is only providing an estimate based on their recollections of previous interactions with the plates, so these minor variances are to be expected; nonetheless, the different accounts provide a generally consistent picture of the *approximate* size of each plate as being around 6–8 inches wide and 7–9 inches long.

---

in the Tabernacle, Salt Lake City, 2 January 1859, *Journal of Discourses* 7:31. See also Poulson to *Deseret News*, 31 July 1878, in Morris, *DHBM*, 453 for an identical description from John Whitmer.

66. W. E. McLellin to S. McLellin, 4 August 1832.
67. *Chicago Tribune*, 17 December 1885; *Chicago Tribune*, 24 January 1888, both in Cook, *David Whitmer Interviews*, 172, 221; Tiffany, "MORMONISM—No. 2," 165, in Morris, *DHBM*, 194; "A witness to the Book of Mormon." *Daily Iowa State Register*, 28 August 1870, online at sidneyrigdon.com (accessed 22 August 2023).
68. "The Golden Bible, or Campbellism Improved," in Morris, *DHBM*, 385.
69. Fayette Lapham, "Interview with the Father of Joseph Smith, the Mormon Prophet, Forty Years Ago. His Account of the Finding of the Sacred Plates," *Historical Magazine* 8, no. 5 (May 1870): 307, in Morris, *DHBM*, 114. In Murdock to *Congregational Observer*, in *EMD* 1:479, William Smith is quoted as estimating the plates to be "eight or ten inches long, less in width." See also the estimate of "about six by nine inches in size" in "David Whitmer," *Kansas City Journal*, 5 June 1881, in Cook, *David Whitmer Interviews*, 64.
70. "Golden Bible, no. 6," in *EMD* 2:249.
71. Mrs. S. F. Anderick, signed statement, 24 June 1887, in *Naked Truths about Mormonism* (Oakland, CA) 1, no. 1 (January 1888), 2, online at sidneyrigdon.com (accessed 15 April 2024).

Ancient metal plates come in a variety of shapes and sizes, including some that are similar in size to the Book of Mormon plates. For example, a set of gold plates found in South Korea, dated to 6th–7th century AD, consisted of plates that measured 17.4 cm long by 14.8 cm wide, which is approximately 7 x 6 inches.[72] In Japan, numerous copper or bronze plates have been found which generally date to the Heian period (AD 794–1185) and measure 21 cm long by 18 cm wide, or about 8 x 7 inches.[73] A trilingual gold tablet from the 6th century BC, found at the ancient site of Ecbatana (modern-day Hamadan, Iran), is close to 8 inches square.[74] Some 6 x 8 inch sheets of gold inscribed with hieroglyphs were recovered from a royal tomb in Egypt.[75] In Yemen, ancient bronze plaques have been found of various sizes, including some that are about 6 x 7 inches, 6 x 8 inches, and 8 x 8 inches.[76] All of these approximate the estimates given by one or more witnesses to the Book of Mormon plates.

The thickness of each individual plate was more difficult for witnesses to estimate, since it was only fractions of an inch. The most common method was to compare it to the thickness of more familiar material,

72. Peter Kornicki and T. H. Barrett, "Buddhist Texts on Gold and Other Metals in East Asia: Preliminary Observations," *Journal of Asian Humanities at Kyushu University* 2 (2017): 115; Park Sang-hyeon, "The Diamond Sutra of the Five-Story Stone Pagoda in Wanggung-Ri is a Relic from the Middle of the 6th Century," *Yonhap News* (Korean), 11 June 2017, online at yna.co.kr (accessed 1 March 2023). These measurements are more precisely 6.85 x 5.83 inches.
73. Kornicki and Barrett, "Buddhist Texts on Gold and Other Metals," 116; Sherry Fowler, "Containers of Sacred Text and Image at Twelfth-Century Choanji in Kyushu," *Artibus Asiae* 74, no. 1 (2014): 50. These measurements are more precisely 8.27 x 7.09 inches.
74. Sidney Smith, "Assyriological Notes," *Journal of the Royal Asiatic Society* 3 (1926): 433 says it "measures about 9 inches square," but Roland G. Kent, "The Recently Published Old Persian Inscriptions," *Journal of the American Oriental Society* 51, no. 3 (1931): 229 says it is 19 x 19 cm, which is about 7.5 inches square.
75. Dennis Forbes, "Cairo Museum in Possession of a Quantity of Gold Which Once Partially Lined the Lid of Coffin from KV 55," *KMT: A Modern Journal of Ancient Egypt* 12, no. 2 (2001): 19–25. It is unclear if these are the original dimensions or if they've been cut/torn to that size in modern times.
76. See Riyāḍ 262F8 (15.5 x 17.5 cm; ca. 6.1 x 6.89 inches); Ja 2195: (20.5 x 14 cm; ca. 8.07 x 5.51 inches); Höfner AF 3: (20 x 13.7 cm; ca. 7.87 x 5.39 inches); FB-wādī Shuḍayf 2: (15.4 x 17 cm; ca. 6.06 x 6.69 inches); Q 905: (20.5 x 19; ca. 8.07 x 7.48 inches), in the Corpus of South Arabian Inscriptions database, online at dasi.cnr.it (accessed 13 September 2023).

usually common tin sheets. Joseph Smith described them as "not quite so thick as common tin," and several others—including each of the Three Witnesses—also compared their thickness to tinplate of their day.[77] The exact thickness of tinplate in the 19th century could vary widely,[78] but the thickness designated as "common" at the time was between 0.012 (ca. 0.03 cm) and 0.0135 inches (ca. 0.034 cm) while the thickest was 0.0239 inches (ca. 0.061 cm).[79] Joseph Smith's brother Samuel estimated that each plate was "about as thick as thin paste board."[80] As with tinplate, the thickness of paste board could vary, but an example of *thin* paste board was the material used to make playing cards of the day. Based on measurements taken by Jerry Grover, 19th century playing cards were between 0.011–0.012 inches (0.028–0.03 cm), a similar thickness to that of "common" tinplate.[81] Other reports compared the thickness of the plates to window glass of their time,[82] which produces much thicker

77. Joseph Smith, "Church History," 707; "The Golden Bible, or Campbellism Improved," in Morris, *DHBM*, 385; Tiffany, "MORMONISM—No. 2," 165, in Morris, *DHBM*, 194; *Chicago Tribune*, 17 December 1885; *Chicago Tribune*, 24 January 1888, both in Cook, *David Whitmer Interviews*, 172, 221; Pratt, "Evidences," *Journal of Discourses* 7:31; "Golden Bible, no. 6," in *EMD* 2:249.
78. Grover, *Ziff, Magic Goggles, and Golden Plates*, 86.
79. Lane Coulter and Maurice Dixon Jr, *New Mexican Tinwork, 1840–1940* (Albuquerque, NM: University of New Mexico Press, 1995), 7 states that thickness of "common" (C) tinplate was 29 gauge (0.0135 inches), while the thickest tinplate available (1XXXX) was 24 gauge (0.0239 inches). According to sizes.com (accessed 15 October 2024), "common" (1C) tinplate was between 0.0117–0.0123 inches thick, most closely approximating 30 gauge (0.012 inches). For conversion of gauges to inches, see custompartnet.com and tinplates.com (both accessed 15 October 2024). Using other sources and his own calculations, Bruce E. Dale, "How Big a Book? Estimating the Total Surface Area of the Book of Mormon Plates," *Interpreter: A Journal of Latter-day Saint Faith and Scholarship* 25 (2017): 262–263 and Bruce E. Dale, "Correction and Additional Calculations for 'How Big a Book?'," comment, 22 June 2017, on Dale, "How Big a Book?," online at journal.interpreterfoundation.org (accessed 26 August 2023) estimated a range of 0.012–0.016 for tinplate in the 19th century. Likewise, Coates, "Combinatorial Approach," 10, 30–35 uses an estimated range of 0.015–0.019 inches, based on his analysis of various historical sources.
80. W. E. McLellin to S. McLellin, 4 August 1832.
81. Jerry Grover, email to author, 16 April 2024. Grover purchased 19th century playing cards and took measurements with a micrometer in December 2023.
82. See Murdock to *Congregational Observer*, in *EMD* 1:479; "Mormonism," *Fredonia Censor*, 7 March 1832, reprinted from the *Franklin Democrat*, ca. March 1832;

estimates—between 0.055 and 0.061 inches (about 0.14 and 0.16 cm).[83]

On one occasion, David Whitmer described them as being "about as thick as parchment."[84] Joseph Smith's wife, Emma, similarly remembered moving the covered plates around, and said they "seemed to be pliable like thick paper, and would rustle with a metallic sound when the edges were moved by the thumb, as one does sometimes thumb the edges of a book."[85] As with tin and paste board, the thickness of paper or parchment varied, but handmade paper created to imitate parchment averaged between 0.0135–0.017 cm (ca. 0.005–0.0067 inches) in thickness during the 19th century while the very thickest paper of the period was around 0.03 cm (ca. 0.011 inches).[86] How thin metal plates have to be to in order to be pliable depends, in part, on their material composition. David Baird, a metallurgist who has made replicas of the Book of Mormon plates, found that thin sheets of brass needed to be between 0.01–0.015 inches (ca. 0.025–0.038 cm) in order to produce a "rustling" sound.[87] Grover ran a series of tests on thin copper plates, and determined that they exhibited "the rustling type sounds described by Emma Smith" at thicknesses between 0.004–0.01 inches (ca. 0.01–0.025 cm), and with a tumbaga plate close to 0.007 inches (0.018 cm).[88]

Overall, this provides a range of 0.005–0.061 inches for the thickness of the plates, with the "pliability" criteria suggesting something closer to the lower end of that spectrum (ca. 0.005–0.015 inches). Inscribed

---

"The Orators of Mormon," *Catholic Telegraph*, 14 April 1832.

83. Grover, *Ziff, Magic Goggles, and Golden Plates*, 86–87.
84. David Whitmer," *Kansas City Journal*, 5 June 1881, in Cook, *David Whitmer Interviews*, 64.
85. "Last Testimony of Sister Emma," *The Saints' Herald*, 1 October 1879, in Morris, *DHBM*, 300.
86. Timothy Barret, Mark Ormsby, and Joseph B. Lang, "Non-Destructive Analysis of 14th–19th Century European Handmade Papers," *Restaurator: International Journal for the Preservation of Library and Archival Material* 37, no. 2 (2016): 107, fig. 10. I have included the highest and lowest points within one standard deviation of the average on the Barret et al. chart.
87. David Baird, Interviewed by Mark Goodman for The Interpreter Foundation, 7 February 2019, 00:28:27.11–00:30:01.8; transcript provided to me courtesy of Daniel C. Peterson and The Interpreter Foundation. An edited version of this interview will eventually be made available on youtube.com.
88. Grover, *Ziff, Magic Goggles, and Golden Plates*, 87–90, quote on p. 89. The tumbaga alloy tested was 85% copper, 12% gold, and 3% silver, which closely approximates what Grover estimates for the plates (see pp. 91–92).

metal plates and ancient sheet metals have been found comparable to all the estimates given by witnesses. The Japanese bronze plates mentioned earlier, which are engraved on both sides, are generally around 0.2 cm (about 0.08 inches) thick, while the engraved gold plates from South Korea mentioned previously, which are only inscribed on a single side, are each 0.15 cm (about 0.06 inches) thick.[89] A large set of copper plates from India, engraved on both sides, are 0.05 inches (0.13 cm).[90] The bronze plates of Roman military diplomas, which are inscribed on both sides, are typically around a millimeter (0.1 cm; about 0.039 in) thick,[91] while the so-called Copper Scroll found at Qumran, inscribed on only one side, is slightly thinner (0.09 cm; about 0.035 inches).[92] In Mesoamerica, gold and gilded copper disks as thin as 0.039–0.062 inches were inscribed with hieroglyphs, battle scenes, and decorative designs.[93] The thickness of any of these metal plates, ranging from 0.035–0.08 inches, might have reasonably been described as comparable to the thickness of window glass (ca. 0.055–0.061 inches) by an 1830s observer.

Closer to the thickness of common tinplate of that era (ca. 0.012–0.0239 inches) is a series of thin tumbaga sheets and polished disks with decorative designs and etchings, recovered from the Nariño, Columbia area, which have an average thickness ranging from 0.033–0.053 cm (about 0.013–0.021 inches).[94] A small tumbaga artifact made out of thin sheeting about 0.03–0.04 cm thick (ca. 0.012–0.016 inches) was

89. Kornicki and Barrett, "Buddhist Texts on Gold and Other Metals," 115–116; Fowler, "Containers of Sacred Text," 50.

90. K. G. Kirshan, *Karandai Tamil Sangam Plates of Rajenrachola I* (New Dehli: Director-General, Archaeological Survey of India, 1984), 2.

91. Welch and Lambert, "Two Ancient Roman Plates," 56.

92. Joan E. Taylor, "Secrets of the Copper Scroll," *Biblical Archaeology Review* 45, no. 4 (2019): 74.

93. See Mary Miller, "Disk G," "Disk H," "Disk F," and Kim N. Richter, "Disk with Ek Chuah," and "Disk," each in *Golden Kingdoms*, 234–237, 245. For more information on the Maya gold and gilded copper disks, see Lothrop, *Metals from the Cenote of Sacrifice*, 28–64, 74–79; Merideth Daniel Paxton, *Gold Disks from the Sacred Cenote at Chichen Itza, Yucatán: Stylistic Analysis and Ethnohistorical Interpretation* (PhD diss.; University of New Mexico, 1975); Coggins and Shane, *Cenote of Sacrifice*, 42–43, 50–51, 94–95, 118–121.

94. Grover, *Ziff, Magic Goggles, and Golden Plates*, 90; David A. Scott, "Depletion Gilding and Surface Treatment of Gold Alloys from the Nariño Area of Ancient Colombia," *Journal of the Historical Metallurgy Society* 17, no. 2 (1983): 104 table 1.

found in Mesoamerica and dated to before AD 500.[95] An equally thin ornamental golden plume found in Peru, dated to between 200 BC and AD 400, was inscribed on both sides with an intricate design.[96] This illustrates that pre-Columbian metalsmiths around the time of Moroni—and perhaps even earlier—were capable of producing gold and tumbaga sheets "not quite so thick as common tin" from the 19th century.

Consistent with Emma's "pliable, like thick paper" descriptor (ca. 0.005–0.011 inches), during the Colonial period "medallions, thin as gold paper" were seen in markets near Tabasco.[97] Bernardino de Sahagún observed goldworkers who could hammer gold "to make it as thin as paper," and in the late 19th-century, Mixtec traders reportedly sold similarly "thin sheets of gold, evidently worked with a hammer … on which were engraved ancient hieroglyphs" to European antiquarians.[98] The discovery of an inscribed Mixtec-style mask made from a thin golden sheet just a tenth of a millimeter thick (0.01 cm; 0.0039 in), with the Nahuatl glyph for "gold" (*teocuitlatl*) engraved over the eyelids, substantially corroborates such reports.[99] Ancient Peruvians also produced gilded copper sheets with "edges that were paper-thin."[100] Tumbaga artifacts from Peru were made of sheets with nearly perfect evenness of 0.02 cm, which converts to slightly less than 0.008 inches.[101] One tumbaga object from Venezuela, dated to the end of the first millennium AD, measures 0.02 cm at the center, but its edges were even thinner—between 0.012–0.017

95. D. M. Pendergast, "Tumbaga Object from the Early Classic Period, Found at Altun Ha, British Honduras (Belize)," *Science* 168 (1970): 116–118.
96. Alicia Boswell, "Ornamental Plume, 200 BC–AD 400," in *Golden Kingdoms*, 158.
97. Román Piña Chan, "Commerce in the Yucatan Peninsula: The Conquest and Colonial Period," in *Mesoamerican Communication Routes and Cultural Contacts*, ed. Thomas A. Lee Jr. and Carlos Navarrete (Provo, UT: New World Archaeological Foundation, Brigham Young University, 1978), 42.
98. José Antinio Gay, *Historia de Oaxaca*, vol. 1 (Mexico, 1881), 62.
99. Stephen Houston, "Essential Luxuries: On Pleasing and Powerful Things among the Maya," in *Golden Kingdoms*, 85, 86 figs. 94–95; Edith Ortiz Diaz, José Luis Ruvalcaba Sil, and Bryan Cockrell, "Mask," in *Golden Kingdoms*, 233; Lothrop, *Metals from the Cenote of Sacrifice*, 64–66; Coggins and Shane, *Cenote of Sacrifice*, 96.
100. Lechtman, "Pre-Columbian Surface Metallurgy," 56.
101. Warwick Bray, "Gold-Working in Ancient America," *Gold Bulletin* 11, no. 4 (1978): 137–138. The conversion of 0.2 mm to the imperial system is more precisely 0.00787 inches.

cm (about 0.005–0.007 inches)—right within the thinness proven to have the pliability needed to "rustle with a metallic sound."[102] The ability of pre-Columbian metalsmiths to create very thin sheets of gold or tumbaga goes back very early, as illustrated by a small tumbaga item from Ecuador, dated to the early first millennium BC, measuring only a tenth of a millimeter at its thickest point.[103] Indeed, "among the earliest worked gold objects from South America" are crown-like diadems, "fabricated of flexible sheet metal that bends easily."[104] Although most of these items were not engraved, in the Old World a silver amulet found in Samaria and engraved on both sides was a mere tenth of a millimeter thick (0.01 cm; 0.0039 in).[105] Tests using tools available to pre-Columbian peoples determined that copper or tumbaga sheets as thin as 0.005 inches could be engraved on both sides without pushing through.[106]

Altogether, it is clear that ancient metalsmiths throughout the world were capable of producing and engraving thin copper and gold plates within the range of thickness estimated for the Book of Mormon plates, based on eyewitness descriptions. Pre-Columbian American metalsmiths, in particular, were capable of making gold, gilded copper, and tumbaga sheets of varying thicknesses, sometimes with engraved or etched designs on the surface, within the range suggested by eyewitness testimony for the Book of Mormon plates (see table 2).

102. Heather Lechtman, "A Tumbaga Object from the High Andes of Venezuela," *American Antiquity* 38, no. 4 (1973): 474. A broken edge was even thinner, 0.003 cm (about 0.001 inches), but this may have been due to the damage to the object.

103. Valdez et al., "Evidencia temprana de metalurigia," 6.

104. Julie Jones, ed., *The Art of Precolumbian Gold: The Jan Mitchell Collection* (New York, NY: The Metropolitan Museum of Art, 1985), 120. Julie Jones and Heidi King, "Gold of the Americas," *Metropolitan Museum of Art Bulletin* 59 (Spring 2002): 13 illustrates an example of such a diadem dating to the early-to-mid first millennium AD.

105. C. Muller-Kessler et al., "An Inscribed Silver Amulet from Samaria," *Palestine Exploration Quarterly* 139, no. 1 (2007): 5–19.

106. Grover, *Ziff, Magic Goggles, and Golden Plates*, 87. On 15 October 2024, Jerry Grover brought a copper sheet only 0.00675 inches thick, electroplated with 10 microns of gold, to the Scripture Central offices. Matt Roper, Jared Riddick, and myself each took turns using a pre-Columbian obsidian awl to engrave 3–4 characters (imitating those found on the "Caractors" document) each on one side. We found it very easy to engrave through the layer of gold without scratching through to the other side of the plate. Grover had also experimented with using a blackening agent to darken one of the characters.

TABLE 2: Thin Metal Plates and Sheets Compared to the Witnesses' Estimates			
Witness Description	**Approximate Measurement**	**Artifacts**	**Thickness Measurement**
About the thickness of window glass	0.055–0.062 inches	Japanese Bronze Plates	0.08 inches
		South Korean Gold Plates	0.06 inches
		Indian Copper Plates	0.05 inches
		Maya Gold/Gilded Copper Disks	0.039–0.062 inches
		Roman Bronze Plates	0.039–0.043 inches
		Qumran Copper Scroll	0.035 inches
About the thickness of common tin	0.012–0.0239 inches	Nariño Tumbaga Disks and Sheets	0.013–0.021 inches
		Honduran Tumbaga Bead	0.012–0.016 inches
		Peruvian Gold Plume	0.012–0.016 inches
Like parchment or thick paper, or paste board; pliable/flexible	0.005–0.011 inches	Mexican Gold Medallions	Like "gold paper"
		Mixtec Gold Sheets	"very thin sheets of gold"
		Moche Gilded Copper Sheets	Edges "paper-thin"
		Golden Diadems	"flexible sheet metal"
		Peruvian Tumbaga Sheets	0.008 inches
		Venezuelan Tumbaga Sheet	0.005–0.007 inches
		Mixtec Gold Mask	0.0039 inches
		Ecuadorian Tumbaga Sheet	0.0039 inches
		Samarian Silver Amulet	0.0039 inches

Height

Joseph Smith recalled that the complete bound set of plates "was something near six inches in thickness."[107] Several other witnesses made similar statements. Oliver Cowdery said they formed "a pile about 6 inches deep,"[108] and Josiah Stowell estimated the stack to be "six inches

107. Joseph Smith, "Church History," 707.
108. "The Golden Bible, or Campbellism Improved," in Morris, *DHBM*, 385.

thick" after handling it while covered.[109] Samuel H. Smith also said they were "alltogether about 6 inches thick,"[110] while William Smith's recollection was that they "made a pile about five or six inches high."[111] Martin Harris gave a slightly smaller estimate, saying that "they were altogether about four inches thick."[112] To better compare this dimension to ancient metal plates, it is helpful to get an estimate of how many plates could be included within a 4–6 inch stack.

On the low end, Read Putnam estimated that there could have been 20 plates-per-inch, based on the assumption that each plate was 0.02 inches (about 0.05 cm) thick and there was about 50% void space between each plate.[113] This would allow for between 80–120 plates in a bound set 4–6 inches high. Robert F. Smith modified Putnam's estimates, suggesting that the plates may have ranged between 0.015–0.02 inches and occupied between 0.03–0.05 inches of space, "allowing for

109. "Mormonism," *New England Christian Herald.*

110. W. E. McLellin to S. McLellin, 4 August 1832.

111. Murdock to *Congregational Observer*, in *EMD* 1:479.

112. Tiffany, "MORMONISM—No. 2," 165, in Morris, *DHBM*, 194; David B. Dille, "Additional Testimony of Martin Harris (One of the Three Witnesses) to the Coming forth of the Book of Mormon," 15 September 1853, in *Millennial Star* 21, no. 34 (August 20, 1859): 545. Francis Gladden Bishop, *A Proclamation from the Lord to His people, scattered throughout all the Earth* (Kirtland, OH, 6 April 1851), 48 also described the plates as being "about four inches in thickness," a detail that Bradley, *Lost 116 Pages*, 141 argues came from Martin Harris. Orson Hyde, *Ein Ruf aus der Wüste (A Cry out of the Wilderness)*, 1842, extract, English translation, p. 25, online at josephsmithpapers.org (accessed 15 October 2024), gives a thicker estimate: "The entire book was approximately 8 inches thick." This outlying estimate is decisively ruled out by a key piece of physical evidence, which may favor the slightly smaller estimates of between 4–5 inches: the chest, owned by Hyrum Smith and handed down to his descendants, which was only "6 ¼ inches deep in the back, sloping to 4 inches deep in the front," according to Andrew H. Hedges, "'All My Endeavors to Preserve Them': Protecting the Plates in Palmyra, 22 September–December 1827," *Journal of Book of Mormon Studies* 8, no. 2 (1999): 21. A set of plates 8 inches high simply could not fit within such a box, while a set 4 or 5 inches high would better fit within such a box than a 6 inch stack would, though it's possible the chest "held the plates for only a short time, perhaps because the plates did not fit into the chest well." See Heidi Bennett, "A True Treasure Chest," 26 February 2016, online at history.churchofjesuschrist.org (accessed 3 September 2023); Baird, Interviewed by Goodman, 00:44:18.24–00:45:48.14.

113. Putnam, "Were the Golden Plates Made of Tumbaga?," 830.

air space and irregularities," resulting in an estimate of 120–200 plates if there were 6 inches worth of plates, and 80–134 plates if there were only 4 inches worth of plates.[114] Using a mathematical model to determine all valid configurations of the plates within the parameters described by the witnesses, Josh Coates concluded that there could be between 187–259 plates, assuming that the plates were between 0.015–0.019 inches thick and there was between 40–60% void space.[115] On the higher end, Jerry Grover concluded that to be pliable, the plates had to be much thinner—between 0.005–0.01 inches thick, as previously discussed—and thus estimates that there could have been between 300–600 total plates in a 6-inch stack (200–400 in a 4-inch stack), with 50% void space due to uneven hammering of the plates.[116] Estimates for the total number of plates in the bound set thus range widely from 80 to 600. Converting these estimates into surface area (for easier comparison) based on a plate size of 6 x 8 inches comes out to a minimum of 7,680 in^2 of plate space and a maximum of 57,600 in^2 (counting both the front and back of each plate).

Most examples of writing on metal plates are relatively short and written on one or two metallic surfaces, and thus even the lower end of this range is somewhat unusual for the ancient world. Binding together multiple plates into a "book," however, is not totally unprecedented, and the total surface area of some metallic documents is comparable to the total surface area estimated for the stack of Book of Mormon plates. The previously mentioned South Korean gold plates are bound by hinges into a book of 19 plates containing the *Diamond Sutra*, a sacred Buddhist text, and three other similarly bound books of Buddhist writings on gold plates have been found in South Korea, one of 16 plates and two of 14 plates each.[117] The so-called "Copper Scroll," found among the Dead Sea

114. Smith, "The 'Golden' Plates," 276.
115. Coates, "Combinatorial Approach," 10–12 (step 4), 13 figs. 3 and 4.
116. Grover, *Ziff, Magic Goggles, and Golden Plates*, 92, scenarios 3 and 4.
117. Kornicki and Barrett, "Buddhist Texts on Gold and Other Metals," 115–117. As noted, the individual plates of the book of 19 plates are very similar in size to those of the Book of Mormon, but they are somewhat smaller than the standardized dimensions of 6 x 8 inches I've assumed for the purposes of determining the potential surface area of the Book of Mormon plates set. At 17.4 x 14.8 cm per plate, the 19 plates have a total surface area of 9785.76 cm^2 (counting both the front and back), or about 1516.8 in^2, which is the equivalent of about 16 standardized 6 x 8 plates.

Scrolls, is actually multiple sheets of copper riveted together to form one long "scroll" that measures about 229 x 29.18 cm (90.16 x 11.49 in)—a total surface area that is equivalent to about 22 Book of Mormon plates (13,421.54 cm^2/2,080.34 in^2, front and back).[118] Although not bound together, 9 bronze tablets were discovered in Italy describing the rituals and sacred decrees of the pre-Roman priestly order *Fratres Atiedii*, akin to the so-called Priestly source in the Pentateuch.[119] Two of the nine tablets have been lost, but the total surface area of the remaining seven tablets is equivalent to approximately 61 Book of Mormon plates (5,849.34 in^2, front and back).[120] The surviving tablets are "probably only a portion of the entire records of the Fratres Atiedii,"[121] suggesting there may have been a far more extensive collection of bronze tablets in antiquity. A Roman legal code from the first century AD was engraved on 10 bronze tablets which, when affixed to the wall side-by-side, spanned nearly 30 feet in length! Each tablet is about 57.5 x 91.5 cm (ca. 22.64 x 36.02 inches), making the total surface area (16,309.86 in^2, counting the front and the back) the equivalent of approximately 170 Book of Mormon

118. Measurements given in Émile Puech, *The Copper Scroll Revisited* (Boston, MA: Brill, 2015), 8. Note that the width is inconsistent, and I've provided an average based on the six measurements she reports. The total surface area was calculated from the dimensions of each individual sheet (not the total) and then added to together. Throughout this section, I provide estimates for the equivalent number of "Book of Mormon plates" by taking the total surface area of the metal document (including both front and back of the artifacts) and dividing by 96, the total surface area (in inches squared) of a single 6 x 8 plate, front and back. All totals are approximate, rounded to the nearest whole number.
119. See Irene Rosenzweig, *Ritual and Cults of Pre-Roman Iguvium* (London: Christophers, 1937); James Wilson Poultney, *The Bronze Tables of Iguvium* (Baltimore, MD: American Philological Association, 1959). Rosenweig notes that early reports state there were originally nine, which is supported by the fact that one of the tablets has an incomplete decree (p. 9).
120. Measurements of all seven surviving tablets are available in Michael Weiss, *Language and Ritual in Sabelli Italy: The Ritual Complex of the Third and Fourth* Tabulae Iguvinae (Boston, MA: Brill, 2010), 4n5. Assuming the missing two tablets are at least as large as the smallest surviving tablet (40 x 28 cm, ca. 15.75 x 11.02 inches), then the complete set of nine—which is still probably only a portion of the ancient records of this religious order—would be equivalent to about 68 Book of Mormon plates.
121. Rosenzweig, *Ritual and Cults of Pre-Roman Iguvium*, 112.

plates—well within the 80–600 range established for the 4–6 inch stack of plates.[122]

Two copies of the Quran have been discovered in China, engraved on gilded copper plates. One is dated to the 15th century, and consists of 30 sets of about 20 plates each, bound together by hinges (604 plates total). Each plate is 11 x 16 cm (ca. 4.33 x 6.3 in), and thus the total surface area is the equivalent of about 343 Book of Mormon plates (212,608 cm^2; 32,954.3 in^2, front and back).[123] Although this example is admittedly quite late, another gold-gilded Quran reportedly dates to 7th or 8th century AD, according to Daniel C. Peterson.[124] It is claimed to have been discovered in a Tang Dynasty (ca. AD 618–907) tomb, and destructive chemical testing performed on the gold gilding support a date between AD 600–1000.[125] This Quran consists of 6 sets of 20 plates each, for a total 120 plates.[126] Each plate is 38 x 24 cm (ca. 14.96 x 9.44 in) for a total surface area equal to about 353 Book of Mormon plates (218,880 cm^2; 33,926.5 in^2, front and back).[127]

As previously noted, thousands of inscribed copper plates from ancient and medieval India have been discovered, many of which contain lengthy texts written across several plates bound together. The largest sets

---

122. Julián Gonzálaz and Michael Crawford, "The Lex Irnitana: A New Copy of the Flavian Municipal Law," *Journal of Roman Studies* 76 (1986): 147–243; Carlos Sánches-Moreno Ellart, "Lex Irnitana," in *Encyclopedia of Ancient History*, ed. Roger S. Bagnall et al. (Blackwell Publishing, 2013), 4040–4042. Ellart reports that the tablets are 57.5 x 91.5 cm, which is equal to 22.64 x 36.02 inches = 815.4928 x 10 = 8154.928 x 2 = 16309.856/96 = 169.89 (~170) plates.

123. Salmah Hj Ahmad, *Gold Tooling Quran: A Scientific (Forensic) Analysis Report on the Ancient Al-Quran Mushaf–A Report on the Writing of Written Copy of Quran on Sheets of Gold Plated Pages* (Bangi, Selangor, Malaysia: National University of Malaysia, 2016); images of this report are available online at worldtopantiques.blogspot.com (accessed 16 October 2024). See also Scripture Central, "Evidence #265: Gold Books," online at scripturecentral.org (accessed 16 October 2024).

124. Daniel C. Peterson, Interviewed by Camrey Bagley Fox for The Interpreter Foundation, "Witnesses of the Book of Mormon Insights, Episode 28: Ancient Metal Plates," min. 5:21–5:45, online at youtube.com (accessed 16 October 2024).

125. Stephen O. Smoot, notes taken 19 January 2024, while examining the plates with an agent of the private owner of these plates. I appreciate Smoot sharing these notes with me.

126. Sorenson, "Metallurgical Plausibility"; Smoot, notes.

127. Individual plate measurements provided in Smoot, notes.

include 21, 31, 57, and 86 plates, all dated to the 10th or 11th century AD.[128] When the total available surface area (front and back) of these copper plates is calculated, the set of 57 plates is equivalent to about 174 Book of Mormon plates, and the set of 86 is equivalent to 258 Book of Mormon plates, bringing both within the range proposed for the 4–6 inch volume described by witnesses.[129] Perhaps most impressive of all, a copy of the *Tevaram*—a sacred corpus of nearly 800 hymns and poems written in the 7th–8th centuries AD—were engraved onto nearly 500 large copper plates discovered in 2023 near Nagapatinam, India.[130] These plates were not bound together, but they nonetheless contain a defined corpus of texts within the Shaiva canon, and are written on a total surface area equivalent to more than 800 Book of Mormon plates (see table 3). Thus, there are examples of sets of metal plates whose total available surface area is comparable to that estimated for the set of plates containing the Book of Mormon.

In addition to these extant examples of large sets of plates, ancient Buddhist historical sources describe even longer sacred texts inscribed on copper and gold. Sources from the 6th–7th centuries AD report that King Kanishka (ca. 127–150 AD), founder of the Kushan Dynasty in

---

128. V. Subrahmanya Aiyer, "The Larger Leiden Plates (Of Rajaraja I)," *Epigraphia Indica* 22 (1933–1934): 213–266; Rao Sahib and H. Krishna Sastri, "The Tiruvalangadu Copper-Plates of the Sixth Year of Rajendra-Chola I," in *South Indian Inscriptions, vol. 3: Miscellaneous Inscriptions in Tamil*, part 3 (Madras, India: Superintendent, Government Press, 1920): 383–439; Kirshan, *Karandai Tamil Sangam Plates*; S. Sankaranarayanan, N. Marxia Gandhi, A. Padmavathy, R. Sivanantham, eds., *Tiruvindalur Copper Plate Charter of Chōḻa King Rajendra II Regnal Year 4 (AD 1058)* (Chenai: Tamilnadu State Department of Archaeology, 2011). For more on these lengthy sets of plates and similarities to the Book of Mormon plates, see Evidence Central, "Book of Mormon Evidence #248: Lengthy Indian Plates," online at evidencecentral.org (accessed 30 August 2023).

129. For measurements on these plates, see the sources from Aiyer, Kirshan, and Sankaranarayanan et al. cited in n.128. Plate size for the Karandai Sangam Plates vary, so multiple dimensions are given with the number of plates that size in parenthesis.

130. "1000-Year-Old Copper Plates And Panchaloha Statues Unearthed in Sattainathar Temple In Nagapattinam District," *The Commune*, 18 April 2023, online at thecommunemag.com (accessed 20 September 2023). The size of each plate is reported to be 68 x 7.5 cm (~26.77 x 2.95 in). For background on the Tevaram, see "Welcome to Digital Tēvāram," online at ifpindia.org (accessed 20 September 2023).

TABLE 3: Surface Area of Large Sets of Metal Plates				
Set of Plates	**Total No. Plates**	**Plate Dimensions**	**Total Surface Area (front and back)**	**Total Book of Mormon Plates Equivalent**
Larger Leiden Plates	21	14 x 5 in	2,940 in^2	~31 plates
Karandai Sangam Plates	57	16.5 x 9.5 in (3) 16.5 x 9 in (21) 13.8 x 9 in (1) 16.3 x 9 in (28) 16 x 8 in (2) 15.2 x 8.3 in (2)	16,710.34 in^2	~174 plates
Tiruvindalur Plates	86	17.3 x 8.3 in	24,697.48 in^2	~258 plates
15th c. Gilded Copper Quran	604	4.33 x 6.3 in	32,954.3 in^2	~343 plates
Tang Dynasty Gilded Copper Quran	120	14.96 x 9.44 in	33,926.5 in^2	~353 plates
Teravam Plates	493	26.8 x 3 in	77,870.84 in^2	~812 plates

northern India, had *The Great Commentary*—the second longest ancient Buddhist text, consisting of 300,000 stanzas and over 1 million verses—copied onto copper plates and stored in stone boxes.[131] The longest Buddhist sutra, *The Perfection of Wisdom*—consisting of 6.4 million Chinese characters—was copied onto leaves of gold by the 8th century monk Shanwuwei, according to his 10th century biographer.[132] The existence of substantial writings on copper and gold from South Asia lends some plausibility to these traditions, but whether or not they are true, they illustrate that some ancient people at least *conceived* of the idea of writing very lengthy religious texts onto metal plates.

131. See Kōgen Mizuno, *Buddhist Sutras: Origin, Development, Transmission* (Tokyo: Kosei Publishing, 1982), 91, 161; Thomas Watters, *On Yuan Chwang's Travels in India 629–645 AD* (London: Royal Asiatic Society, 1904), 271. See also Evidence Central, "Book of Mormon Evidence #242: Large Collections of Metal Plates," online at evidencecentral.org (accessed 30 August 2023).

132. See David B. Honey and Michael P. Lyon, "An Inscribed Chinese Gold Plate in Its Context: Glimpses of the Sacred Center," in *The Disciple as Scholar: Essays on Scripture and the Ancient World in Honor of Richard Lloyd Anderson*, ed. Stephen D. Ricks, Donald W. Parry, and Andrew H. Hedges (Provo, UT: FARMS, 2000), 42. For additional background on Shanwuwei, see "Shan-wu-wei," Nichiren Buddhism Library, online at nichirenlibrary.org (accessed 30 August 2023). On Zanning, see "Zanning," online at encyclopedia.com (accessed 30 August 2023).

Sizable archives of metal documents have also been discovered or reported in historical sources. An archive of 2,289 copper plates was found in India containing the lifetime works (~13,000 compositions) of a single 15th century Hindu saint, poet, and musical composer.[133] The ancient Roman historian Suetonius described an archive of more than 3,000 bronze tablets that was destroyed by fire in the first century AD.[134] Roman archival documents on bronze likely numbered in the hundreds of thousands, although only a small percentage of them have survived. For example, between 800–1,200 bronze military diplomas have been recovered, but scholars estimate that as many as 100,000 were issued by the Roman Empire between the 1st–3rd centuries AD.[135] Duplicates of these diplomas were made and archived in Rome itself "for more than two hundred years." Yet according to Werner Eck, "Of this enormous mass of bronze documents not a single small piece has been found in Rome—nothing at all."[136] These examples illustrate that not only is a metallic record of 6 x 8 inch plates stacked 4–6 inches in depth not beyond the scope of attested historical precedents, but even larger collections of writings were archived on metal plates in the ancient world, similar to the larger repository of metallic records alluded to in the Book of Mormon (see Words of Mormon 1:3; 4 Nephi 1:48; Mormon 1:1–4; 4:23; 6:6).[137]

---

133. Velcheru Narayana Rao and David Shulman, trans., *God on the Hill: Temple Poems from Turpati* (New York, NY: Oxford University Press, 2005), 104–105.

134. *The Life of Vespasian*, 8:5, in C. Suetonius Tranquillas, *The Lives of the Twelve Caesars*, trans. J. C. Rolfe (1913–1914), online penelope.uchicago.edu (accessed 30 August 2023).

135. See Leman Altuntas, "A 2000-year-old Bronze Military Diploma was Discovered in Turkey's Perre Ancient City," *Arkeo News*, 2 January 2022, online at arkeonews.net (accessed 30 August 2023); "Roman Military Diploma On-Line," at romancoins.info (accessed 30 August 2023).

136. Werner Eck, "Documents on Bronze: A Phenomenon of the Roman West?" in *Ancient Documents and their Contexts: First North American Congress of Greek and Latin Epigraphy (2011)*, ed. John Bodel and Nora Dimitrova (Boston, MA: Brill, 2015), 130.

137. While we should not assume that everything in the larger Nephite record repository was written on metal plates, several records are described as such, including the plates of brass (1 Nephi 5:10–19; Alma 37:3–5), both the large and small plates of Nephi (1 Nephi 6:1; 9:2–4; 19:1–7; 2 Nephi 5:30–32; Jacob 1:1–4; 3:13–14; Words of Mormon 1:3–7; Alma 37:2; 3 Nephi 5:10), the plates of Zeniff (Mosiah 8:5), the plates of Ether (Mosiah 8:9; 28:11; Ether 1:2), and the plates of

Weight

Joseph Smith told his neighbor Willard Chase "he should think [the plates] would weigh sixty pounds, and was sure it would weigh forty."[138] Martin Harris said, "I hefted the plates many times, and should think they weighed forty or fifty pounds."[139] On another occasion, Martin described the plates as "weighing altogether, from forty to sixty lbs."[140] William Smith, who hefted them while covered, said on multiple occasions that they "weighed about sixty pounds."[141] In a late recollection, Fayette Lapham said that Joseph Smith Sr. judged the plates to have "weighed thirty pounds."[142] In total, these estimates provide a range from 30–60 pounds, with most of the estimates favoring something above 40 pounds.

A solid block of gold or even copper the size of the plates would weigh substantially more, but thin sheets of metal would have to be hammered in antiquity, and thus typically were not perfectly even, leaving void space in between individual plates in a stack. The Korean gold plates, for instance, are visibly uneven, and images of them piled on top of each other show gaps which are sometimes thicker than the plates themselves. Jerry Grover has noted that thin tumbaga disks and sheets from near Nariño, Columbia, dated to AD 800–1200, had a thickness variation ranging between 5–39%, which could create void space as high as 78% if they were stacked on top of each other. Grover thus surmises that there could have been an average of 50% void space between the

---

Mormon (Mormon 8:14; these are the plates given to Joseph Smith).

138. Testimony of Willard Chase, 11 December 1833, in Howe, *Mormonism Unvailed*, 246, in Morris, *DHMB*, 72.

139. Tiffany, "MORMONISM—No. 2," 166, in Morris, *DHBM*, 194.

140. "A witness to the Book of Mormon." *Daily Iowa State Register*, 28 August 1870, online at sidneyrigdon.com (accessed 26 August 2023).

141. William Smith, *William Smith on Mormonism* (Lamoni, IA: Herald Steam Book and Job Office, 1883), 12; "The Old Soldier's Testimony," 644; Peterson, "Wm. B. Smith's Last Statement," 6, in *EMD* 1:511.

142. Lapham, "Interview with the Father of Joseph Smith," 307, in Morris, *DHBM*, 114. Cornelious Blatchly, a New York newspaper editor, had heard that the plates weighed around 30 pounds as early as December 1829, though his source for this is not stated. See Cornelious C. Blatchly, "The New Bible," *Gospel Luminary* 2, no. 49 (10 December 1829): 194, in Morris, *DHBM*, 495; Cornelious C. Blatchly, "Caution Against the Golden Bible," *New-York Telescope* 6, no. 38 (20 February 1830):150, in Morris, *DHBM*, 501.

plates.[143] More recently, Josh Coates conducted an experiment wherein he stacked 165 copper discs, with an average thickness of 0.020 inches, and found that "the calculated resting void is approximately 55%." When compression was applied to the stack, the void space was reduced to approximately 42%.[144]

Read Putnam calculated that tumbaga plates with 8-karat gold and 50% air space between the plates would have weighed about 53 pounds, while tumbaga plates with 12-karat gold would have weighed just under 87 pounds.[145] More recently, Grover accounted for several more variables in estimating the weight of the plates and considered four possible scenarios, adjusting for variations in void space and plate thickness. The first two scenarios Grover considered employed an average of 12% and 30% void space, respectively, but the weight of the plates significantly exceeded the 60-pound limit given by the witnesses.[146] In his last two scenarios, he estimated an average of 50% void space and assumed the plates were gilded copper between 0.005 and 0.01 inches thick—resulting in calculations of 57.9 pounds and 53.6 pounds, respectively.[147] Under this final scenario, 60 pound tumbaga plates would have to consist of around 85.2–87.6% copper, 11.4–11.8% gold (about 3-karats), and between 0.6–3.4% silver.[148] Using the density of tumbaga with these ratios, Bruce Dale calculated how many plates between 0.008–0.016 inches thick would add up to the 20–30 pounds consisting of the unsealed portion.[149] Doubling his estimates to account for the full set of plates indicates that somewhere between 140–418 tumbaga plates would have weighed between 40–60 pounds.[150]

---

143. Grover, *Ziff, Magic Goggles, and Golden Plates*, 90, with calculations based on the data in Scott, "Depletion Gilding and Surface Treatment of Gold Alloys," 104 table 1. Jerry Grover, personal communication, 27 September 2023, explained that if "at least one maximum deflection abutted another maximum deflection on the adjacent plates," it would create a void space of 78% (39 x 2).

144. Coates, "Combinatorial Approach," 30 (appendix D).

145. Putnam, "Were the Golden Plates Made of Tumbaga?," 830–831.

146. Grover, *Ziff, Magic Goggles, and Golden Plates*, 91–92, scenarios 1 and 2.

147. Grover, *Ziff, Magic Goggles, and Golden Plates*, 92, scenarios 3 and 4.

148. Grover, *Ziff, Magic Goggles, and Golden Plates*, 92–93.

149. Dale, "How Big a Book?," 264–265.

150. Dale, "Correction and Additional Calculations," comment on "How Big a Book?," estimates a maximum of 209 plates 0.008 inches thick within a 30 pound stack and minimum of 69.7 plates 0.016 inches thick within a 20 pound stack.

Both Putnam and Grover based their calculations on the assumption that the bound set of plates was 6 inches thick. Since witness statements actually provide a range of 4–6 inches for the height of the bound volume (see previous section), reducing the weight calculations by one-third gives an approximation of how much the plates would weigh in each scenario if the volume of plates was closer to only 4 inches thick. Interestingly, when this adjustment is made the weight range of the plates across the six different scenarios proposed by either Putnam or Grover is 35–66 pounds, fairly close to the 30–60 pound range provided by the witnesses (see table 4).

Adjustments to other variables—such as the copper-to-gold ratio, the average void space, and the thickness of the individual plates—could also be explored. Coates used an algorithm to calculate literally billions of possible configurations based on incremental adjustments to all known variables, but found that when the void space is assumed to be between 40–60% (a number derived from his experiment, mentioned above), then a 5.5–6.25 inch stack of tumbaga plates with less than 20% gold-alloy content would come out to be at least 55 pounds.[151] For my purposes, these various calculations sufficiently illustrate that a set of plates made from either tumbaga or gilded copper stacked between 4–6 inches high could have fallen within the estimated weight range provided by the witnesses.

In terms of real world examples, the large sets of copper plates from India weigh substantially more than the weight estimated for the golden plates—the set of 86 copper plates weighs over 330 pounds, and the set of 57 copper plates weighs almost 250, while the smaller set of 31 plates weighs just over 200 pounds.[152] The recently discovered *Tevaram* plates individually weigh just less than a pound (~14.1 oz.), with the whole set weighing more than 430 pounds.[153] These are much heavier than the

151. Coates, "Combinatorial Approach," 13 fig. 4.

152. N. Marxia Gandhi, "Thiru Indalur Copper Plate: A Study," *Bulletin of the Department of Museums, Chennai: Tourism Endowment Lecture* (Chennai: The Director, Museums Department, 2016), 3. Exact weight is given in kilograms as 150 (330.7 lbs.), 111.73 (246.3 lbs.), and 92 (202.8 lbs.), respectively.

153. The weight of the Tevaram plates is reported in "1000-Year-Old Copper Plates" as 400 grams (~14.1 oz) per plate. 400 x 493 = 197,200 grams for the whole set, or about 434.75 lbs. Interestingly, since the surface area of the 493 plates is equivalent to 811.15 Book of Mormon plates, dividing 434.75/811.15 = 0.536 pounds per Book of Mormon plate, or about 8.5 oz. The number of plates this

TABLE 4: Estimated Weight of 4–6 inch Stack of Tumbaga Plates		
Scenario	**6-inch**	**4-inch**
Putnam, 8-karat scenario (50% void space, 0.02 in plates)	53.44 lbs.	35.63 lbs.
Putnam, 12-karat scenario (50% void space, 0.02 in plates)	86.83 lbs.	57.9 lbs.
Grover, scenario 1 (12% void space, 0.005 in plates)	99.3 lbs.	66.2 lbs.
Grover, scenario 2 (30% void space, 0.005 in plates)	79.7 lbs.	53.14 lbs.
Grover, scenario 3 (50% void space, 0.005 in plates)	57.9 lbs.	38.6 lbs.
Grover, scenario 4 (50% void space, 0.01 in plates)	53.6 lbs.	35.73 lbs.

estimated weight of the Book of Mormon plates—likely because the individual plates were thicker than the leaves of the golden plates—and thus they serve to illustrate that 30–60 pounds worth of inscribed metal plates is well within the range of historical precedents.

Characters

Witnesses also provided various details about the characters they saw on the plates, from identifying its script, to how small, compact, and densely written it was, to the color of the characters against the golden backdrop of the plates. Once again, these are also features that can be compared to various examples of ancient inscriptions on metal and other surfaces.

Script

The Book of Mormon reports that the original text was written in Egyptian (1 Nephi 1:2), or "reformed Egyptian," and states that the writers also knew Hebrew (Mormon 9:32). This likely influenced how the witnesses interpreted the script they saw on the plates, since none of them could have had more than a passing familiarity with ancient languages. Thus, Oliver Cowdery described the plates' script as "ancient Egyptian characters" or "reformed Egyptian characters," closely adhering to the text's own statements.[154] Similarly, Samuel H. Smith said the plates had "engravings of reformed Egyptian Hieroglyphical characters."[155] In 1842,

would allow for in 40–60 pounds is between 75–113, which closely approximates the 80–120 plates derived from Putnam's estimates for the Book of Mormon plates.

154. Cowdery to Blatchly, 9 November 1829, in Morris, *DHBM*, 375; A. W. B., "Mormonites," *Evangelical Magazine and Gospel Advocate* 2, no. 15 (9 April 1831): 120, in Morris, *DHBM*, 349.

155. W. E. McLellin to S. McLellin, 4 August 1832.

Joseph Smith also said that the plates "were filled with engravings, in Egyptian characters,"[156] but in earlier sources he and others in his family seem to simply refer the script on the plates as "hieroglyphics," a term that was frequently used more generically to refer to ancient scripts in the early 1800s.[157] By 1842, however, Joseph had studied the hieratic script on the Joseph Smith Papyri, so perhaps he had recognized a similarity to the Book of Mormon script that gave him more confidence in identifying the characters as Egyptian.[158] Indeed, Oliver Cowdery observed a resemblance between the hieratic script of the papyri and "a number of characters … which were previously copied from the plates."[159]

Curiously, others related the script to languages never mentioned in the text. For instance, Hyrum Smith and William McLellin said the plates had "Arabic characters inscribed on them" while preaching together in Illinois,[160] and Fayette Lapham recalled Joseph Smith Sr. saying that "with few exceptions, the characters were Arabic."[161] Martin Harris described the characters as a mixture of four different languages:

156. Joseph Smith, "Church History," 707.

157. Jesse Smith to Hyrum Smith, 17 June 1829, in Morris, *DHBM*, 366; Hadley, "Golden Bible," in Morris, *DHBM*, 238. Morris, *DHBM*, 228 notes that "hieroglyphics" could be used "to refer to ancient writing in general" in that period. Blatchly, "The New Bible," in Morris, *DHBM*, 494 distinguishes between hieroglyphics and Egyptian characters.

158. For accessible introductions to and images of the Joseph Smith Papyri, see John Gee, *A Guide to the Joseph Smith Papyri* (Provo, UT: FARMS, 2000); John Gee, *An Introduction to the Book of Abraham* (Salt Lake City, UT: Deseret Book; Provo, UT: Religious Studies Center, Brigham Young University, 2017), 13–42, 57–81; Stephen O. Smoot et al., *A Guide to the Book of Abraham* (Provo, UT: BYU Studies, 2022), 13–28. For academic editions of the papyri, see Michael D. Rhoads, *The Hor Book of Breathings: A Translation and Commentary*, Studies in the Book of Abraham 2 (Provo, UT: FARMS, 2002); Michael D. Rhoads, *Books of the Dead Belonging to Tshemmin and Neferirnub: A Translation and Commentary*, Studies in the Book of Abraham 4 (Provo, UT: Neal A. Maxwell Institute, 2010); Robin Scott Jensen and Brian M. Hauglid, eds., *Revelations and Translations, vol. 4: Book of Abraham and Related Manuscripts*, The Joseph Smith Papers (Salt Lake City, UT: Church Historian's Press, 2018).

159. Oliver Cowdery to William Frye, 22 December 1835, in "Egyptian Mummies—Ancient Records," *Latter-day Saint Messenger and Advocate* 2, no. 3 (December 1835): 235.

160. "Mormonism," in Kirkham, *New Witness*, 2: 405.

161. Lapham, "Interview with the Father of Joseph Smith," 307, in Morris, *DHBM*, 114.

"Arabic, Chaldaic, Syriac, and Egyptian."[162] These unexpected statements were most likely influenced by Martin's conversations about the characters with Charles Anthon and other scholars in 1828.[163] Indeed, Martin specifically cited Anthon as his source for linking the script to each of the languages he mentioned, and Joseph Sr. had apparently heard that it was "the most learned man then in [New York] city" who said the script was Arabic.[164] Anthon later denied providing such an assessment, but it is unlikely Martin would have associated the Book of Mormon characters with all these languages without the influence of Anthon or another scholar well versed in the contemporary linguistic studies of the time.[165]

162. Tiffany, "MORMONISM—No. 2," 162, in Morris, *DHBM*, 192.

163. See Richard E. Bennett, "'Read This I Pray Thee': Martin Harris and the Three Wise Men of the East," *Journal of Mormon History* 36, no. 1 (2010): 178–216; Richard E. Bennett, "Martin Harris's 1828 Visit to Luther Bradish, Charles Anthon, and Samuel Mitchill," in *The Coming Forth of the Book of Mormon*, 103–115; Michael Hubbard MacKay and Gerrit J. Dirkmaat, *From Darkness Unto Light: Joseph Smith's Translation and Publication of the Book of Mormon* (Salt Lake City, UT: Deseret Book; Provo, UT: Religious Studies Center, Brigham Young University, 2015), 39–59.

164. See Joseph Smith, History Draft, ca. June 1839–ca. 1841 [Draft 2], p. 9; Dille, "Additional Testimony of Martin Harris," 545; Lapham, "Interview with the Father of Joseph Smith," 307, in Morris, *DHBM*, 114.

165. Anthon to Howe; Anthon to Coit; Charles Anthon to William E. Vibbert, 12 August 1844, in "A Fact in the Mormon Imposture," *New York Observer* 23, no. 69 (3 May 1845), each in Morris, *DHBM*, 230–236. It is possible that some of the other scholars and "learned men" Martin talked to made some of the associations he remembered, and later stories conflated what he learned from others with what Anthon said. For example, some accounts indicate that Luther Bradish compared the transcribed characters to his Turkish Passport, which would have used a variant of Arabic (the Ottoman Turkish script), and an early (but third-hand) source said it was actually Samuel Mitchill who compared the script with Egyptian. See Richard E. Bennett, "'A Very Particular Friend': Luther Bradish," in *Approaching Antiquity*, 63–82; Richard E. Bennett, "'A Nation Now Extinct,' American Origin Theories as of 1820: Samuel L. Mitchill, Martin Harris, and the New York Theory," *Journal of Book of Mormon and Other Restoration Scripture* 20, no. 2 (2011): 30–51. Anthon admitted to seeing a resemblance to Hebrew (see n.170). So the recollection of the characters being compared to Arabic, Egyptian, and Chaldaic (Aramaic/Hebrew script) could be an amalgamation of what Martin heard from Bradish, Mitchill, and Anthon combined.

In the early 1800s, "Chaldaic" or "Chaldean" was used to refer to the Aramaic script, which was also commonly used to write Hebrew, and academic sources known to Anthon at the time compared demotic Egyptian to Arabic and Syriac.[166] W. W. Phelps had heard from Martin that Anthon identified the script as "the ancient shorthand Egyptian," a contemporary academic term for hieratic, also likely known to Anthon.[167] Thus, the languages Martin remembers Anthon (or perhaps another scholar) mentioning suggest that someone with an academic background in ancient languages did see a resemblance to both Hebrew and Egyptian (i.e., demotic and hieratic) scripts.[168] This is consistent with William Smith's understanding that Anthon "pronounced the characters to be ancient Hebrew corrupted, and the language to be degenerate Hebrew with a mixture of Egyptian."[169] Interestingly, even in his denials Anthon did grant that some of the characters looked like "rude imitations of Hebrew," or Hebrew letters "more or less distorted," but maintained that it was mixed with similarly distorted Greek, rather than Egyptian.[170]

It is noteworthy that texts using a combination of Hebrew and Egyptian script have been discovered in ancient Israel, including a few examples of Hebrew and hieratic signs inscribed onto bronze weights.[171] Two

---

166. See Evidence Central, "Book of Mormon Evidence #219: The Anthon Account," online at evidencecentral.org (accessed 9 September 2023).
167. W. W. Phelps to E. D. Howe, 15 January 1831, in Morris, *DHBM*, 240; Evidence Central, "Anthon Account."
168. Based on the account canonized as Joseph Smith—History 1:64, John S. Thompson, "Looking Again at the Anthon Transcript(s)," *Interpreter: A Journal of Latter-day Saint Faith and Scholarship* 63 (2025): 353–366, argues that Anthon was shown a transcript of two sets of characters, one that he pronounced as Egyptian that had been correctly translated and then another that he compared to Egyptian, Chaldaic, Assyriac, and Arabic. Thompson reasons that Anthon was struggling to identify the "reformed Egyptian" script from the large plates (and hence compared it to various languages) but correctly identified the script from the small plates as "short-hand Egyptian," i.e., hieratic.
169. Murdock to *Congregational Observer*, in *EMD* 1:479.
170. Anthon to Vibbert, in Morris, *DHBM*, 235; Anthon to Coit, in Morris, *DHBM* 232.
171. See Stefan Wimmer, *Palästiniches Hieratisch: Die Zahl- und Sonderzeichen in der althebräishen Schrift* (Wiesbaden: Harraossowitz, 2008); David Calabro, "The Hieratic Scribal Tradition in Preexilic Judah," in *Evolving Egypt: Innovation, Appropriation, and Reinterpretation in Ancient Egypt*, ed. Kerry Muhlestein and John Gee (Oxford, Eng.: Archaeopress, 2012), 77–85. For previous studies

small silver scrolls inscribed in Hebrew and dated to about the time of Lehi also include hieratic signs representing a cartouche demarcating the divine name (YHWH).[172] While these inscriptions only use minor Egyptian elements, they nonetheless illustrate that Israelites in the early first millennium BC were indeed mixing Hebrew with hieratic Egyptian in metallic inscriptions. Inscribed gold and silver amulets from the Israelites' neighbors, the Phoenicians, more prominently feature Egyptian iconography and hieroglyphs alongside short prayers inscribed in Phoenician (a Semitic language closely related to Hebrew).[173]

In addition to the witnesses' descriptions, a small sample of characters copied from the plates has survived to the present-day in the form of the "Caractors" document and a few other sources.[174] Researchers have compared these surviving examples of Book of Mormon script to both Old and New World scripts, with the most detailed studies by Ariel L. Crowley and (more recently) Jerry Grover finding a strong resemblance to demotic and/or hieratic.[175] Some prominent non-Latter-day Saint

---

applying these findings to the Book of Mormon, see Stephen D. Ricks and John A. Tvedtnes, "Jewish and Other Semitic Texts Written in Egyptian Characters," *Journal of Book of Mormon Studies* 5, no. 2 (1996): 156–163; John S. Thompson, "Lehi and Egypt," in *Glimpses of Lehi's Jerusalem*, ed. John W. Welch, David Rolph Seely, and Jo Ann H. Seely (Provo, UT: FARMS, 2004), 259–276; Neal Rappleye, "Learning Nephi's Language: Creating a Context for 1 Nephi 1:2," *Interpreter: A Journal of Mormon Scripture* 16 (2015): 151–159. On the bronze weights with Hebrew and hieratic signs, see Wimmer, *Palästiniches Hieratisch*, 162–166, 168.

172. Wimmer, *Palästiniches Hieratisch*, 144–146.

173. Günter Hölbl, *Ägyptisches Kulturgut im Phönikischen und Punischen Sardinien I* (Leiden: E. J. Brill, 1986), 345–358; Carolina López-Ruiz, "Near Eastern Precedents of the 'Orphic' Gold Tablets: The Phoenician Missing Link," *Journal of Ancient Near Eastern Religions* 15 (2015): 63–70.

174. See Jerry D. Grover Jr., *Translation of the "Caractors" Document*, revised and updated (Provo, UT: Challex Scientific Publications, 2019), 21–23 for description of the additional copies of Book of Mormon characters.

175. See R. C. Webb, "Egyptology and the Book of Mormon," *Improvement Era* 26, no. 6 (1923): 546–554; Ariel L. Crowley, "The Anthon Transcript II: The Identification of the Characters as Egyptian," *Improvement Era* 45, no. 2 (1942): 76–80, 124–125; Grover, *Translation of the "Caractors" Document*. For comparisons to New World scripts, see Carl Hugh Jones, "The 'Anthon Transcript' and Two Mesoamerican Seals," *Newsletter and Proceedings of the SEHA* 122 (September 1970): 1–8. Note, however, that according to John E. Clark, "Exposing Book of Mormon Plagiarism: A Proposed Solution to the Book's

Egyptologists have even expressed the view that the document could, in fact, be copies of either a hieratic or demotic text. For example, William C. Hays said, "The inscription … could conceivably have been an inaccurate copy of an Egyptian account or something of the sort written in hieratic script."[176] In a meeting with Stanley Kimball, Hays even identified the beginning sequence as a date formula, and transcribed what it would look like in hieroglyphs.[177] Another Egyptologist, Richard Parker, assisted Crowley with his hieratic and demotic identifications, and told an avid anti-Mormon, "I have seen copies of the signs purportedly from the Book of Mormon and they could well be the latest form of the written [Egyptian] language—demotic characters."[178] In addition, Hugh Nibley saw a striking resemblance between the Book of Mormon characters and meroitic cursive—a script adapted (or "reformed") from demotic to write the non-Egyptian language spoken anciently in Sudan.[179]

It should come as no surprise that the Nephite script is not a perfect match to either hieratic or demotic since the available inventory of hieratic and demotic texts engraved on metal is limited,[180] and "the ductus of hieratic (and demotic) that has been engraved is altered from that

---

Authorship," in *Remembrance and Return: Papers in Honor of Louis C. Midgley*, ed. Ted Vaggalis and Daniel C. Peterson (Orem, UT: Interpreter Foundation; Salt Lake City, UT: Eborn Books, 2019), 244 the Tlatilco seal has been dated to 900 BC, and so would pre-date the arrival the Nephites' Egyptian writing system in the Americas.

176. William C. Hays to Paul M. Hanson, 8 June 1956, in Paul M. Hanson, "The Transcript from the Plates of the Book of Mormon," *Sants' Herald* 103 (12 November 1956): 1098. Hanson also received letters from Alan H. Gardiner and John A. Wilson, both of whom did not believe the script resembled any form of Egyptian.
177. Stanley B. Kimball, "A Visit with Dr. Hayes," *Sunstone* 123 (July 2002): 12–13; Stanley B. Kimball to John W. Welch, 1 November 1994.
178. Richard A. Parker to Marvin W. Cowen, 22 March 1966; FARMS Staff, "Martin Harris's Visit with Charles Anthon: Collected Documents on the Anthon Transcript and 'Shorthand Egyptian'" (FARMS Papers, 1990), 7, citing personal correspondence with Richard Bushman.
179. Hugh Nibley, *Since Cumorah*, 3rd ed. (Salt Lake City, UT: Deseret Book; Provo, UT: FARMS, 1988), 149–150; Hugh Nibley, *The Prophetic Book of Mormon* (Salt Lake City, UT: Deseret Book; Provo, UT: FARMS, 1989), 386–387.
180. See Evidence Central, "Book of Mormon Evidence #316: Egyptian Inscriptions on Metal Plates," online at evidencecentral.org (accessed 11 September 2023).

found on papyrus."[181] Furthermore, the Nephite script underwent about a thousand years of its own evolution independent of (and isolated from) other Egyptian scripts, likely influenced by the Nephites' New World linguistic milieu—which not only means we should expect differences with other forms of Egyptian script, but it also contributes to the difficulty in interpreting the small sample of surviving script, favorable comparisons to hieratic and demotic notwithstanding.[182] In this respect, the Book of Mormon "Caractors" are similar to another "reformed Egyptian" script which survives in a limited corpus of texts inscribed onto bronze and stone: the so-call Byblos script or Byblos syllabic inscriptions.[183] As William J. Hamblin often observed, "it would not be unreasonable to describe the Byblos Syllabic texts as a Semitic language written on metal plates in reformed Egyptian characters, which is precisely what the Book of Mormon describes."[184] Despite the fact that these inscriptions display a strong affinity to Egyptian and many interpretations have been offered based on their presumed relationship, "the script must still be considered as undeciphered."[185] Like the Byblos script, the available sample of Book of Mormon characters is plausibly a copy of a script derived from Egyptian, consistent with both the claims of the text and the testimony

181. John Gee, "Two Notes on Egyptian Script," *Journal of Book of Mormon Studies* 5, no. 1 (1996): 164–165.

182. The best attempt to deal with these issues and provide a translation of the "Caractors" document is Grover, *Translation of the "Caractors" Document*, which provides much useful commentary and analysis of the surviving samples of Book of Mormon script. Nonetheless, the Book of Mormon script is generally considered undeciphered by most Book of Mormon scholars. For a general comment on some of the difficulties in attempting to translate it, see John Gee, "Some Notes on the Anthon Transcript," *FARMS Review of Books* 12, no. 1 (2000): 7–8.

183. See George E. Mendenhall, "Languages, Byblos Syllabic Inscriptions," in *The Anchor Bible Dictionary*, 6 vols., ed. David Noel Freedman (New York, NY: Double Day, 1992), 4:178–180; Fred C. Woudhuizen, "On the Byblos Script," *Ugarit-Forschungen* 39 (2007): 689–756; Juan-Pablo Vita and José-Ángel Zamora, "The Byblos Script," in *Paths in Script Formation in the Ancient Mediterranean*, ed. Silvia Ferrar and Miguel Valério (Rome: Edizioni Quasar, 2018), 75–102.

184. William J. Hamblin, "Reformed Egyptian," *FARMS Review* 19, no. 1 (2007): 33. See also Hamblin, "Sacred Writing on Metal Plates," 43; Hamblin, "Metal Plates and the Book of Mormon," 21.

185. Vita and Zamora, "Byblos Script," 75.

of those who saw the plates or a more extensive but now lost transcript of their characters.

Size and Density

According to Joseph Smith, each plate was "filled with engravings" which were "small, and beautifully engraved."[186] One of the Whitmers may have indicated that the characters actually varied in size, describing them as "divers and wonderful *characters*; some of them large and some small."[187] Fayette Lapham recalled Joseph Smith Sr. saying that the plates "were closely written over in characters."[188] John Whitmer said each plate had "fine engravings on both sides."[189] Martin Harris reportedly described the record as "metallic plates covered with characters."[190] A Palmyra resident who knew Martin Harris and Joseph Smith had heard that "each leaf or plate was filled on both sides with engravings of finely-drawn characters."[191] Echoing what the witnesses reported, Parley P. Pratt also said that the plates "were filled with engravings on both sides."[192]

What constitutes "small" or "large" engravings is obviously a subjective judgment, but the overall impression one gets from these sources is that the space on each plate was maximized to its fullest extent. The Book of Mormon itself frequently gives the impression that the scribes were often concerned about limited space on the plates and took measures (such as choosing a more concise writing system) to ensure the maximum amount of text possible could fit onto each plate.[193]

---

186. Joseph Smith, "Church History," 707.
187. "Golden Bible, no. 6," in *EMD* 2:249. Size variation in script could be due to some scribes writing in a smaller, more cramped script when they were running out of space (Jarom 1:2; Omni 1:30; Mormon 8:5; 9:32–33).
188. Lapham, "Interview with the Father of Joseph Smith," 307, in Morris, *DHBM*, 114.
189. Theodore Turley Memoranda, ca. February 1845, Historian's Office, Joseph Smith History Documents (1839–1860), Church History Library, CR 100-396.
190. John A. Clark, *Gleanings By the Way* (Philadelphia: W. J. & J. K. Simon, 1842), 226, in Morris, *DHBM*, 91.
191. Pomeroy Tucker, *Origin, Rise, and Progress of Mormonism: Biography of Its Founders and History of Its Church* (New York, NY: D. Appleton and Co., 1867), 34, in Morris, *DHBM*, 199.
192. Parley P. Pratt, "Discovery of an Ancient Record in America," *Millennial Star* 1, no. 2 (1840): 30.
193. See 1 Nephi 6:1–2; 19:6; 2 Nephi 5:4; Jacob 1:2–3; 4:1–2; Jarom 1:2, 14; Omni 1:30; Words of Mormon 1:5; Mormon 8:5; 9:32–33.

The exact size of the inscribed characters on each plate cannot be known with certainty, but we do know that the source text of the entire Book of Mormon, plus that of the lost manuscript, must have fit on the unsealed portion of the plates. The original English text of the Book of Mormon consisted of 269,528 words.[194] The number of English words in the lost manuscript can be estimated from the number of words-per-page in the original manuscript, which was about 554–555 words based on an estimated 486 pages.[195] This means there would have been about 64,332 words on the 116 lost pages,[196] and thus the total number of words in the English translation of the unsealed plates must be around 333,860.

As determined earlier, estimates for the total number of plates range widely from 80–600. This would allow for a maximum number of 400 unsealed plates (assuming 600 total plates, with one-third being sealed), and a minimum of 27 plates (assuming 80 total plates, with two-thirds being sealed). If there were 400 plates, this would mean about 835 English words were derived from one plate (front and back) on average, whereas if the source text were only inscribed onto 27 plates, it would come out to about 12,365 English words per plate. Assuming the plates were 6 x 8 inches, these figures would indicate that there was somewhere

---

194. Royal Skousen, ed., *The Book of Mormon: The Earliest Text* (New Haven, CT: Yale University Press, 2022), xii states that the word total is 270,012, from which I have subtracted the 484 words (by my count) that are part of the witnesses' statements.

195. Royal Skousen and Robin Scott Jensen, eds., *Joseph Smith Papers—Revelations and Translations, vol. 5: Original Manuscript of the Book of Mormon* (Salt Lake City, UT: Church Historian's Press, 2021), 3 place the total at 488, from which I have subtracted 2 to account for the two pages which likely had the witnesses statements on them, per Royal Skousen, ed., *The Original Manuscript of the Book of Mormon* (Provo, UT: FARMS, 2001), 36.

196. 269,528/486 = 554.584 words per page; 554.584 x 116 ≈ 64,332. While there is some evidence to suggest that the lost manuscript was actually more than 116 pages, this remains a subject of some debate among scholars. See Bradley, *Lost 116 Pages*, 84–101; Clifford P. Jones, "'That Which You Have Translated, Which You Have Retained'," *Interpreter: A Journal of Latter-day Saint Faith and Scholarship* 43 (2021): 47–61. Coates, "Combinatorial Approach," 17–18, 36–37 (appendix F) argues that the lost manuscript was actually *shorter* than 1 Nephi–Omni. For the purposes of just getting a minimum estimated number of words-per-plate, I am content to use the standard number of lost pages (116). Interested readers are welcome to explore calculations using larger (or smaller) numbers of assumed lost pages.

between 8.7 to 128.8 translated words per square inch of the plates. Obviously, we do not know the exact relationship between the translation and the original text, but the clear implication is that this was a very compactly written text.

The extreme end of this spectrum—cramming the entire source text of the Book of Mormon onto a mere 27 plates—may seem implausible, but in 1923 Janne M. Sjodahl had Henry Miller, a Jewish convert, write out a Hebrew translation of 2 Nephi 5:20–11:3 onto a single 7 x 8 inch sheet of paper—the approximate dimensions of the Book of Mormon plates, according to some sources (see the section on Individual Plates). Based on this, Sjodahl calculated that the entire Book of Mormon could have fit on 21 plates.[197] Factoring in the additional text of the lost manuscript brings the plate total to 26, just under the 27 plates estimated as the *minimum* number of plates.[198] Miller wrote using modern Hebrew script, but when he re-did the experiment using the paleo-Hebrew script contemporary with Lehi, he was only able to fit half as much text onto a single 7 x 8 sheet, and thus Sjodahl calculated this would require 41 plates to fit the entire Book of Mormon text.[199] When the text of the lost manuscript is accounted for, this comes out to about 51 plates—still on the lower end of the estimated range of available plates.[200] Nonetheless, in 2001 John Gee argued that the type of Hebrew script is less important than the *size* of the characters. Comparing Miller's 1.5 mm characters in his original transcript to engraved pre-exilic Hebrew inscriptions, Gee

---

197. Janne M. Sjodahl, "The Book of Mormon Plates," *Improvement Era* 26, no. 6 (1923): 541–545; reprinted in *Journal of Book of Mormon Studies* 10, no. 1 (2001): 22–24, 79. See also Janne M. Sjodahl, *An Introduction to the Study of the Book of Mormon* (Salt Lake City, UT: Deseret News Press, 1927), 35–46.

198. If these numbers are adjusted to the slightly smaller plate size (6 x 8 inches) assumed in my calculations on the number of plates, it brings the total number of plates to just over 30, but keeping in mind (1) that "reformed Egyptian" was said to be *more* compact than the Nephites' Hebrew (Mormon 9:32–33), and (2) the portion sealed is merely an estimate from witnesses, not an exact measurement, I still think this reasonably supports the bare minimum number of plates potentially available.

199. Sjodahl, *Introduction*, 40–41. This second time he used a Hebrew translation of 2 Nephi 11:4–16:9.

200. Once again, adjusting these numbers for the slightly smaller plate size (6 x 8 inches), the total number of plates comes out to just under 60.

found "the characters used anciently are about the same size as those that Sjodahl's scribe used."[201]

A hundred years after Sjodahl's experiment, we now can more directly examine the writing density of actual examples of metallic epigraphy to get a better measurement of how small and compact such texts could be. Arguably, given the languages mentioned in the text and by witnesses (see the section on Script) the most relevant comparisons would be to metallic inscriptions in cursive Egyptian scripts (hieratic and demotic), and the next most relevant would be pre-exilic Hebrew. Existing examples of both are fairly limited—but what we do have suggests that scribes using both scripts could write small, high-density texts on limited metallic space.

A number of silver and bronze votive objects from the Dendera temple in Egypt, dated to between 30 BC to AD 14, were inscribed with both demotic and hieroglyphic texts.[202] One bronze plate about 20.75 x 8.75 inches contains a demotic inscription with 58 lines, which requires each line to be about one-third of an inch (just under a centimeter) in height.[203] There is considerable damage along the edges of the tablet, and thus the translation is incomplete, but based on the total surface area of the extant portions of the text, this yields about 9.1 translated words per square inch.[204] This comes in just above the minimum words per square

201. John Gee, "Epigraphic Considerations on Janne Sjodahl's Experiment with Nephite Writing," *Journal of Book of Mormon Studies* 10, no. 1 (2001): 25.

202. A. F. Shore, "Votive Objects from Dendera of the Greaco-Roman Period," in *Glimpses of Ancient Egypt: Studies in Honour of H. W. Fairman*, ed. John Ruffle, G. A. Gaballa, and Kenneth A. Kitchen (Warminster, Eng.: Aris and Phillips, 1979), 138–159.

203. Shore, "Votive Objects from Dendera," 141. The bottom inch of the tablet is blank, so the 58 lines fit length-wise onto 19.75 inches. 19.75/58 ≈ 0.34 inches (ca. 0.87 cm) per line.

204. Shore, "Votive Objects from Dendera," 146–149 provides a transliteration and translation, and includes the number of inches missing for each line. The total surface area of the 58 lines is 172.8125 in^2 (19.75 x 8.75). Six lines are too damaged to yield any translation at all, so when the approximate surface area of these lines is subtracted (6 x 0.34052 = 2.43 x 8.75 = 17.876 in^2) there remains 154.94 in^2 for 52 lines of text. Adding the measurements for the missing portions of each line given by Shore and multiplying it by the height of each line (199.5 x 0.34052 = 67.94) reduces the surface area of the surviving text to about 87 in^2. The surviving text is translated by Shore into 772 English words. To this, I add 19 more to make up for 19 lacunae that are not measured (and therefore their

inch (8.7) required for the Book of Mormon text, and at this density the entire Book of Mormon could have fit onto about 383 plates.

The signs of this demotic text, however, are actually comparatively large. Hebrew inscriptions found on two small silver scrolls at Ketef Hinnom, dated to about 600 BC, illustrate that scribes in Jerusalem at Lehi's time could inscribe very small Hebrew letters onto metal surfaces.[205] The first scroll is the larger of the two, at 2.7 x 9.7 cm (about 1.06 x 3.82 inches). It has 18 lines of text with 126 Hebrew characters on it. The average size of each character is 5 mm (less than 0.2 inches), while the smallest is 1.7 mm (about 0.067 inches).[206] The second scroll is only 1.1 x 3.9 cm (about 0.43 x 1.54 inches), has 12 lines with 102 Hebrew characters, the largest of which is only 3.5 mm (less than 0.14 inches).[207]

The text of the first scroll translates into 59 English words, but damage to the scroll makes portions illegible (or completely missing).[208] Based on the average number of words in the extant lines, the full original text would probably translate into about 71 English words.[209] Since the scroll is 4.06 inches squared, there are about 17.5 translated words per square inch, well above the minimum 8.7 required for the Book of Mormon text to fit onto the plates. If the Book of Mormon text were written at that same word density, it would require just under 200 plates.[210] The second, smaller scroll is even more compact, translating

---

space has not been subtracted from the total), assuming each accounts for about 1 missing word. 791/87.006 = 9.09 translated words per square inch.

205. See Gabriel Barkay, "The Priestly Benediction in Silver Plaques from Ketef Hinnom in Jerusalem," *Tel Aviv* 19, no. 2 (1992): 139–192; Gabriel Barkay et al., "The Amulets from Ketef Hinnom: A New Edition and Evaluation," *Bulletin of the American Schools of Oriental Research* 334 (2004): 41–71; Jeremy D. Smoak, *The Priestly Blessing in Inscription and Scripture* (New York, NY: Oxford University Press, 2016); Jeremy D. Smoak, "Words Unseen," *Biblical Archaeology Review* 44, no. 1 (2018): 52–59, 70.

206. Barkay, "Priestly Benediction in Silver," 149.

207. Barkay, "Priestly Benediction in Silver," 151.

208. See the translations in Barkay et al., "Amulets from Ketef Hinnom," 61; Smoak, "Words Unseen," 55.

209. I arrived at this number by first adding 4 words to the total of 59 because there is at least 1 missing word from lines 3 and 8, and a minimum of two words missing from line 1. Then, dividing 63 by the number of extant lines (16) comes to about 4 words per line; I then added 8 to 63 to account for lines 2 and 7, which are completely missing.

210. This was determined by multiplying 17.49 x 96 (square inches of each plate,

to 38 English words.[211] Again accounting for damaged portions of the text using the average words per extant line, the full original text would likely translate to around 41 words,[212] all from text inscribed on a meager 0.668 inches squared—coming out to 61.37 translated words per square inch. At this word density, the Book of Mormon text could have fit onto about 57 plates.[213] Thus, based on the only sample of metallic epigraphy from Lehi's Jerusalem, the Book of Mormon text could have fit on anywhere from 57–200 plates. Taking the average translated words per square inch between the two inscriptions (39.43), the Book of Mormon text could have fit onto about 89 plates.[214] If we include the translated words per square inch of the demotic text from the temple of Dendera (9.1), then the average between the three (29.32) would yield about 119 plates needed to fit the Book of Mormon.[215] Either calculation fits comfortably within the estimate range of available plates (27–400), but both are admittedly based on a fairly small sample size.

To get a larger sample size for comparison, we can draw on other inscriptions written in ancient Near Eastern languages, starting with those from closely related Northwest Semitic texts. A small gold scroll from the sixth century BC contains a short inscription in the closely related Phoenician language written in characters 1–3 mm in size and running a total length of 6.5 cm.[216] It translates into 18 English words, which extrapolates to about 58.6 translated words per square inch.[217] Two small metallic scrolls—one of gold and one of silver—inscribed

---

front and back) = 1679.04 words per plate, and then dividing 333,860/1679.04 = 198.84 (~199) plates.

211. See the translations in Barkay et al., "Amulets from Ketef Hinnom," 68; Smoak, "Words Unseen," 55.

212. This scroll was only missing a single line of text, so I simply divided 38 by the number of extant lines (11), which comes out to just under 3.5. Rounding down, for the sake of being conservative, brings us to 41 words.

213. 61.37 x 96 = 5891.52; 333,860/5891.52 = 56.67 (~57) plates.

214. 17.49 + 61.37 = 78.86/2 = 39.43 x 96 = 3785.28; 333860/3785.28 = 88.2 (~89) plates.

215. 17.49 + 61.37 + 9.09 = 87.95/3 = 29.32 x 96 = 2814.4; 333860/2814.4 = 118.63 (~119) plates.

216. López-Ruiz, "Near Eastern Precedents of the 'Orphic' Gold Tablets," 68–69, fig. 4; Maria Giulia Amadasi Guzzo, "Une Lamelle Magique a Inscription Phenicienne," *Vicino Oriente* 13 (2007): 197n3.

217. 6.5 x 0.3 cm = 2.56 x 0.12 inches = 0.307 inches squared. 18/0.307 = 58.63 words per square inch.

with Jewish texts in Aramaic from late antiquity (ca. 5th–6th century AD) have similar word densities, coming out to about 56–57 translated words per square inch.[218] These additional examples of northwest Semitic inscribed on metal are closer to the higher end of the spectrum exemplified in the Ketef Hinnom scrolls. An even more compact example from late antiquity (ca. 5th–7th century AD) is a 52-line inscription found in Iran, written in Mandaic (an eastern dialect of Aramaic) and inscribed on both sides of a small gold scroll just barely larger than an inch squared.[219] The individual characters are close to 1.5 mm, and the 26 lines of text on each side translates into more than 100 words—with second side translating into a whopping 127 words![220] The translated words per square inch of this inscription ranges from about 84.5 to 105.2, with an average of 94.86. If the Book of Mormon were written at a similar density, it could have fit onto as few as 33 plates, with the average based on both sides requiring only a few more (~37) plates.[221] Based on the average translated words per square inch of all six samples of northwest Semitic written on metal (~57.6), the entire Book of Mormon could have been

218. See Roy Kotansky, "Two Inscribed Jewish Aramaic Amulets from Syria," *Israel Exploration Journal* 41, no. 4 (1991): 267–281. The gold scroll is 2.3 x 3.2 cm (ca. 0.906 x 1.25 inches), which is about 1.14 in^2 and its English translation has 65 words (counting the "words" in the untranslatable sequence in parts of lines 6–8 that are merely transliterated). 65/1.14 = 57.02 translated words per square inch. The silver scroll is 2.1 x 4.8 cm (ca. 0.83 x 1.157 inches), which is about 1.57 in^2 and its English translation comes out to 88 words. 88/1.57 = 56.05 translated words per square inch.

219. Christa Müller-Kessler, "A Mandaic Gold Amulet in the British Museum," *Bulletin of the American Schools of Oriental Research* 311 (August 1998): 83–88. The measurements given on the British Museum website, britishmuseum.org (accessed 1 October 2023) for this scroll are 4.1 x 1.9 cm, ca. 1.61 x 0.75 inches and approximately 1.2 in^2.

220. Based on the translation in Müller-Kessler, "Mandaic Gold Amulet," 83–88. At 41 mm long with 26 lines on each side, the average line height is 1.58 mm.

221. The obverse translates into 102 words: 102/1.207 = 84.507 (words per square inch) x 96 = 8,112.672; 333,860/8,112.672 = 41.15 total plates. The reverse translates into 127 words: 127/1.207 = 105.2196 (words per square inch) x 96 = 10,101.082; 333,860/10,101.082 = 33.05 total plates. Taking the total 229 words and total surface area of both sides (2.414 in^2): 229/2.414 = 94.863 (words per square inch) x 96 = 9,106.848; 333,860/9,106.848 = 36.66 total plates. Thus, at the writing density of this text, the Book of Mormon could have fit on 33–41 plates, with the average pointing to about 37 plates.

written on about 61 plates.[222]

Although the examples of such metal amulets inscribed with Semitic languages are fairly rare,[223] according Roy Kotansky, "the practice must have enjoyed a long, perhaps unbroken history" starting "as early as the seventh to fifth centuries B.C.E." and going on into late antiquity.[224] Thus, it seems that for well over a thousand years many scribes in the Syro-Palestine area were capable of inscribing exceptionally small text onto metal surfaces. Even when incorporating Greek—a much less compact language and script—with Hebrew/Aramaic, ancient Jewish scribes could still write texts that translate to 24.5–28.9 words per square inch on a metal surface—well within the range of density needed to accommodate the entire Book of Mormon text on less than 150 plates.[225] In fact, one unusually large silver amulet found in Egypt, and dating to the fifth century AD, includes a lengthy, 38-line inscription in small Greek and Aramaic characters (about 1.6 mm) that translates to about 88 words per square inch—an average that goes up to almost 106 if only the Aramaic portions are considered. Such compact writing could accommodate the entire Book of Mormon within 41 plates (see table 5).[226]

---

222. 17.49 + 61.37 + 58.63 + 57.02 + 56.05 + 94.86 = 345.42/6 = 57.57 x 96 = 5,526.72; 333,860/5,526.72 = 60.4 (~61) plates.

223. Kotansky, "Inscribed Copper Amulet," 81. Greek examples are more prevalent. See Roy Kotansky, *Greek Magical Amulets: The Inscribed Gold, Silver, Copper, and Bronze Lamellae, Part I: Published Texts of Known Provenance* (Westdeutscher Verlag, 1994).

224. Kotansky, "Two Inscribed Jewish Aramaic Amulets," 267.

225. See Kotansky, "Inscribed Copper Amulet," 81–87; Roy D. Kotansky, "A Bilingual Graeco-Aramaic Silver *Lamella* from Jerusalem," *Le Museon* 134, nos. 1–2 (2021): 13–34. The copper amulet, written in Hebrew and Greek, is 4.3 x 7.8 cm, ca. 1.69 x 3.07 inches, so it's about 5.19 inches squared and has 15 lines with 127 words in its English translation. 127/5.1883 = 24.478 words per square inch. The silver amulet is in Aramaic and Greek, 9.5 x 3.8 cm, ca. 3.74 x 1.5 inches, thus about 5.61 inches squared, and has 15 lines with 162 words. 162/5.61 = 28.87 words per square inch.

226. R. Kotansky, J. Naveh, and S. Shaked, "A Greek-Aramaic Silver Amulet from Egypt in the Ashmolean Museum," *Le Muséon* 105 (1992): 5–24. The amulet measures 12 x 6 cm (4.724 x 2.363 in), and is thus 11.15 inches squared. It's 38 lines are written out long ways, and are thus crammed length-wise into the short, 2.362 inches of width, for an average line height of 1.58 mm. The Greek portions from 1–6 and most of lines 29–37 are generally untranslatable magic signs, words, and syllables. "Words" were counted for these lines based on the

While less closely related to the languages and scripts Book of Mormon writers mentioned using, there are numerous examples of Akkadian texts written in cuneiform on gold, silver, and bronze foundation tablets from the late second and early first millennium BC,[227] which also serve to illustrate that ancient Semitic texts could be written at a high density on metal surfaces. Like the metal amulet scrolls, many of these tablets are quite small, yet are covered, front and back, with several lines of cuneiform signs about 3–4 mm in size. The gold tablet of Shalmaneser I (ca. 1273–1244 BC) is 3.45 x 2.41 cm (about 1.36 x 0.95 inches), and yet has 20 lines of text that translate into 64 English words.[228] A similarly sized gold tablet (4 x 2.6 cm, ca. 1.57 x 1.02 inches) of Tukulti-Ninutra I (ca. 1243–1207 BC) contains 21 lines of text, which translate into 87 English words.[229] Shalmaneser III (ca. 859–824 BC) had a small gold tablet about 4.1 x 2.9 cm (ca. 1.61 x 1.14 inches) inscribed with 24 lines of text that translate to 99 English words.[230] Perhaps most impressive of

transliteration and spacing of the signs, with each string of "magic signs" simply counted as one word. As per usually, a word was also added for each lacunae. The Aramaic lines 7–28 are largely intact and smoothly translated, though again occasional lacunae have been accounted for by adding an additional word. The Aramaic portion translates to 651 words, plus 32 lacunae, for 683 words total. Just calculating the surface area of those lines (1.58 mm x 120 mm = 189.47 mm^2 per line; multiplied by 22 lines comes to 3,978.87 mm^2 = 6.461 in^2. 683/6.461 = 105.711 words per square inch). My best estimate for the total words of the whole inscription, based on how transliteration of the Greek portions (and counting the lacunae) is 981. 981/11.15 = 87.982 x 96 = 8446.278; 333,860/8446.278 = 39.527 (~40) plates. If we just used the Aramaic text, the whole Book of Mormon would fit onto about 33 plates (105.711 x 96 = 10,148.256; 333,860/10.148.256 = 32.898).

227. See H. Curtis Wright, "Ancient Burials of Metal Documents in Stone Boxes—Their Implications for Library History," *Journal of Library History* 16, no. 1 (1981): 48–70; H. Curtis Wright, "Ancient Burials of Metallic Foundation Documents in Stone Boxes," *University of Illinois Occasional Papers* 157 (1982).

228. A. Kirk Grayson, *Assyrian Rulers of the Third and Second Millennia BC (to 1115 BC)* (Toronto: University of Toronto Press, 1987), 196; Richard S. Ellis, *Foundation Deposits in Ancient Mesopotamia* (New Haven, CT: Yale University Press, 1968), 97; Laurie E. Pearce, "Materials of Writing and Materiality of Knowledge," in *Gazing on the Deep: Ancient Near Eastern and Other Studies in Honor of Tzvi Abusch*, ed. Jeffrey Stackert, Barbara Nevling Porter, and David P. Wright (Bethesda, MD: CDL Press, 2010), 172.

229. Grayson, *Assyrian Rulers of the Third and Second Millennia BC*, 260–261.

230. A. Kirk Grayson, *Assyrian Rulers of the Early First Millennium BC II (858–745*

TABLE 5: Writing Density of NW Semitic, Demotic, Greek, and Latin Texts on Metallic Surfaces				
Inscription	**Measurements**	**Lines/English Words**	**English Words Per Square Inch**	**Total Book of Mormon Plates**
Northwest Semitic				
Ketef Hinnom I (Silver, Heb.)	1.06 x 3.82 in	18/~71	17.49	~199
Ketef Hinnom II (Silver, Heb.)	0.43 x 1.54 in	12/~41	61.37	~57
Gold Phoenician Amulet	2.56 x 0.12 in	1/18	58.63	~60
Gold Aramaic Amulet	0.906 x 1.26 in	11/65	57.02	~61
Silver Aramaic Amulet	0.83 x 1.89 in	11/88	56.05	~62
Gold Mandaic Amulet	0.75 x 1.61 in	52/229	94.86	~37
Egyptian Demotic				
Bronze Demotic Plate	20.75 x 8.75 in	58/~1,571	9.09	~383
Bilingual (Semitic and Greek)				
Hebrew/Greek Copper Amulet	1.69 x 3.07 in	15/127	24.48	~142
Aramaic/Greek Silver Amulet	3.74 x 1.5 in	15/162	28.87	~121
Egyptian Aramaic/Greek Silver Amulet	4.72 x 2.36 in	38/~981	87.98	~40
Greek and Latin				
Greek Gold Amulet	1.65 x 0.79 in	31/85	65.3	~54
Latin Silver Amulet	1.38 x 0.35	18/74	151.64	~23

these is the gold tablet of Ashurnasirpal II (ca. 883–859 BC), which is about 4.1 x 2.1 cm (ca. 1.61 x 0.83 inches), but contains 18 lines that translate into 122 words.[231] Overall, the writing density of all the metallic

BC) (Toronto: University of Toronto Press, 1996), 99–100.

231. A. Kirk Grayson, *Assyrian Rulers of the Early First Millennium BC I (1114–859 BC)* (Toronto: University of Toronto Press, 1991), 341–342; Ellis, *Foundation Deposits*, 100, 193.

cuneiform tablets ranges from 8.7–45.7 translated words per square inch (see table 6).

Although Indo-European languages are even further removed from the Book of Mormon's linguistic milieu, it is worth considering how compactly even Greek and Latin inscriptions could be written. Unlike the Semitic scripts focused on thus far, these writing systems required writing out both consonants and vowels, and so were less compact than most ancient Near Eastern scripts. Nonetheless, skilled ancient scribes could also inscribe Greek and Latin texts onto metal surfaces in very small script (see table 5). For instance, a third century AD Judeo-Christian text, written in Greek onto a small gold amulet, was inscribed using "almost microscopic size" script, with characters averaging less than 1.4 mm tall and a writing density that could fit the entire Book of Mormon onto just 54 plates.[232] A recently discovered silver amulet, dated to ca. AD 230–270, contains a Christian inscription consisting of 18-lines and 55 Latin words inscribed onto *less than half an inch squared*![233] Multiple translations exist of this text, with different word counts, and depending on which translation is accepted, this text yields between 143 and 170 translated words per square inch—small enough fit the entire Book of Mormon onto as few as 21–25 plates![234]

232. Roy Kotansky, "Two Amulets in the Getty Museum: A Gold Amulet for Aurelia's Epilepsy; An Inscribed Magical-Stone for Fever, 'Chills', and Headache," *J. Paul Getty Museum Journal* 8 (1980): 181–184. The amulet measures 4.2 x 2.0 cm (1.654 x 0.787 inches) and is thus only 1.3 inches squared with 31 lines written length-wise (42 mm/31 = 1.36 mm average line height). It translates to 85 words, with no lacunae, which comes to 65.3 words per square inch (85/1.3). 65.3 x 96 = 6,269.207; 333,860/6,269.207 = 53.25, or about 54 plates.

233. "Der älteste Christ nördlich der Alpen war Frankfurter," *Hessenschau*, December 11, 2024, online at hessenschau.de (accessed June 1, 2025); "Additional information on the Frankfurt silver inscription," *Archaeologisches Museum Frankfurt*, online at archaeologisches-museum-frankfurt.ed (accessed June 1, 2025). The amulet is listed as 35 x 9 mm, which comes out to about 1.38 x 0.35 inches and a total surface area of 0.488 inches squared. 18 lines along the length of 35 mm means that the characters, on average, would be less than 2 mm in size (35/18 = 1.94).

234. "University of Bonn Researcher Involved in Sensational Find in Frankfurt," December 13, 2024, online at uni-bonn.de (accessed June 1, 2025) shows a German translation that consists of 70 words. 70/0.488 in^2 = 143.44 translated words per square inch; 143.44 x 96 = 13,770.24; 333,860/13,770.24 = 24.245 (~25) plates required to fit the Book of Mormon at that rate. Tim Newcomb,

The miniscule writing in many of these examples is no doubt necessitated by the small size of the metallic surfaces being inscribed, but there is no inherent reason why scribes writing on larger metal plates could not also use small script, especially if they were concerned about having sufficient space. In fact, even some longer texts written on larger surfaces still used a fairly small and compact script comparable to what is required to fit the entire Book of Mormon onto the estimated range of plates. For example, a number of Akkadian tablets more than twice the size of the above examples still use compact signs between 2–5 mm in size, and yield between 14.5–21.7 translated words per square inch (see table 6). The bronze cuneiform tablet of Sargon II (ca. 722–705 BC) is approximately the size of a Book of Mormon plate at 19 x 12 cm (ca. 7 x 5 inches) and has 60 lines of text that translate into more than 600 words.[235] The previously mentioned Greek-Aramaic amulet found in Egypt translates to nearly a thousand words, inscribed in characters smaller than 2 mm on a surface nearly one-fourth the size of a Book of Mormon plate. If the full text of the previously mentioned demotic inscription from the Dendera temple had been preserved, it probably would have translated into

---

"Archaeologists Found a Skeleton Wearing an Amulet That May Change the History of Christianity," Popular Mechanics, May 21, 2025, online at popularmechanics.com (accessed June 1, 2025) includes an English translation that consists of 74 words. 74/0.488 in^2 = 151.64 translated words per square inch; 151.64 x 96 = 14,557.44; 333,860/14,557.44 = 22.934 (~23) plates required to fit the Book of Mormon at that rate. Lastly, "Frankfurt silver inscription," *Archaeologisches Museum Frankfurt*, online at archaeologisches-museum-frankfurt.ed (accessed June 1, 2025) includes an English translation that consists of 83 words. 83/0.488 in^2 = 170.08 translated words per square inch; 170.08 x 96 = 16,327.68; 333,860/16,327.68 = 20.447 (~21) plates required to fit the Book of Mormon at that rate.

235. Grant Frame, *The Royal Inscriptions of the Neo-Assyrian Period, vol. 2: The Royal Inscriptions of Sargon II, King of Assyria (721–705 BC)* (University Park, PA: Eisenbrauns, 2021), 231–234. Lines 31–32 are completely untranslated, and lines 40–46 are highly fragmentary. I thus estimate the total number of words based on the number of words translated from lines 1–30, 33–39, and 47–60, which comes out to 519 words, plus 3 to account for at least one missing word on lines 33, 35, and 51, bringing the total to 522. Dividing this by the total number of translated lines (51) provides an average of 10.24 words per line, multiplied by 9 to account for the untranslated/fragmentary lines provides a total 92.16, added to the 522 for approximately 614 words.

more than 1,500 English words.[236] The Hittite treaty between the Great King Tuthaliya IV and Kurunta was engraved onto a bronze plate in cuneiform signs generally around 3.5 mm in height—the same approximate size as the writing on the smaller of the two silver scrolls found at Ketef Hinnom.[237] The treaty translates into approximately 4,000 English words and yields a density of approximately 17.7 translated words per square inch.[238] Although Hittite, an Indo-European language, is less closely related to the Book of Mormon's presumed Semitic and Egyptian linguistic background, this nonetheless serves to illustrate that even lengthy texts inscribed onto larger metal surfaces (a bronze tablet 35 x 24 cm, ca. 13.8 x 9.5 inches) were sometimes written in a small script, compact enough to fit the entire text of the Book of Mormon on about 200 plates. Another lengthy example coming from the Indo-European linguistic sphere is the previously mentioned Roman legal code *Lex Irnitata*. This code, which translates to approximately 20,000 words, was scrawled across 30-feet worth of large bronze tablets in Latin script 4–6 mm in size.[239] For context, the Hebrew writing on the larger of the two

---

236. This estimate is derived from taking the total surface area of the inscribed portion of the text (19.75 x 8.75 = 172.8125) and multiplying it by 9.09 (the words per square inch of the surviving portion of the tablet), which comes to 1,570.87.

237. The line height of Ketef Hinnom II is about 3.25 mm (39mm/12 lines), and the largest character is 3.5 mm. Note that Ketef Hinnom II yields a much higher words per square inch than this Hittite treaty (61.37 vs. 17.67—more comparable to Ketef Hinnom I at 17.49), indicating that pre-exilic Hebrew was evidently a more compact written language than Hittite was. This thus treaty actually serves as evidence that ancient scribes did, in fact, write lengthy texts in characters small enough to fit the entire Book of Mormon on about 57 plates if it was originally written in Hebrew.

238. See Harry A. Hoffner Jr. "The Treaty of Tudḫaliya IV with Kurunta of Tarḫuntašša on the Bronze Tablet Found in Ḫattuša," in *The Context of Scripture*, 4 vols., ed. William W. Hallo and K. Lawson Younger Jr. (Boston, MA: Brill, 2003–2017), 2:100–106; Thomas Zimmermann, et al., "The Metal Tablet from Bogazkoy-Hattusa: First Archaeometroc Impressions," *Journal of Near Eastern Studies* 69, no. 2 (2010): 225. According to Zimmermann et al., the bronze tablet is 35 x 24 cm (~13.78 x 9.45 inches), which provides 130.221 in^2 for a single side. Since the second side is not completely filled, translated words per square inch were calculated using only the front side translation, which comes out to 2,301 words in Hoffner's translation. 2,301/130.221 = 17.67 words per square inch. There are also 98–102 lines per "full" column, so taking 35 cm = 350 mm/100 = 3.5 mm as the average height of each line and approximately the max size for the signs.

239. See Gonzálaz and Crawford, "Lex Irnitana," 147–243. The extant portion is

Ketef Hinnom inscriptions was an average of 5 mm, illustrating once again that sometimes lengthy texts written on large metallic surfaces were written in small script comparable to those used on these small Semitic amulets and foundation tablets.[240]

Taken together, the 24 examples found in tables 5 and 6 illustrate that all across the ancient Near East over the course of more than two millennia, scribes working in a variety of different languages and scripts and writing texts of varying lengths were capable of inscribing small, compact text onto metals. When translated into English, these densely written texts yield between 8.7–151.6 translated words per square inch (see tables 5 and 6).[241] This completely overlaps with the range estimated for the translated words per square inch on the Book of Mormon plates (ca. 8.7–128.8). Assuming the that the English translation of the Book of Mormon relates to the original text in a way that approximates the academic translations of these ancient Near Eastern texts, then the Book of Mormon could have fit onto somewhere between 23–400 plates; with the average translated words per square inch of all twenty-four sample texts (40.4) yielding an estimated 86 plates for the entire text of the Book

---

translated into 13,297 English words, and is estimated to be 2/3 of the original; thus the original inscription would have translated into nearly 20,000 words (13,297/0.6667 ≈ 19,945).

240. Ketef Hinnom I is 97mm and has 18 lines, resulting in 5.4 mm per line. Remember that this text yielded about 17.5 translated words per square inch. Thus, based on the word density of Ketef Hinnom I, if the surface area of the Roman bronze tablets (16,309.856 in^2) were engraved on both sides in pre-exilic Hebrew consisting of characters the same average size as the Latin script used on the tablets (~5 mm), it could fit a text longer than the current Book of Mormon (269,528) by more than 15,700 words (17.49 x 16,309.856 = 285,259.38). So it seems there is at least one instance where a metallic engraving used a small enough script size on a large enough surface (if we use a script more closely related to the presumed original text of the Book of Mormon) to fit the entire source text for the current Book of Mormon (though not the full lost manuscript).

241. For the information on each of the Assyrian inscriptions in table 6 see Grayson, *Assyrian Rulers of the Third and Second Millennia BC*, 196, 253–257, 259–261, 264–265; Grayson, *Assyrian Rulers of the Early First Millennium BC I*, 341–342; Grayson, *Assyrian Rulers of the Early First Millennium BC II*, 99–100; Frame, *Royal Inscriptions of the Neo-Assyrian Period 2*, 231–238. Calculations of translated words per square inch and estimated number of plates the Book of Mormon would fit on at that word density are my own, according to the mathematical procedures explained in nn.209, 214–215.

TABLE 6: Writing Density of Cuneiform Epigraphy on Metallic Surfaces				
Inscription	**Measurements**	**Lines/ English Words**	**English Words Per Square Inch**	**Total Book of Mormon Plates**
Gold Tablet of Shalmaneser I	1.36 x 0.95 in	20/64	24.8	~141
Gold Tablet of Tukulti-Ninutra I 1	3.5 x 1.96 in	81/230	16.76	~208
Gold Tablet of Tukulti-Ninutra I 2	2.26 x 1.12 in	26/90	17.79	~196
Silver Tablet of Tukulti-Ninutra I	3.43 x 2.05 in	43/213	15.15	~230
Gold Tablet of Tukulti-Ninutra I 3	1.57 x 1.02 in	21/87	27.19	~128
Gold Tablet of Tukulti-Ninutra I 4	2.4 x 1.65 in	35/166	20.96	~166
Gold Tablet of Ashurnasirpal II	1.61 x 0.83 in	18/122	45.69	~76
Gold Tablet of Shalmaneser III	1.61 x 1.14 in	24/99	26.98	~129
Bronze Tablet of Sargon II	7.48 x 4.72 in	60/~614	8.7	~400
Silver Tablet of Sargon II	4.65 x 2.36 in	51/319	14.53	~240
Gold Tablet of Sargon II	2.76 x 1.65 in	40/198	21.73	~160
Bronze Tablet of Tuthaliya IV	13.78 x 9.45 in	352/~4,000	17.67	~198

of Mormon, including the portion on the lost manuscript.[242] The estimated range of available plates based on physical properties of the record (27–400) substantially overlaps with these numbers, suggesting that the entire Book of Mormon and lost manuscript could indeed have fit onto

242. Dale, "How Big A Book?" 265–267 arrived at 129 plates (86 ft^2) using a calculation based on space needed to write the entire Quran in Arabic, though Dale does not factor in the lost manuscript, which would require adding another 31 plates to his total, for 160 total plates. Alternatively, Jerry D. Grover Jr., *The Swords of Shule: Jaredite Land Northward Chronology, Geography, and Culture in Mesoamerica* (Provo, UT: Challex Scientific Publishing, 2018), 294 provides an estimated 146 plates required for the entire Book of Mormon plus the lost 116 pages, based on an assumed word density of 23.87 words per square inch, which he derived from his own proposed translation of the "Caractors" document (on which, see n.182) and the assumption that the size of the script on that document represents the approximate size of the script on the plates. Clearly, both of these estimates fit within the range of plates and writing density established from samples of ancient Near Eastern plates, and there are some individual samples (see tables 5 and 6) that come close to these same numbers.

the space available on the unsealed portion of the plates. This is especially so when we remember that the Nephites actually wrote in a script that was *more compact* and space saving than their Hebrew (Mormon 9:32–33).[243] If parts of the translation are more dynamic, interpretive, or even expansive (as some scholars have suggested),[244] then that would imply even fewer plates were required to contain the original text.

Stained Black

This detail is not as well attested as all the others, but William I. Appleby, who joined the Church in 1840, heard Orson Pratt describe the characters on the plates as "filled with black cement" in a sermon in 1839.[245] About twenty years later, Pratt himself said that it was the Eight Witnesses who described the "fine engravings" on the plates as "stained with a black, hard stain, so as to make the letters more legible and easier

243. Coates, "Combinatorial Approach," 14–15, 17, 22–25 (appendix B) notes that, based on the Masoretic Hebrew of Genesis and the King James English translation, the ratio of English to Hebrew characters in translation is ~2.4:1. Using an academic translation of Egyptian texts written in hieratic and demotic, he found the English to hieratic character ratio to be ~2.6:1, while the English to demotic ratio was ~3.1:1. For comparative purposes, Coates also notes that English to Chinese translation character ratio is ~3.9:1. Assuming that "reformed Egyptian" would have a higher translation ratio than Hebrew, based on Mormon 9:32–33, Coates uses a range from 3:1 to 5:1 and script sizes ranging from 2.5–5.4 mm, which fits well within historically attested inscriptions, as documented above. Within these parameters, Coates found millions of valid scenarios (p. 17, 18 fig. 7). In his examples of valid configurations (pp. 38–39, appendix G), Coates finds that if the characters were 2.5 mm with a translation density of 3.0 (comparable to demotic), the entire Book of Mormon could have fit onto about 70 unsealed plates (206 total plates, with 66% sealed), while at 5.4 mm with a translation density of 5.0, it could have fit onto about 161 unsealed plates (241 total plates, with 33% sealed). These numbers fit comfortably within the range established above based on translated words per square inch of actual ancient metal inscriptions.

244. See Brant A. Gardner, *By the Gift and Power: Translating the Book of Mormon* (Salt Lake City: Greg Kofford Books, 2011); Blake T. Ostler, "The Book of Mormon as a Modern Expansion of an Ancient Source," *Dialogue: A Journal of Mormon Thought* 20, no. 1 (1987): 66–123.

245. W. I. Appleby, *A Dissertation on Nebuchadnezzar's Dream* (Philadelphia, PA: Brown, Bicking, and Guilbert, 1844), 23; "Biography and Journal of William I. Appleby, Elder in the Church of Latter Day Saints," 1848, 32, in *EMD* 1:148.

to be read."[246] A source close to Martin Harris similarly claimed that the characters on the plates were "rubbed over with a black substance so as to fill them up, in order that the dazzling of the gold between the characters would not prevent their being readily seen."[247]

While these sources assume the characters were *deliberately* blackened, to make the text more legible, it is possible that after 1400 years in the ground, the characters were blackened as a result of corrosion. Although oxidized copper often produces bluish-greenish corrosion products, as previously discussed, dark brown or black corrosion products are also known to occur, particularly with high-copper tumbaga alloys.[248] Thus, if the plates were made of tumbaga or gilded copper, and the engravings pierced through the thin layer of gold, then the copper or silver in the underlying alloy could have corroded over with a dark brown or black substance. Jerry Grover considers this possibility, but argues that it is more likely the characters were deliberately blackened, either to increase legibility or perhaps to protect the underlying alloy from exposure and corrosion.[249]

Something similar may have been done on some ancient inscriptions, though in the examples I have found it is not clear if this was done deliberately or the result of corrosion. Grover has pointed out that in photographs of the famous gold plate of King Darius, dated to around 515 BC, "the engravings [appear to] have a black/brown coloration to them," but it is unclear if this is due the gold plate lying underneath a silver plate covered in black corrosion products that could have fallen into and collected in the engravings.[250] Images of both the gold and silver tablets of Ashurnasirpal II (ca. 883–859 BC) also clearly show that the cuneiform signs are filled with some kind of black or dark brown patina that helps them stand out strikingly, especially against the golden background.[251] In the New World, the lines of an inscribed design on a

246. Pratt, "Evidences," *Journal of Discourses* 7:31.

247. Bishop, *Proclamation from the Lord*, 48; Bradley, *Lost 116 Pages*, 5, 141 argues that Bishop gleaned this detail from Martin Harris.

248. See Fleming, "Confounding the Conquistadors," 6–7; Scott, "Deterioration of Gold Alloys," 200.

249. See Grover, *Ziff, Magic Goggles, and Golden Plates*, 74–76.

250. Grover, *Ziff, Magic Goggles, and Golden Plates*, 79.

251. See Yale Peabody Museum, catalogue no. 016992, online at collections.peabody.yale.edu (silver) and Yale Peabody Museum, catalogue no. 016991, online at collections.peabody.yale.edu (gold), both accessed 15 September 2023.

thin golden sheet from Peru, dating to Book of Mormon times, appear to have a black substance in them that helps the design stand out more clearly.[252] To my knowledge, no analysis has been done on any of these objects to determine if this was a deliberately created patina or a corrosion by-product.[253]

Regardless of whether these inscriptions were deliberately blackened or not, there were methods and techniques used anciently in both the Old and New Worlds to achieve a deliberately blackened color on copper and gold surfaces. For example, metallurgist David Baird points to an etching process used anciently wherein a mixture of tar and wax called "pitch" is rubbed over the surface of a metal, and then the writing or designs could be scratched through the pitch and then treated with acid and other chemical processes, resulting in "characters with a dark black crusty appearance."[254] Grover also mentions an acid etching technique called "black matte," used in both the Old and New Worlds "to create a black color on gold … as well [as] on tumbaga discs," but believes it is unlikely this technique was used on the Book of Mormon plates.[255] Alternatively, Grover discusses a method used to create "black copper" in both Egypt and Japan, which often involved an object made of a copper-gold alloy that was deliberately treated to create bi-colored gold and black designs.[256]

In the New World, tumbaga disks from Nariño, Columbia, exhibit an alternating black and gold design that was likely created deliberately.[257] According to Bryan Cockrell, this differing coloration was created by using resins to protect portions of the disks during the depletion gild-

252. See the images of both sides of this "ornamental plume" online at the metmuseum.org (accessed 14 April 2024). See also Jones and King, "Gold of the Americas," 31. A similar affect can be seen on the shaft of a golden earspool from Peru, dated to twelfth to fifteenth centuries in Jones and King, "Gold of the Americas," 17.

253. In addition to these, Paul R. Cheesman, "External Evidences of the Book of Mormon," in *By Study and Also by Faith*, 2:81, reports seeing various specimen of "a base metal covered with gold, with enameled black writing" on them while visiting various museums, but does not provide any references that can be verified.

254. Baird, Interviewed by Goodman, 00:30:01.08–00.32:08.23.

255. Grover, *Ziff, Magic Goggles, and Golden Plates*, 80–81.

256. See Grover, *Ziff, Magic Goggles, and Golden Plates*, 76–79.

257. See Grover, *Ziff, Magic Goggles, and Golden Plates*, 82; Bray, "Techniques of Gilding," plate 16.1; Scott, "Review of Gilding Techniques," 212.

ing process.[258] Experiments conducted by Mark Grimwade, a goldsmith, and Teresa del Solar, an archaeology grad student, confirmed that this black-and-gold effect could be achieved by covering certain portions of the tumbaga alloy during the depletion gilding process, and then burnishing and heating the undepleted portions to create a brown/black "oxidized silver" finish.[259] As Grover has pointed out, one of Grimwade and del Solar's experimental plates has the appearance of a golden surface with a black engraving, illustrating that this process could have been used to blacken the engravings on the Book of Mormon plates.[260] Through his own experimentation, Josh Coates found that washing an engraved tumbaga plate in a solution of lye, water, and salt—all materials known to pre-Columbian cultures—would turn the engravings black without affecting the golden finish.[261] Thus, the materials and techniques needed to create a blackened text set against a golden backdrop on tumbaga plates were accessible in ancient America.

Conclusion

Considering the description of the golden plates within the broader comparative context of ancient metallic epigraphy, we find precedents for nearly every single detail described by the witnesses—from their material appearance, binding, and partial sealing, to the dimensions and size of the individual plates and volume as a whole (based on weight and estimated surface area), to the size and appearance of the engraved characters. The Book of Mormon plates, as described by eyewitnesses, fit well within the scope of diverse precedents of ancient metallic epigraphy. Nonetheless, it must be recognized that no other singular example is quite like the golden plates. Similarities to the plates' physical characteristics are found scattered throughout the ancient world, from a variety of different artifacts, contexts, and cultures. The lack of any other lengthy golden codices having ever been discovered in a pre-Columbian American context ensures that if the golden plates were available today, they would be considered an unprecedented discovery in American archaeology. Some may feel that this makes it unlikely or improbable that such an extraordinary artifact was ever real.

---

258. Bryan Cockrell, "Disk," in *Golden Kingdoms*, 185.
259. Grimwade, "Surface Enrichment," 20.
260. Grover, *Ziff, Magic Goggles, and Golden Plates*, 81.
261. Josh Coates, personal communication, 20 October 2024.

Yet it can hardly be denied that Joseph Smith had a real set of plates. A plethora of witnesses saw, handled, and hefted them, and left behind descriptions of their encounters with this artifact. Their testimonies do not square well with a crude forgery made of tin or early 19th-century printing plates used as a prop: tin does not resemble gold nor does it turn green when it oxidizes, and it is difficult to engrave; while printing plates are not golden, are not bound by rings, and are relatively thick and too stiff—they would make more of a clanking sound as opposed to the metallic rustling of thin, pliable, paper-like metal sheets described by some witnesses. The attempts of several modern metallurgists to create replicas conforming to the descriptions given by the witnesses attests to the tremendous amount of work and skill required to create a believable forgery.[262] For instance, David Baird, who has made several replicas of the golden plates, notes that the process of making believable "pages of gold plates, regardless of whatever the metal was, to make it thin consistently, to cut it and shape it, and then to engrave and etch on it would have been extremely difficult. … If [Joseph Smith] was to make his gold plates, it would have taken him quite a while. … I don't think there's any evidence that he had any of the skills required to do that."[263] The Kinderhook plates, which are much smaller and simpler than the plates described by the Book of Mormon witnesses, involved the efforts of three different people, including a blacksmith, and required knowing how to use wax and acids to etch the characters onto the plates and to make them look aged with rust—not to mention the fact that some of the conspirators began admitting to the hoax fairly soon after the fact.[264] In my view, the

262. Shanna Butler, "A Golden Opportunity," *New Era* (February 2006): 34–37; Steven Pratt, "A Model of the Plates," *New Era* (July 2007).

263. Baird, Interviewed by Goodman, 00:41:57.27–00:43:04.10, 00:43:49.17–00:44:15.22.

264. On the Kinderhook plates, see Jason Frederick Peters, "The Kinderhook Plates: Examining a Nineteenth-Century Hoax," *Journal of the Illinois State Historical Society* 96, no. 2 (2003): 130–145; Don Bradley and Mark Ashurst-McGee, "'President Joseph Has Translated a Portion': Joseph Smith and the Mistranslation of the Kinderhook Plates," in *Producing Ancient Scripture: Joseph Smith's Translation Projects in the Development of Mormon Christianity*, ed. Michael Hubbard MacKay, Mark Ashurst-McGee, and Brian M. Hauglid (Salt Lake City, UT: University of Utah, 2020), 452–523. Although the fact that it was a hoax was not widely known until 1879, one of the original witnesses to their discovery in 1843 reported in 1855 that he had been informed that they

plates *as described by the witnesses* cannot be satisfactorily accounted for as a modern artifact.[265]

Without a compelling *modern* explanation for the plates, the prospect that they were an *ancient* artifact deserves to be taken seriously. To do so, I contend that it is necessary to take the full range of ancient historical metal-writing practices attested throughout the world into consideration—failure to do so risks overlooking potential evidence and coming away with a skewed view of what is possible or even likely. When the full breadth of the ancient evidence is taken into account, we find that nothing about the physical description of the plates is beyond the scope of ancient practices and capabilities; and while no other golden codex has yet come forth from pre-Columbian America, it does appear that the metallurgical technology required to create thin sheets of tumbaga or gilded copper inscribed with blackened characters did exist in Central and South America by the mid-first millennium AD. Therefore, I find it entirely plausible that the witnesses were describing a real encounter with an *ancient* artifact and not a modern prop. Put simply, the plates described by the witnesses are far too impressive of an artifact to be a forgery made by Joseph Smith, and yet their descriptions seem to be more realistic than one might expect for a fanciful artifact of nineteenth century imagination.

Considering the descriptions of the Book of Mormon plates within the broader context of pre-modern metallic epigraphy also helps us better appreciate those plates as a real, tangible artifact, made by real people who painstakingly worked the metal and engraved their sacred words for us today. There can be little doubt that the creation of this metallic record was an expensive and labor-intensive process that required exceptional skill and craftsmanship. The more I have personally researched this topic, the more I've been impressed with what ancient metal workers and scribes were capable of more generally, and with those ancient authors and forgers of the Book of Mormon record in particular. Gordon Andrus, a silversmith who created a replica of the plates for the Church History Museum, concluded from his experience that "monumental determination was needed for the making of such a record. … The ancient metal

were fake by the blacksmith who made them sometime before 1850 (see Peters, "Kinderhook Plates," 140).

265. See also Richard Lyman Bushman, *Joseph Smith's Gold Plates: A Cultural History* (New York, NY: Oxford University Press, 2023), 135–156.

smiths who recorded their history and spiritual teachings on plates were highly skilled in the art of refining, shaping and marking alloys of copper (and gold) as evidenced in the artifacts they left behind."[266]

Rather than causing doubt or skepticism, the extraordinary and unprecedented nature of this artifact deepens my appreciation for the plates not only as a physical object attesting to the Book of Mormon's reality, but as a monument of faith in and of itself—a testament to the ancient prophets who painstakingly worked to create and preserve this one-of-a-kind record with a singular purpose to testify of Christ. As the prophet Jacob wrote, "We labor diligently to engraven these words upon plates, hoping that our beloved brethren and our children will receive them with thankful hearts. … For, for this intent have we written these things, that they may know that we knew of Christ, and we had a hope of his glory many hundred years before his coming" (Jacob 4:3–4).

Acknowledgements: I owe thanks to Matt Roper for his great research on metal plates for Evidence Central, and Jerry Grover for his previous work on the metallurgical composition of the plates, plus his assistance on some technical metallurgical questions, and his sharing some his experimentation on gilded copper with me; their work was foundational for this paper. I also appreciate Josh Coates sharing his mathematical modeling and some of his experimentation with tumbaga plates with me. I would also like to thank Spencer Kraus for his diligent research assistance, and Kerry Hull for assisting me with some questions and source material on tumbaga. Jasmin Rappleye assisted in organizing and presenting a preliminary version of this paper, and Brant Gardner, John Thompson, and Ryan Dahle provided feedback on that early presentation of this material, for which I am grateful.

266. Gordon Andrus, in R. Scott Lloyd, "Recreating the golden plates: Artist tells how he replicated Nephite record for museum display," *Church News*, 27 September 2017, online at thechurchnews.com (accessed 19 September 2023).

5

Greater Portion of the Word

The Decisive Book of Mormon in the Debates on War and Peace

Morgan Deane

As a relatively new major scripture, the Book of Mormon is often neglected in discussions of Just War principles. Latter-day Saint scholars have not helped by rarely engaging with seminal Just War thinkers. Their engagement often becomes a perfunctory review serving as a platform to dismiss Just War theories and theorists as insufficient—either in favor of preferred theories and a handful of proof texts, or due to a chauvinistic attitude that disregards non-Restoration texts. This is tragic, given the Lord's command to seek ye out of the best books [and] words of wisdom (Doctrine and Covenants 88:118), and because the Book of Mormon not only aligns with Just War beliefs but offers important commentary and insights. In contrast to Just War theorists who derived their insights through expertly reasoned—but extrabiblical—theorizing, the Book of Mormon's insights come within holy text and thus warrant greater importance. Studying the Book of Mormon's engagement with Just War Theory reveals how it resolves the apparent contradiction of how a soldier with a peaceful heart can wield the sword and be a peacemaker (or renounce war). This, in turn, forms a stronger foundation for understanding war and peace.

The Latter-day Saint study of war and peace could be greatly enhanced by engagement with the seminal thinkers on the subject, but unfortunately, little of that study has been done.[1] Several common reasons are given for ignoring these theorists. These include Restoration scriptures creating a "higher bar" that some scholars see as "neither broad

1. Morgan Deane, *To Stop a Slaughter: Just War and the Book of Mormon* (self-published, 2024), 5–15.

nor comprehensive enough" for Just War sources.[2] Others contend that Just War theories are 'obviously insufficient.'[3] Also suggested is the idea that Latter-day Saints should not be beholden to medieval Catholic theologians who – it is implied – are too narrow, old, or small-minded to provide helpful insights in the modern age.[4]

It is true that Latter-Saints are blessed with the Restored Gospel and that modern problems may seem a difficult wrestle, but there have been vanishingly few examinations of how Restoration scripture can help solve these problems.[5] Latter-day Saint thought – and the interactions of that thought with Just War theorists – would benefit immensely from utilizing those thousand-year-old texts and not ignoring or minimizing them. We are commanded by the Lord to "seek ye out of the best books" [and] "words of wisdom" (Doctrine and Covenants 88:118). The great thinkers

2. Patrick Q. Mason and J. David Pulsipher, *Proclaim Peace: The Restoration's Answer to an Age of Conflict* (Provo, UT: Neal A. Maxwell Institute for Religious Scholarship; Salt Lake City: Deseret Book, 2021), 135. "
3. Duane Boyce, *Even Unto Bloodshed: An LDS Perspective on War* (Salt Lake City: Greg Kofford Books, 2015), 223. Boyce states "modern just war framework… makes no explicit use of scripture…it seems obvious that it cannot be sufficient to address the concerns of Latter-day Saints."
4. Mark Henshaw, "Towards an LDS *Jus Post Bellum*," in *National Security in an Era of Global Upheaval: Perspectives from Latter-day Saint Professionals*, ed. Eric Jensen and Kerry Kartchner (Provo, UT: David M. Kennedy Center for International Studies, forthcoming).
5. Kyle McKay Brown, "'Whatsoever Evil We Cannot Resist with Our Words': An Exploration of Mormon Just War Theory" (master's thesis, University of Edinburgh, 2012); Duane Boyce, *Even Unto Bloodshed: An LDS Perspective on War* (Salt Lake City: Greg Kofford Books, 2015); Kerry M. Kartchner and Valerie M. Hudson, eds., *Wielding the Sword While Proclaiming Peace: Views from the LDS Community on Reconciling the Demands of National Security with the Imperatives of Revealed Truth* (Provo, UT: David M. Kennedy Center for International Studies, 2003); Valerie M. Hudson, Eric Talbot Jensen, and Kerry M. Kartchner, eds., *A Time of War, A Time of Peace: Latter-Day Saint Ethics of War and Diplomacy* (Provo, UT: David M. Kennedy Center for International Studies, 2018); Duane Boyce, "Captain Moroni and the Sermon on the Mount: Resolving a Scriptural Tension," *BYU Studies Quarterly* 60, no. 2 (2021): 127–62; J. David Pulsipher, "Defend Your Families and Love Your Enemies: A New Look at the Book of Mormon's Patterns of Protection," *BYU Studies Quarterly* 60, no. 2 (2021): 163–84; Patrick Q. Mason and J. David Pulsipher, *Proclaim Peace: The Restoration's Answer to an Age of Conflict* (Provo, UT: Neal A. Maxwell Institute for Religious Scholarship; Salt Lake City: Deseret Book, 2021).

have wrestled for centuries with these questions, such as the importance of the heart, the morality of preemptive war, and how Biblical principles interact with the creation and nuances of international law. Comparatively, Latter-day Saint thinkers have only been able to briefly consider them for the last few decades.

In important ways, those seminal texts and ideas benefit from engagement with the Book of Mormon. It does not simply show congruency with Just War beliefs; the interaction of ideas between the Nephite text and seminal thinkers produces important commentary and stronger insights. For added benefit, in contrast to Just War theorists who often had to establish and ground their thinking through extrabiblical theorizing, these new insights derive from holy scripture and should thus assume stronger importance.

Many of these conversations are found in my book *"To Stop a Slaughter": Just War and the Book of Mormon*. One of the most important is how the Book of Mormon settles the debate regarding how a soldier with a peaceful heart that desires to turn the other cheek (or renounce war as Latter-day Saints would say) can also wield the sword. That answer, established by Christian theorists and decisively solidified by the Book of Mormon, provides a stronger foundation for discernment between matters of war and peace.

The heart of a sincere believer is the origin of one's faith, but it is also the center of the debate surrounding the use of force. The pacifist impulse stems most strongly from the Sermon on the Mount and the Savior's setting aside of past laws, proclaiming that one must turn the other cheek and be a peacemaker (Matthew 5:9; 38-40; see also 3 Nephi 12:44). Frequently without knowing, Latter-day Saints follow the same contours of the debate between pacifism and Just War, but do so often utilizing a different scripture where the Lord commands his people to renounce war and proclaim peace (Doctrine and Covenants 98:16).[6] If justifying the use of force, many Latter-day Saints will fall back on Book of Mormon verses such as Alma 43:14 and Alma 48:15, where the Lord commands the Nephites to defend their families "even unto bloodshed."

Debates among the broader Christian community involve the utilization of Biblical scriptures. The example of the Good Samaritan is

6. Duane Boyce has done an excellent job of showing how unworkable that section is as a guide to foreign policy. Duane Boyce, *Even Unto Bloodshed: An LDS Perspective on War* (Salt Lake City: Greg Kofford Books, 2015), 156–57.

probably the most important, but the Savior's cleansing the temple, and John the Baptist and Jesus' commands to soldiers are pertinent as well (Luke 3:14; Luke 10:30-37).

Both sides often talk past one another with very little interaction.[7] Latter-day Saints have neither recognized the assumptions their arguments are founded upon, nor have they thought about a way to reconcile the two viewpoints. But there are basic logical assumptions and a vast body of historic thought that shows how there is no contradiction between peacemakers and warring soldiers.

Careful examinations of New Testament passages by many Christian thinkers regarding the role of force eventually determined that the supposed contradiction is resolved by soldiers that wield the sword with a peaceful, loving heart. Jesus violently cleansed the temple in Matthew 21:12-13 and John 2:14-17, and notably, when struck, didn't turn the other cheek himself (John 18:23), which suggests the Prince of Peace at least found a situation when turning the other cheek was not the right course.

Some scholars have contended that the Sermon on the Mount directs inner attitudes - not external behaviors - and certainly does not convey instructions to guide foreign policy. In reviewing the Church Fathers, David Corey and Daryl Charles summarized that most of them commented on the general nature of Christians to be peaceable, content, and conciliatory as said by Justin Martyr.[8]

Contrary to popular perception, the Fathers did not reject soldiering, but objected - as did Tertullian - to the pagan ceremonies often associated with military service. Many Church Fathers cited Jesus and John the Baptist's words to soldiers. The Savior did not tell a Roman soldier to put down his sword, but instead Matthew 8:8-10 records how Jesus praised one's faith. John the Baptist did not tell the soldier to put down his sword and follow the Prince of Peace, but to be just and stop extorting the people (Luke 3:14). When some Latter-day Saints claim that members should reject nationalism and military service, they reject these clear scriptures.

---

7. See Patrick Q. Mason, J. David Pulsipher, and Richard L. Bushman, eds., *War and Peace in Our Time: Mormon Perspectives* (Salt Lake City: Greg Kofford Books, 2012) for some of the limited engagement thus far.
8. David D. Corey and J. Daryl Charles, *The Just War Tradition: An Introduction* (Wilmington, DE: ISI Books, 2012), 29.

As before mentioned, Tertullian recorded that Christians fought as Roman soldiers, but he rejected the danger of idolatrous military ceremonies. Clement supported the state's right to use force and prayed for the success of the emperor's army. After hundreds of years of early Christian thought, the summary of the two positions to be peaceful and to fight in wars was described as a "vengeful spirit that is denounced" but not force itself.[9] This idea may have been inspired by a reading of Romans 12:19: "Dearly beloved, avenge not yourselves, but rather give place unto wrath: for it is written, Vengeance is mine; I will repay, saith the Lord." One of the sins of the Nephite armies, which made Mormon refuse to lead them, was their desire to "avenge themselves of the blood of their brethren who had been slain" (Mormon 3:9).

Like the Nephites of Alma 48:21-23, St. Augustine seemed as concerned about where the souls of dead soldiers would go as he was about warfare itself. He summarized the idea of soldiers with a loving heart wielding the sword by using the term "benevolent harshness" which, according to Augustine, could sometimes be seen in God himself.[10] The medieval monk Gratian warned that force should be used for the love of justice, not for the love of inflicting punishment.[11] St. Thomas Aquinas said that war is waged for a peace, so those fighting "are not opposed to peace, except evil peace."[12] It may seem a contradiction in terms, but Aquinas would use the example of a parent punishing a child. That punishment may be harsh, but is done out of love.[13] Martin Luther compared

9. Corey and Charles, *The Just War Tradition*, 47.

10. Augustine, *On the Sermon on the Mount*, 1.19.59, 1.20.63, 1.22.77, in *Nicene and Post-Nicene Fathers: First Series*, vol. 6, ed. Philip Schaff, trans. William Findlay (Peabody, MA: Hendrickson, 2004), citing Proverbs 3:12.

11. Corey and Charles, *The Just War Tradition*, 73.

12. Thomas Aquinas, Summa Theologiae, II–II, q. 40, a. 1, reply to obj. 3, accessed September 5, 2021, online at newadvent.org.

13. To be clear, the culture in which Augustine lived (and, thus, Augustine) viewed corporal punishment as appropriate for children and others in society — this was the type of physical punishment that Augustine had in mind in his example. In most societies in today's world corporal punishment involving inflicting pain on children with an object such as a strap, switch, or cane is considered child abuse. Disapproving of parenting approaches utilized in Augustine's time doesn't mean that one should ignore the arguments put forward by him or others of his time, however. The example may be viewed as inappropriate, but one should not ignore or throw out the entire argument because one doesn't like the example used.

the use of force by a loving soldier to a doctor that must save the patient by amputating a limb:

> For a good physician, when the disease is so deep and virulent that he has to cut off and destroy hand, foot, eye, or ear in order to save the body, seems, when we consider the limb that he cuts off, a terrible, merciless man, yet considering the body that he thus tries to save, he is in truth an excellent, faithful man, and is doing a good.[14]

The Salamanca School scholar, Francisco de Vitoria, wrote that a leader should come to the necessity of war only reluctantly and under compulsion.[15] John Locke focused on natural rights more than scripture but came to the same conclusions: it was permissible to defend against aggression, but force should only be used as calm reason and conscience dictate, and not in extravagant passion.[16]

Perhaps the most important summary of the need for a loving use of force comes from the Parable of the Good Samaritan (Luke 10:25-37), used by the Savior as an example of true Christian love for one's neighbor. The twentieth-century theologian Paul Ramsey asked, what if the Good Samaritan had come across the beaten traveler during the attack?[17] It would be ridiculous to think that the Good Samaritan would turn the other cheek of the beaten traveler, renounce war, proclaim peace, and stand idly by, waiting until the traveler was attacked three times, or questioning the legitimacy of action by citing long-standing ethnic tension in the region, or perhaps the culpability of the traveler. The love of the Good Samaritan for his neighbor would compel intervention, perhaps violent intervention, on his behalf.

That is an impressive array of Christian scholars, but they mostly appeal to reason and astute observations about holy scripture, instead of holy scripture itself. By noting their points, readers see the Book of Mormon is filled with examples that show the importance of a loving heart in wielding the sword. In the discussion of Nephite warfare during

---

14. Martin Luther, Whether Soldiers, Too, Can Be Saved (1526), trans. anon., 3, accessed September 5, 2021, online at opensiuc.lib.siu.edu.
15. Francisco de Vitoria, *The Principles of Political and International Law in the Work of Francisco de Vitoria*, trans. Antonio Truyol Serra (Madrid: Ediciones Cultura Hispánica, 1946), 98.
16. Corey and Charles, *The Just War Tradition*, 147.
17. Paul Ramsey, *The Just War: Force and Political Responsibility* (New York: Scribner, 1968; reprint, Lanham, MD: Rowman & Littlefield Publishers, 2002), 143.

their terminal period, Mormon wrote that "it is the wicked that stir up the hearts of the children of men unto bloodshed" and described the origin of their indescribable sins, that "every [Nephite] heart was hardened, so that they delighted in the shedding of blood continually" (Mormon 4:5, 11).

In multiple descriptions of Captain Moroni, Mormon emphasized that not delighting in bloodshed was more important than strategy. Alma 48:14 says that the Nephites were taught "never to raise the sword except it were against an enemy, except it were to preserve their lives," and that Moroni "did not delight in murder or bloodshed, but he delighted in the saving of his people from destruction; and for this cause he might not bring upon him injustice" (Alma 55:19).

The opening of Mormon 7:4, "know ye that ye must lay down your weapons of war," is used by some as a pacifistic command to lay down arms.[18] But reading the verse in its entirety suggests that it is the heart wielding the sword, that was more important than the sword itself. "Delight no more in the shedding of blood," the text says, "and take them not again, save it be that God shall command you."

When establishing the church around the Waters of Mormon - in one of my favorite verses - Alma the Elder stressed that the people obtained peace because they had "hearts...knit together in unity" (Mosiah 18:21). This verse becomes even stronger as it calls to mind a Chinese poem called the Peach Blossom Spring that describes a Daoist version of heaven, and suggests that a peaceful heart can create a peaceful, heavenly existence out of their environment, as exemplified by those around the Waters of Mormon.[19]

Alma 43 and 44 repeatedly set up a dichotomy between the Nephites and Lamanites, which centered the better goals and heartfelt attitudes of the Nephites. Alma 43:45 quotes the better cause of the Nephites as defending "their homes and their liberties, their wives and their children, and...for their rites of worship and their church." Now, the Nephites here could be akin to Laman and Lemuel in 1 Nephi 17:21, which describes how the two think their homes are simply about enjoying their possessions, but this verse is more likely a reference to the same feelings we have for our brothers and sisters in Ukraine. We care because we have

18. Mason and Pulsipher, *Proclaim Peace*, xxiii–xxiv.
19. Cyril Birch, ed., *Anthology of Chinese Literature*, vol. 1: *From Early Times to the Fourteenth Century* (New York: Grove Press, 1965), 167–68.

compassion for them, because so many of their homes and liberties are being trampled. The Nephites were commanded to have compassion, or love "even unto bloodshed" (Alma 43:14).

In contrast, we might compare the Nephites' loving attitude and "better cause" with the Lamanites, who are recorded as "rejoicing over the blood of the Nephites" and inflicting "barbarous cruelty" (Alma 48:24-25).[20] In Alma 43:7-8 the Lamanites are inspired by hatred and anger, and verse 45 of the same chapter adds that the Lamanites were fighting for monarchy and power.

The difference is summarized and highlighted in two key verses. In Alma 48:21-23, the Nephites were reluctantly compelled to fight against the Lamanites and were "sorry to take up arms," both of which describe the primacy of the heart. After the personal ministry of Jesus "there was no contention in the land, because of the love of God which did dwell in the hearts of the people" (4 Nephi 1:15).

In summary, the seminal texts from brilliant Christian thinkers show Latter-day Saints where to look within their own scriptures. The Book of Mormon responds with strong and repeated indications that it was the loving, peaceful heart of the soldier that mattered more than the tragic necessity to wield the sword. When talking about the Great Apostasy, it is commonly asserted that those without the light of the restored gospel often did their best to explain principles. We can see that in this case seminal Christian thinkers did very well. But without the weight of scriptures their words could be equivocated away and often ignored as insufficient. In fact, in a caution to us, this often happens when discussing even the clearest Restoration scriptures. For those that are interested in learning, the conversation between leading historic thinkers and the Book of Mormon enhances and solidifies the understanding of the most important part of war and peace. There is no contradiction between turning the other cheek and renouncing war or wielding the sword. The loving Christian heart knows when they are compelled to wield the sword, as Psalms 82:4 said, to deliver the poor and the needy, or as Alma 48:24-25 said, to prevent barbarous cruelty being inflicted on their loved ones. There are many things that Latter-day Saints can learn from the interaction between Christian Just War Theory and Restoration scrip-

20. This could be an ethnocentric stereotype about the Lamanites but given the number of destructive invasions the Nephites suffered it seems like a legitimate description.

ture. In many other cases, the Restoration texts are in discussion with those thinkers that produce additional and needed insights. It is our duty to find and understand them.

6

The Restoration of Relational Grace Through the Book of Mormon

Brent Schmidt

While most modern Christian theologians have concluded that grace is an unconditional pass guaranteeing salvation or a mystical abstraction, few know that the principle of grace (hen in Hebrew or charis in Greek, meaning "a gift") was relational in antiquity. Unfortunately, the active, relational, covenantal nuances of grace were lost during the apostasy but were remarkably restored in the Book of Mormon. In its original Mediterranean context, grace was an obliging, reciprocal, and relational gift. Ancient Greek and Hebrew writers in 600 BC expected gift-giving to form relationships, creating a binding expectation of future reciprocity. Archaic gift-giving forged alliances and covenants and inspired ongoing exchange in the Near East that gradually empowered both giver and recipient. However, in late antiquity and during the Reformation, Christian intellectuals transformed this covenantal gift into an emotional, one-directional freebie allegedly offering immediate salvation. In contrast, the Book of Mormon clarifies that God's grace encourages action, invites, obliges, enables, and empowers disciples to restore broken covenant relationships and become like Heavenly Father because of His Son's obliging, atoning gift.

The Meaning of Grace

While most Christian theologians have long concluded that grace is an unconditional pass guaranteeing salvation or some kind of mystical abstraction, few know that the conventional concept of grace in antiquity (*hen*: Hebrew or *charis:* Greek=meaning a gift) created covenantal obligations. Unfortunately, the relational, covenantal nuances of grace (or *hen* and *charis*) were lost during the apostasy but were remarkably reinstated by the Book of Mormon. This paper summarizes the main findings of my book *Relational Grace: The Reciprocal and Binding Covenant of Charis* and seeks to provide further insights about how the Book of Mormon restores the relational, covenantal principle of grace. Grace began as an ancient practice of gift-giving in both Hebrew (*hen*) and Greek (*charis*). Ancient gift-giving created obligations and reciprocity in its original, ancient, Mediterranean context. Through cycles of gift-giving, ancient Hebrews and Greeks in the Mediterranean formed relationships with others. However, in late-antiquity and during the Reformation, Christian intellectuals transformed this covenant-inspiring meaning of grace into an emotional, one-directional freebie that provided immediate salvation. In contrast, the Book of Mormon restores the plain and precious doctrine that God's grace encourages, obliges, enables and empowers disciples to make and keep covenants.

Reciprocal Gift-Giving

The disciplines of anthropology and sociology have long theorized that Near Eastern and Indo-European tribes millennia ago were often threatened by war and disunity so, in order to survive, beneficial, reciprocal relationships enabled early human societies to take shape and then prosper through gift-giving. Gifts led to the rise of peaceful relationships and the formation of alliances with other potentially dangerous groups, thereby avoiding conflict and war. These gifts or favors given to others who were less prosperous commonly included friendship, marriage, protection, security, land, tools, food, and weapons. Prized objects circulated because of the obligations that formed through gift-giving. These objects became obliging gifts that one received and then were returned, and then again were received and returned, as gifts slowly moved in a cycle of reciprocity and thereby established mutually beneficial relationships, inevitably producing the social networks of vibrant societies.[1] Until the 1960s, the concept of reciprocity was not widely studied in anthropology.[2] Marcel Mauss's seminal sociological essay "The Gift" (1924), which only became popular decades later, explained the ubiquitous practice

1. Annette B. Weiner, "A Replacement for Reciprocity," *American Ethnologist* 7 (February 1980): 79.
2. Geoffrey MacCormack, "Reciprocity," *Man* 1 (March 1976): 97. Marcel Mauss's popular essay was turned into a work entitled *The Gift: Forms and Functions of Exchange in Archaic Societies* (New York: Norton Press, 1967); Mary Douglas, *The World of Goods* (New York: Routledge, 1996), 118.

of gift exchange in all societies. Mauss persuasively argued there are three parts to gift-giving: the obligation to make a gift, the obligation to receive it, and the obligation to repay it; thus gift-giving creates reciprocal relationships.[3] *Hen* and *charis* are the ancient Hebrew and Greek nouns respectively used to describe this universal norm that established and cemented covenants in the ancient Mediterranean.[4]

Uses of Hen *in the Old Testament*

The Hebrew noun *hen* (derived from *hanan*) in the Torah is later translated as the Greek noun *charis* in the Septuagint. Meanings of *hen* include favor, a gracious gift, beauty, and goodwill, which are instrumental in bringing about a special covenant relationship [*hesed*]. For example, when Lot's life is preserved, he says, "Behold, your servant has found favor [*hen*] in your sight, and you have shown me great kindness [*hesed*] in saving my life" (Genesis 19:19). Scholars have long noted that the portrayal of Joseph of Egypt's life in Genesis is one of reciprocal grace.[5] Joseph strengthened his relationship with God by always keeping his commandments. As Jacob neared death, he asked Joseph, "If I have found grace [*hen*] in thy sight, put, I pray thee, thy hand under my thigh, and deal kindly [*hesed*] and truly with me; bury me not, I pray thee, in Egypt" (Genesis 47:29). Joseph then appealed to Pharaoh, asking, "If now I have found grace [*hen*] in your eyes," and only then asked for permission to bury his father (Genesis 50:4). Both of these early Hebrew requests draw on the norm of covenantal reciprocity: because of the relational bond that existed between these people, they could ask for favors that were granted with mercy by means of covenant relationships. In Numbers 32, the children of Reuben who had numerous herds of cattle wanted a favor (Hebrew *hen*; Septuagint *charin*) from Moses (Numbers 32:5). They wanted to inherit the land of Gilead, a land to the east of the Jordan river, because this was a land more suitable for their

3. Geoffrey MacCormack, "Reciprocity," *Man* 1 (March 1976): 97. Marcel Mauss, *The Gift: Forms and Functions of Exchange in Archaic Societies* (New York: Norton Press, 1967).
4. Carolyn Osiek, "The Politics of Patronage and the Politics of Kinship: The Meeting of the Ways," *Biblical Theology Bulletin: A Journal of Bible and Theology* 39 (2009): 144.
5. For more analysis on the reciprocity in this passage, see William L. Reed, "Some Implications of *Hēn* for Old Testament Religion," *Journal of Biblical Literature* 73 (March 1954): 36–41.

cattle (Numbers 32:1–5). However, most of the Israelites were planning on going to war with the enemies of Israel on the west side of the Jordan. Moses asked the Reubenites and Gadites if they would go to war on the west side of the Jordan while they simultaneously settled on the east in the land of Gilead. In response to Moses' question, the sons of Reuben and Gad offered to go to war if, at the end of the war, they would receive Gilead for their inheritance (Numbers 32:16–19). Moses promised to give them this land if they would go to war (Numbers 32:20–29). The children of Gad and Reuben employed the convention of *hen/charis* to make a covenant with the servant of the Lord (Numbers 32:31) and only then became involved in this military expedition. Because they kept the covenant with the Lord through his servant Moses, they eventually inherited the land of Gilead. The conventional practice in the ancient Hebrew and archaic Greek world of individuals or groups granting and receiving favors and gifts invited and obligated covenantal obligations.

Uses of Charis *in Archaic and Classical Greece*

Moving west, the Greek word *charis* was derived from the Indo-European root **gher* "having and receiving" pleasure from gift-giving in contexts of public relationships, honor, and obligation.[6] *Charis* expresses the norm of receiving and later reciprocating gifts, the formation of relationships, and a reciprocal obligation because of the beauty of a gift, the joy of receiving the gift, or the gift's usefulness.[7] In archaic Greek literature of the seventh-century BC, Homer's *Iliad* contains the phrase *charin oida,* meaning "I recognize the favor," and this recognition exhibited a tangible, active force; it was not a mere passive expression of appreciation.[8] Throughout the *Iliad,* the nuances of *charis* bound ancient people together by instilling in the recipient some sense of favor that was expected to be returned in some way.[9] A key element of strife in the *Iliad* is that the warrior Achilles performed labor or a *charis* for King Agamemnon, yet Agamemnon disappointingly failed to return any

6. Don Ringe, *From Proto-Indo-European to Proto-Germanic* (Oxford: Oxford University Press, 2006), 63.
7. Simon Pulleyn, *Prayer in Greek Religion* (Oxford: Clarendon Press, 1997), 4; quoted in M. P. Knowles, "Reciprocity and 'Favour' in the Parable of the Undeserving Servant (Luke 17.7–10)," *New Testament Studies* 49, no. 2 (2003), 256.
8. Bonnie MacLachlan, *The Age of Grace* (Princeton University Press, 1993), 5-6.
9. Homer, *Iliad* 14.233–35.

appropriate favors (*charis*) to Achilles. Agamemnon's decision to withhold obligatory *charis* to demonstrate gratitude for Achilles' bellicose labors, his leadership, and his loyalty provoked Achilles' wrath. In anger, Achilles withdrew from the battlefield (*Iliad* 9.316), with serious consequences for those with him. Achilles was wrathful not only because of the material gains he should have received, but more importantly, because Agamemnon's failure to reciprocate was an insult to Achilles' honor. Strong, reciprocal, binding relationships bestowed honor for service to one's king and companions during war. The Greek gods also expected reciprocal gratitude in literature of this period or shame would result. In *Olympian Ode* 8, Pindar, an archaic Greek poet, wrote "Accomplishment is granted to the prayers of men in gratitude (*charis*) for their piety." The Greek gods were proverbially pleased with athletes who prayed to them while demonstrating gratitude through sacrifice, and these gods granted victory and honor as a reward. Hesiod, another archaic poet, stressed that one was always expected to "remember good deeds" through reciprocating *charis*.[10]

Grace in the First-Century World of the New Testament

It is especially notable that New Testament writers like the apostle Paul chose the same Greek noun *charis* to express the inviting gift of the atonement of Jesus Christ that the Book of Mormon restores. Paul's Gentile readers innately understood that the *charis* of Jesus' atonement obligated them to cultivate a relationship with God the Father through Jesus Christ's gifts by means of covenantal faithfulness.[11] Gratefully receiving Jesus' atoning gift also granted other future gifts like those of the Spirit as received in covenant relationships by means of continuous cycles of reciprocity (1 Corinthians 12-13; Galatians 5).Therefore, these obliging gifts obligated the ancient Christian disciple to demonstrate gratitude by gradually developing a personal relationship with God the Father and his Son Jesus Christ. Paul wrote, "By the grace [*charis*] of God I am what I am: and his grace [*charis*] which was bestowed upon me was not in vain; but I laboured more abundantly than they all: yet not I, but the grace [*charis*] of God which was with me," (1 Corinthians 15:10). Paul credits

10. Hesiod, *Theogony*, 503–05.
11. Brent J. Schmidt, *Relational Faith* (Provo: BYU Studies, 2022).

his becoming an effective apostle to the gift of obliging grace [*charis*] since it was reciprocated and not received in vain when Paul became motivated and empowered to labor among the Gentiles. Instead of promoting the later doctrine of salvation just by an abstract, one-directional feeling of grace alone, Paul taught empowerment through reciprocating with God the Father through covenants. Paul did not mean in Romans 3:24 to speak of, "being justified freely by his grace" (KJV) but he only stressed being justified through fulfilling covenantal responsibilities, "as a *gift*" (Greek: δωρεὰν, *dorean*) by his obliging grace. Joseph Smith brilliantly changed "freely" to "only" in the JST which reflected the nature of Jesus' inviting, empowering gift. Paul's first-century, Gentile audience certainly would have understood *charis* as a relational, reciprocal gift with expectations of covenantal faithfulness. God's further gifts (*charis*) of the Holy Spirit provide sanctification that gradually empowered individuals to make and keep covenants through faithfulness. Grace motivated them to provide continuing rounds of covenantal, gift-giving. Prophets in the Book of Mormon stressed that faithfulness and sanctification result from gradually receiving many gifts of the Spirit made possible because of Christ's atoning gift.[12] Two-way, reciprocal gift-giving also results in the binding covenants of Christ's church and kingdom.[13]

Grace Becomes Passive and Irresistible During the Apostasy

Early Christian theologians during the apostasy attempted to make the gospel respectable to worldly Gentiles by interpreting Christian doctrines such as the Trinity and moral agency through Neo-Platonism. In the Neo-Platonism of the third century AD, the One (an incomprehensible, all-transcending, abstract Oneness considered to be God) mystically gives everything by an act of all-encompassing love and grace to all things with no-strings-attached (Plotinus, *Enneads* VI.7.35.30–34a). Neo-Platonism rejected traditional expectations of *charis* because mankind was already a low emanation of this One and of this same substance. Therefore, no gifts could be exchanged and no personal relationship with the

12. Brent J. Schmidt, *Relational Faith* (Provo: BYU Studies, 2022), 242-52.
13. Alvin W. Gouldner, "The Norm of Reciprocity: A Preliminary Statement," *American Sociological Review* 25 (April 1960): 161–62; Georg Simmel, *The Sociology of Georg Simmel*, trans. and ed. Kurt H. Wolff (Glencoe, Ill: Free Press, 1950), 387; Howard Becker, *Man in Reciprocity* (New York: Prager, 1956), 1.

"One" god became possible. The pagan Plotinus (AD 204-270) argued that humans could not resist the grace of the One, formerly represented by the distant Greek gods, and so grace (*charis*) could no longer be reciprocated within covenant relationships. Augustine (AD 354-430), the most influential western church father, admired Plotinus even though he was not a Christian and Augustine conveniently interpreted the doctrine of grace through Neo-Platonism instead of traditional archaic, classical, or hellenistic lenses. Moreover, active, relational grace was incompatible with an incomprehensible "Oneness" or God of the creeds of the fourth century AD which neither expected nor required anything. Like Plotinus, Augustine asserted that *charis* was not relational, neither did receiving it oblige any action, loyalty, covenantal faithfulness, nor any kind of reciprocity.[14] Augustine argued for the irresistibility of God's abstract grace, effectively severing the link between covenants, reciprocity, and obligations of traditional grace (*charis*). "It is not to be doubted," wrote Augustine, "that the human will cannot resist the will of God," by turning grace into a mystical emotion that only a completely sovereign God would grant to some through negating human agency and thereby rendering the doctrine of grace completely passive.[15]

Further distortions of relational grace began during the Reformation. Martin Luther (1483-1546), an Augustinian monk, further distorted the relational nature of grace when he professed his gladness that "God has taken my salvation out of my hands [and] into his, making it depend on his choice and not mine, and has promised to save me not by my own work or exertion but by his grace and mercy," exhibiting later Augustinian and Neo-Platonist influences of a passive and mystical notion of grace.[16] John Calvin's (1509-1564) followers summarized his teachings on grace as "irresistible" because grace would automatically save only the elect and then force them to persevere to be saved with no action or covenant relationship with God. Centuries later, Joseph Smith's Christian contemporaries continued to hold these Augustinian and Reformers'

14. Augustine, *De Predestinatione* 100.18; see Blake T. Ostler, "The Concept of Grace in Christian Thought," *Dialogue* 23 (Winter 1990): 13–43, for a discussion on this topic.
15. Augustine, *De Corruptione et Gratia* 14; Augustine, *Enchiridion* 100.2; see Ostler, "Concept of Grace in Christian Thought," for more discussion on this topic.
16. Martin Luther, *On the Bondage of the Will* (LW 33:289), in Philip Cary, *Inner Grace* (Oxford: Oxford University Press, 2008), 85.

understandings of passive, emotional, and mystical grace. The loss of grace's covenantal nuances provides evidence that a universal apostasy occurred because passive, cheap grace distorts the necessity of making and keeping covenants (1 Nephi 13:26). Fortunately, active, covenantal understandings of grace were restored by the Book of Mormon.

Joseph Smith Restores Relational Grace

Joseph Smith's translation of the Book of Mormon restores the ancient nuances of obliging grace as grace again invites, encourages, and promotes faithfulness by teaching how to have a genuine relationship with God. The proper way to demonstrate gratitude for the gifts of God in the Book of Mormon was through repentance and keeping commandments within a covenant by actively accepting Jesus Christ's atoning grace and furthering a relationship with Heavenly Father. The Book of Mormon's depiction of grace is remarkably in harmony with the social sciences and parallels ancient Mediterranean conventions of *hen* and *charis*. Its depictions of relational grace are naturally at home in the seventh-century BC, Near Eastern and Mediterranean cultures, and the later Hellenistic world of Paul. Furthermore, it corrects the divergent and erroneous modern Protestant beliefs of abstract, incongruous, one-directional grace. In particular, the Book of Mormon's usages of grace parallel the reciprocal meanings of *hesed* (mercy) and *hen* (gift) from the Old Testament since all gifts give rise to reciprocal obligations to repent and become faithful within a covenantal relationship with God.

Grace as described in the Book of Mormon remarkably enables and encourages disciples to restore broken covenant relationships. These relationships eventually permit admittance to God's presence. The sermons of Jacob and Nephi in 2 Nephi 10 and 2 Nephi 25 restore active, relational, and covenantal grace. Later in the text, Nephi explains why he works so hard to persuade his posterity and his *brethren*, faithful or recalcitrant, "to believe in Christ," the Messiah, and, "to be *reconciled to God*," preserving and restoring their good standing within the covenantal relationship forged between them and the Lord because of grace as we read, "for we know that it is *by grace that we are saved*, *after all we can do*" (2 Nephi 25:23). Here Nephi's famous words echo the words of his brother Jacob in 2 Nephi 10:24, where Jacob encouraged *the brethren* to reconcile themselves to the will of God and to remember that "*after* ye are *reconciled unto God,* that it is only in and *through the grace of God that you are saved.*" Nephi's phrase, "be reconciled to God," is a shortened allusion to Jacob's slightly longer phrases, "reconcile yourselves to *the will of* God" and "after ye are reconciled to God" since grace necessitated accomplishing His will. When Nephi says, "*We know that* it is by grace that we are saved," he speaks not only for himself, but he also implicitly recognizes Jacob as the source of this expression of their belief. Moreover, when Nephi refers to "*after* all we can do," he would expect his readers to recall what Jacob had previously said, when Jacob explained that salvation can operate through the grace of God only after one is reconciled to God through restoring a proper covenantal relationship. "After all we can do" is then an elliptical reference to Jacob's, "after ye are reconciled unto God," thereby maintaining the covenantal relationship through Jesus' Atonement and human reconciliation of any infractions.

The doctrine of relational grace allows justice, wisdom, power, mercy, and greatness of God to be received in stages as further reciprocal gifts in a cycle of empowering grace so that the recipients "are saved" (2 Nephi 10:24; 2 Nephi 25:23). Besides being an astonishing example of intertextuality in the Book of Mormon, Nephi's description of 2 Nephi 25 invokes the ancient covenantal understanding of obliging grace that was conventional in the pre-classical, Mediterranean world. Furthermore, it is significant that Jacob's sermon was delivered in a setting of a temple dedication to situate Nephi's concept of covenantal grace. In order that this salvific, covenantal relationship might materialize, those bound to God through his covenant, as Jacob taught, must reconcile themselves through grace-enabled relationships. This intriguing Book of Mormon passage corrects false notions of abstract, mystical grace that flourished during late antiquity, the Middle Ages, the Reformation, and are still very popular in many circles of Christendom today. In another passage, the Book of Mormon clarified that being born again comes by choosing to receive the obliging gift of the Spirit of God through the ordinance of baptism as stressed by Jesus Christ himself in 3 Nephi 11:32-35.[17] Making and keeping covenants, beginning with the covenant of baptism (4 Nephi 1:1), empowers disciples to fully receive the temporal and spiritual blessings of the Savior's atoning gift (4 Nephi 1:1-18).

17. "History, 1838–1856, volume C-1 [2 November 1838–31 July 1842]," addenda, p. 13, online at josephsmithpapers.org.

At the end of his ministry, Mormon delivered a message about the obligatory, reciprocal nature of the gift of God through exhorting his son Moroni. This graceful gift specifically resulted in the "gift of his calling" that enabled him to be willing to communicate with all (Moroni 7:2). This grace obligated and thereby empowered Mormon to magnify his calling as a prophetic writer to speak to future readers of the Book of Mormon. He reminded his son to remember the grace of Jesus which invites faith and repentance followed by receiving the covenant of baptism. Furthermore, Jesus' graceful gift progressively brings about a knowledge of His infinite goodness that should obligate Moroni to gain "endurance of faith on his name to the end" (Moroni 8:3). By means of actively encouraging Moroni and the future reader to understand and choose to accept this obliging grace and the covenantal obligations that this relationship entails, the reader might have God the Father's grace to "abide with him forever" (Moroni 9:26). In order for grace to abide forever in a cycle of gift-giving reciprocity, one must choose to come to Jesus Christ, be perfected in him, deny all ungodliness, completely love God and only thereby would his grace become "sufficient" for all in order to complete future cycles of grace (Moroni 10:32). This special gift of reciprocal grace obligates disciples to be perfect in a relationship with Jesus, making it impossible to "deny the power of God" (Moroni 10:32). By means of enabling cycles of relational grace, the faithful may become "sanctified in Christ by the grace of God" and empowered "in the covenant of the Father unto the remission of your sins" to gradually and eventually become completely holy (Moroni 10:33). These uses of grace remarkably parallel those of the ancient, archaic Old World.

Book of Mormon passages also explain in detail what *hen/charis* gifts are and how their acceptance will empower disciples to become faithful. Jesus's atonement is described as an infinite gift which continually invites repentance (2 Nephi 9:7; Alma 34:8-12). Jesus' graceful gift of "tender mercies" are characterized in the first chapter of the Book of Mormon as a gift to the chosen faithful (1 Nephi 1:20) that may "make them mighty even unto the power of deliverance." Finally, at the conclusion of the Book of Mormon, Moroni invites the reader to remember "how merciful the Lord hath been unto the children of men, from the creation of Adam even down until the time that ye shall receive these things, and ponder it in your hearts" (Moroni 10:3), inspiring action of receiving and internalizing Jesus' graceful gift of mercy to result in empowering knowledge of the truthfulness of the Book of Mormon. This grace-encouraging knowledge facilitates the ability to become faithful in covenant relationships. As disciples choose to strive to keep these covenants and remain loyal, they will in due course receive more empowering gifts from God the Father, including the enabling gift of the Holy Ghost to become converted in time, and thus ensure their faithful relationship with God the Father and His Son Jesus Christ is strengthened. Jesus taught that if his people "always remember me," that they would in turn have his Spirit to be with them (3 Nephi 18:11). Through enduring to the end (2 Nephi 31:20), as necessitated by the covenant relationship of obliging grace, disciples come closer to God and even become able to become like Him. Jesus also became like the Father "grace for grace" as all disciples may do so (Helaman 12:24; Doctrine and Covenants 93:12). Even though Jesus did not receive a fulness of God the Father's gifts at first, he continued "grace to grace" (Doctrine and Covenants 93:13) in a cycle of graceful, gift-giving until he did eventually receive their fulness.

In summary, the Book of Mormon's presentation of the doctrine of grace beautifully restores its lost ancient understandings. Grace in the Book of Mormon inspires individuals to faithfully act and thereby receive more gifts of God that progressively enable covenantal faithfulness. Through reading the Book of Mormon, I have been able appreciate the necessity of the Restoration upon realizing how Christ's atoning gift brings about the empowering gift of the Holy Ghost to take full advantage of all of God the Father's amazing gifts. These gifts, favors, and blessings assist us to remain on and progress along the covenant path. Disciples qualify for future spiritual gifts by loyal, faithful service and increasingly receive more divine gifts, especially the gifts of the Holy Ghost, until they receive a fulness of these gifts like Jesus Christ did.

7

The Lehites' God-Imposed Affliction by the Red Sea

A New Solution to the Puzzling 2 Nephi 19:1

Spencer R. Marsh and Spencer Kraus

Among the more puzzling passages in the Book of Mormon is 2 Nephi 19:1. It is a quotation of Isaiah 9:1 as contained in the King James Bible with slight differences. The textual differences in 2 Nephi 19:1 have long been puzzling for textual critics and other students of the Book of Mormon and a point of attack among critics of Joseph Smith. Several solutions have been proposed for the questions that have arisen, but each is found wanting given various considerations including the historical context of both Isaiah and Nephi's writing and the correlative correct translation of Isaiah 9:1. Any solution to "The Red Sea Problem" in 2 Nephi 19:1 must account for all data presented in Isaiah 9:1 and 2 Nephi 19:1. This paper critiques the solutions on offer and proposes a new solution that accounts for all the data.

One of the more puzzling passages in the Book of Mormon is 2 Nephi 19:1. The verse is a quotation of Isaiah 9:1 with some seemingly minor textual differences. In the current Latter-day Saint edition of the King James Bible, Isaiah 9:1 reads as follows:

> Nevertheless the dimness *shall* not *be* such as *was* in her vexation, when at the first he lightly afflicted the land of Zebulun and the land of Naphtali, and afterward did more grievously afflict *her by* the way of the sea, beyond Jordan, in Galilee of the nations. (italics retained from KJV)

In the 2013 ed. of the Book of Mormon, 2 Nephi 19:1 reads as follows:

> Nevertheless, the dimness shall not be such as was in her vexation, when at first he lightly afflicted the land of Zebulun, and the

> land of Naphtali, and afterwards did more grievously afflict by the way of the Red Sea beyond Jordan in Galilee of the nations.

Beyond changes in punctuation and the minor change of *afterward* to *afterwards*, the italicized *her* present in Isaiah 9:1 is absent in 2 Nephi 19:1 and the word "red" is added before "sea." Both "red" and "sea" are capitalized—making the passage read "more grievously afflict by the way of the Red Sea."

According to Latter-day Saint scholar John A. Tvedtnes, the absence of the italicized *her* makes sense since it is not contained in the Masoretic Text from which the King James Version of Isaiah is translated. But the presence of "red" before "sea" makes this passage confusing since the Red Sea is not "'beyond Jordan, in Galilee' nor near the tribes of Zebulun and Naphtali."[1] In addition, the Savior quotes this passage in Matthew 4:14–15 and does not mention the Red Sea. Nor is mention of the Red Sea contained in any extant ancient manuscripts of Isaiah 9:1.

It is somewhat difficult to understand what has become troubling about the textual differences between KJV Isaiah 9:1 and 2 Nephi 19:1 to modern readers of and believers in the Book of Mormon.[2] A possibility is that some see in these differences potential evidence of Joseph Smith trying to bolster the credibility of the Book of Mormon as an ancient document by inserting something that would appear to preserve a more ancient version of Isaiah. Thus, Joseph Smith becomes something of a trigger-happy and reckless reviser of the biblical text in his supposed fabrication of the Book of Mormon. Also, if the Book of Mormon is wrong on this point, it could have bearing on the question of whether the Book of Mormon can be considered, as taught by Joseph Smith, "the most correct of any Book on earth."[3]

Several solutions have been proposed for the problem of 2 Nephi 19:1. This paper will review and critique them and then present a new solution to this problem. We will first lay some groundwork to adequately

---

1. John Tvedtnes, "The Isaiah Variants in the Book of Mormon," *FARMS Preliminary Reports* (1981): 45, available online on the Scripture Central Library.
2. For his part, Jeremy Runnells includes this question in a discussion of King James italics in the Book of Mormon. This is puzzling in itself since the main difference in wording from the KJV does not occur near italicized words. See Jeremy Runnells, *CES Letter: A Search for Answers to My Mormon Doubts* (n.p.: CES Letter Foundation, 2017), 14.
3. Remarks, 28 November 1841, p. 112, online at josephsmithpapers.org.

and quickly critique the solutions proposed to this problem later on. These considerations cumulatively constitute what we believe are desiderata for any proposed solution to the problem of 2 Nephi 19:1.

Part of creating an adequate solution to the problem of 2 Nephi 19:1 and responsibly critiquing the potential solutions currently on offer is just how many moving parts must be nailed down. Thus, we have tried to proceed carefully and judiciously in evaluating and documenting these points.

Various Considerations Calibrating a Solution

A Proper Translation of Isaiah 9:1

One of the first things to consider is a proper translation of the Hebrew of Isaiah 9:1 since specific translations can lead to interpreting the text of Isaiah in different ways. Kraus translates this verse from the Masoretic Text as follows:

> For there will be no gloom to her who is distressed, when at the first time He afflicted the land of Zebulon and the land of Naphtali, and afterwards He has made glorious the Way of the Sea across from the Jordan; Galilee of the Nations.

KJV Isaiah 9:1 (and the corresponding passage in 2 Nephi 19:1) varies from Kraus' translation in two potentially important ways given that they may reflect translation errors on the part of the King James translators (or, perhaps more accurately, their translator predecessors):[4]

1. "Nevertheless, the dimness shall not be such as was in her vexation;"
2. "more grievously afflict."

4. As observed in Stan Spencer, "Missing Words: King James Bible Italics, the Translation of the Book of Mormon, and Joseph Smith as an Unlearned Reader," *Interpreter: A Journal of Latter-day Saint Faith and Scholarship* 38 (2020): 47, the King James Version is a conservative revision of the Bishop's Bible. The original, 1568 edition of the Bishop's Bible in Isaiah 9:1 reads "Neuerthelesse [sic], the darknesse shall not be suche as was in her vexation, when at the first he lightly afflicted the lande Zabulon, and the lande of Nephthali, and afterwarde dyd more greeuously afflict her by the way of the sea beyond Iordane in Galilee of the heathen." Since the King James translators failed to correct for this error, perhaps it is accurate to say that they made a translation error. However it is perhaps most accurate to say the King James translators made a *revision error* since they did not catch the translation error of the Bishop's Bible translators.

Regarding the first phrase, Kraus' translation states that there will be *no gloom* for the future inhabitants of Israel and Judah whereas, in the KJV, the text seems to suggest that the darkness will not be *of the same degree* as it was at the time of the Assyrian invasion. The degree of significance of this translation difference may be seen ranging from little to moderate. We do not see this as strictly an error and thus will not give it further attention.

For the second variation, Kraus rendered the verb *hikbîd* (הכביד) as "honor" rather than "more grievously afflict." This verb comes from the root *kbd*, which could be translated either as "glorify/honor" or as "make heavy," often with a negative connotation.[5] Given the context of this verse, however, "honor" appears to be the correct translation as Isaiah begins, in verse 2 and onward, to prophecy of the future glorious reunification of Israel through a new Davidic king.[6] As such, "more grievously afflict" could be considered a "King James Version translation error" found in the Book of Mormon. However, as we will argue, the dual meaning of the verb *hikbîd* (הכביד) may have been used creatively by Nephi to describe afflictions he and his family experienced and, as such, this may not be an error in the *Book of Mormon;* but it may be considered a translation error for *KJV Isaiah specifically.*[7]

---

5. See, for example, how this verb is used in Exodus 8:11; 1 Kings 12:10, 14; Isaiah 6:10; and Lamentations 3:7. See Ludwig Koehler and Walter Baumgartner, *The Hebrew and Aramaic Lexicon of the Old Testament*, trans. M. E. J. Richardson, study edition, 2 vols. (Leiden: Brill, 2001), s.v. כבד. Hereafter cited as *HALOT.* Scholars that follow the translation of the Hebrew *hikbîd* (הכביד) as something akin to "more grievously afflict" are uncertain as to the exact identity of the two rulers that make the two military passes on Israel. See Robert S. Boylan, "Ben McGuire on the use of 'Red Sea' in 2 Nephi 19:1," *Scriptural Mormonism*, July 6, 2018, online at scripturalmormonism.blogspot.com. This is a repost of an archived website hosted by FAIR found at https://web.archive.org/web/19990224085409/http://www.fair-lds.org:80/Questions/Answers/AN01010.html.
6. Latter-day Saint linguist Royal Skousen likewise agrees that this translation is preferable in Royal Skousen, *The History of the Text of the Book of Mormon, Part Five: King James Quotations in the Book of Mormon* (Provo, UT: FARMS, 2019), 216. This translation has support from a significant number of modern, popular, English translations of the Bible. See "Isaiah 9:1," BibleHub, accessed December 3, 2023, https://biblehub.com/parallel/isaiah/9-1.htm.
7. The meaning of this verb is briefly discussed in Boylan, "Ben McGuire."

These translational considerations delimit our options for interpreting Isaiah 9:1 and providing solutions to 2 Nephi 19:1, as do other historical considerations that we now discuss.

Isaiah 9:1 in Historical Context

Isaiah 9:1 is part of a set of passages that discuss Isaiah's visits with King Ahaz of Judah, prior to Judah negotiating with Israel and Syria to militarily oppose Assyria's pending invasion of the southern Levant. Isaiah prophesies the impending doom of Judah if they unite with King Pekah of Israel and King Rezin of Syria.

In the chapters previous to Isaiah 9, it is specified that the Lord is the one who, through Assyria, will punish Judah if they form alliances with Israel and Syria (Isaiah 7:17–20; 8:5–8).[8] The Chronicler likewise sees God as a driving force behind the Assyrian invasion (1 Chronicles 5:26). However, in Isaiah 9:1, hope is introduced since those whom Isaiah sees as being conquered in the future (Israel and Judah) are promised a lifting of their gloom and frustration and a future restoration brought about by a new Davidic king (Isaiah 9:1–6).[9]

Most biblical interpreters have seen the mention of "the way of the sea" as a reference to the well-known highway *Via Maris*-–the coastal trade route that stretches along the Mediterranean Sea.[10]

Messianic Interpretation of Isaiah 9

Many potential solutions to the problem of 2 Nephi 19:1 have involved messianic interpretation. We are told by Nephi that Isaiah saw Christ (2 Nephi 11:2), and that "all the holy prophets" had "a hope of [Christ's] glory many hundred years before his coming" (Jacob 4:4). That

---

8. Affirmed in G.G.D. Kilpatrick, "The Book of Isaiah," in *The Interpreter's Bible*, 12 vols. (New York: Abingdon Press, 1956), 5:220–21; John Barton and John Muddiman, eds., *The Oxford Bible Commentary* (New York: Oxford University Press, 2001), 445.
9. For excellent treatments on the historical nature of this prophecy regarding a future Davidic king, see J. J. M. Roberts, *First Isaiah: A Commentary* in *Hermeneia: A Critical and Historical Commentary on the Bible* ed. Peter Machinist et al. (Minneapolis, MI: Fortress Press, 2015), 144–154 and Joseph Blenkinsopp, *Isaiah 1–39: A New Translation with Introduction and Commentary* in *The Anchor Bible* vol. 19 (New York, NY: Doubleday, 2000), 245–251.
10. As argued by Roberts, "way of the sea" is probably referring to "the coastal area south of Mount Carmel that became the Assyrian province of Dūʾru." See Roberts, *First Isaiah*, 147; cf. Blenkinsopp, *Isaiah*, 247.

would naturally include Isaiah. It would thus be logical to fit both Isaiah and Nephi's version of Isaiah into a messianic framework.

On the other hand, there are some potential challenges to reading any text of the Old Testament (such as this Isaiah passage included in the Book of Mormon) through a messianic lens. Some of these challenges have been presented by scholar Joseph M. Spencer in relation to Isaiah 9 particularly. Following many scholars, Spencer sees this chapter as likely referring to the historical King Hezekiah–a contemporary of Isaiah. However, other scholars believe that Isaiah's prophecy has a dual fulfillment, allowing this prophecy to refer to Jesus as well as to Isaiah's more immediate context.[11]

The debate over whether Christ is present in Isaiah 9 continues to be heated. Given how debatable messianism is in Isaiah 9, we believe that the most satisfying solution to the problems of 2 Nephi 19:1 is one that does not rely on messianism and thus avoids the debate altogether. The solution thus, in its own way, becomes robust against criticism from either side of that debate.

The Joseph Smith Translation of Isaiah 9:1

The Joseph Smith Translation (JST) of Isaiah 9:1 is fascinating. It was completed by Joseph Smith with Frederick G. Williams as his scribe

---

11. Joseph M. Spencer, *The Vision of All: 25 Lectures on Isaiah in Nephi's Record* (Salt Lake City: Greg Kofford Books, 2016), 203–08; 10–12. Informed pushback is presented in John Gee, "How Not to Read Isaiah," *Interpreter: A Journal of Latter-day Saint Faith and Scholarship* 37 (2020): 29–40 and Donald W. Parry, "An Approach to Isaiah Studies," *Interpreter: A Journal of Latter-day Saint Faith and Scholarship* 34 (2020): 245–264. Specifically, they argue that the consensus of scholarship views this chapter as Messianic in an eschatological sense and that Isaiah 9 does not describe a mere human king contemporary to Isaiah. It appears one of the main differences in Spencer's approach to Gee's and Parry's is that the former views this prophecy primarily as historical, which has been likened to the Messiah by later interpreters, whereas the latter both see this prophecy primarily as Isaiah waxing messianic while still crafting it in such a way that it has present meaning to Isaiah's specific historical context as well. A response to Parry's review of Spencer is found in Joshua M. Sears, "An Other Approach to Isaiah Studies," *Interpreter: A Journal of Latter-day Saint Faith and Scholarship* 37 (2020): 1–20. Parry has responded that, in many ways, Sears' response misreads Parry's authorial intent. See Donald W. Parry, "The Importance of Authorial Intent," *Interpreter: A Journal of Latter-day Saint Faith and Scholarship* 37 (2020): 21–28.

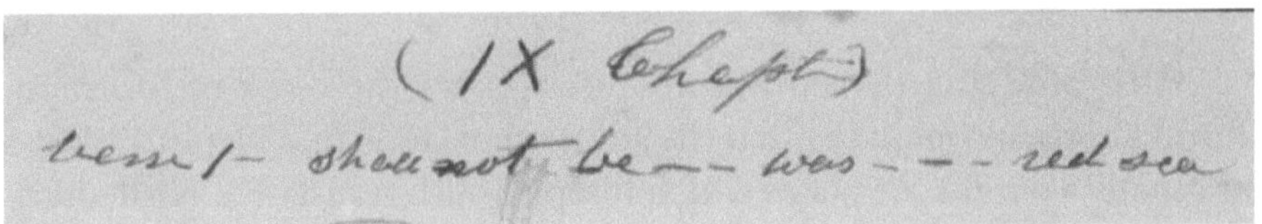
(IX Chapt)
verse 1— shall not be — was — — red sea

Joseph Smith's proposed revisions of Isaiah 9:1 in the handwriting of his scribe Frederick G. Williams.

sometime between late July 1832 and July 2, 1833.[12] Above is an image of the translation taken from the Joseph Smith Papers.[13]

One will see that Joseph Smith seems to target the words "shall," "not," "be," and "was" in his revision. He also intentionally adds "red" before "sea." "Not" seems to have an aborted strikethrough going through at least that word's first letter. It appears that the word "be" was written after the "t" in "not" but that also looks like it was aborted and like the ink used to write it was wiped off. "Be" was then written separately from "not." It may be of note that "shall," "be," and "was" are italicized words in the King James Version of the Bible that Joseph Smith was working from.[14] Fascinatingly, the italicized *her* does *not* appear to be targeted in JST Isaiah 9:1 as it seems to have been in the Book of Mormon's rendering of Isaiah 9:1.

Along with this data from the JST, it is known that Joseph Smith made edits to the text of the Book of Mormon for its 1837 and 1840 editions, and it is highly unlikely that he would have let an error persist after three separate examinations of the text. We are unaware of any other source contemporary to Joseph that translates Isaiah 9:1 with "red" before "sea."[15] The minimal inference that can be made from this data is that Joseph Smith was comfortable with the appearance of "red" in the Book of Mormon. Any solution to the problem of 2 Nephi 19:1's addition of "red" must be consistent with that clearly-supported inference.

12. Scott H. Faulring, Kent P. Jackson, and Robert J. Matthews, *Joseph Smith's New Translation of the Bible: Original Manuscripts* (Provo, UT: Religious Studies Center, Brigham Young University, 2004), 59.
13. Old Testament Revision 2, p. 100, The Joseph Smith Papers, online at josephsmithpapers.org.
14. See Faulring, Jackson, and Matthews, *New Translation*, 794.
15. We mention Targum Jonathan in this paper, but the earliest English translation we could locate of it did not appear until 1871–close to 30 years after Joseph Smith's death and 41 years after the publication of the Book of Mormon.

Skousen's Textual Criticism of 2 Nephi 19:1

After studying the earliest manuscripts for the Book of Mormon, Royal Skousen concluded that the addition of "red" in 2 Nephi 19:1 was originally a part of the plates which Joseph Smith translated. He deduces this from the fact the phrase "way of the Red sea [sic]" appears four times in the King James Version.[16] Also, out of 82 occurrences of the word "sea" in the Book of Mormon, there is no early manuscript evidence that "red" was added to the text and then later deleted. Therefore, according to Skousen, this variant was likely either introduced by Nephi or was present in a supposed ancient version of Isaiah quoted by Nephi.[17]

Regarding the four references to the "way of the Red sea" in the Bible, each literally translates the same phrase: *derek yam sûp* (דרך ים־סוף).[18] Commentators indicate that that phrase can have reference to the King's Highway or some other nonspecific route leading to the Red Sea.[19]

It is worth noting that the English phrase "by way of the X" in Joseph Smith's and the King James translators' time could have been interpreted as signifying "by a route which passes through or over (a specified place)."[20] Similarly, the expression "by the way" could refer to being "[a]longside or near the road; by the roadside" in both the King

16. Numbers 14:25; 21:4; Deuteronomy 1:40; 2:1.
17. Royal Skousen, *Analysis of Textual Variants of the Book of Mormon Part Two: 2 Nephi 11 – Mosiah 16* (Provo, UT: FARMS, 2014), 732–33. Because of the support for this phrase in the manuscript evidence, Skousen has retained it in his reconstruction of "the earliest text" of the Book of Mormon. See 2 Nephi 19:1 in Royal Skousen, ed., *The Book of Mormon: The Earliest Text* (New Haven, CT: Yale University Press, 2009), 119; Royal Skousen, ed., *The Book of Mormon: The Earliest Text*, 2nd ed. (New Haven, CT: Yale University Press, 2022), 119.
18. While the Hebrew would literally read "way of the Sea of Reeds," Kraus has translated the name of this sea as the traditional "Red Sea " out of convenience to show the connection to the Book of Mormon text more clearly.
19. For commentators arguing for a nonspecific route, see Michael D. Coogan, ed., *The New Oxford Annotated Bible*, 5th ed. (New York: Oxford University Press, 2018), 212-13, 223, 252-53. While we do not know how Nephi composed his record or in what language it was preserved in, the underlying Hebrew with which Nephi would have been familiar is an illuminating source to understand the Book of Mormon more fully. For the purposes of this paper, we will assume that Nephi had this same phrase in mind with all of the nuances available in the Hebrew language.
20. *Oxford English Dictionary*; s.v. "by way of; by the way of."

James translators' timeframe and that of Joseph Smith.[21] The Hebrew *derek* has been understood in the same broad way, including travel *near* a given place. As such, the phrase "by the way of the Red Sea", as it appears in 2 Nephi 19:1 (and translated in part from the Hebrew word *derek*), *could* refer to the King's Highway; but it does not necessarily do so. It could refer to any path *to*, *near*, or even *over* the Red Sea. Depending on the translation of the Hebrew and on the interpretive choices one makes with the English text of KJV Isaiah, one can interpret the English phrase "by way of the Red Sea" in 2 Nephi 19:1 in one of four ways:

1. As referring to traveling *towards* the Red Sea
2. As referring to traveling *near* the Red Sea.
3. As referring to traveling *over* or *through* the Red Sea
4. As referring to traveling by the Way of the Red Sea or the King's Highway.

These considerations will help us to provide an interpretive solution consistent with the data presented by both KJV Isaiah 9:1 and 2 Nephi 19:1.

The Current Solutions to the Problem of 2 Nephi 19:1

We now present the current solutions on offer from various commentators on 2 Nephi 19:1. One will see that the theorists differ as to exactly *who* is responsible for the textual differences between the 2 Nephi 19:1 and KJV Isaiah 9:1 as well as *why* the differences exist. They also differ in whether the differences constitute an error in either translation or discernment of fact. With our preliminary considerations in place, we can now present and critique the various theories quickly. Our critiques will focus on the different solutions' *plausibility* and/or their *desirability*.

Oliver Overcorrecting

John Tvedtnes suggests that the addition of "red" before "sea" is an example of Oliver Cowdery, Joseph's scribe during this portion of the Book of Mormon translation, "over-hearing" (our term) *Red* and inserting it into the Book of Mormon. That is, Joseph Smith supposedly

21. *Oxford English Dictionary*; s.v. "by the way." Worth noting is that the expression "by way" could refer to being in the journey *towards* a given place. See "by way of; by the way of."

dictated the word "sea" and Oliver understood that to be a reference to the Red Sea given prior mention of it in the Book of Mormon text (e.g. 1 Nephi 4:2). The addition of "red" is therefore an error and attributable to Oliver Cowdery. Whether Tvedtnes believes this insertion was more deliberate or accidental is unclear. The problems with Tvedtnes' theory are twofold. First, it does not account for the likely translation error in KJV Isaiah 9:1 and 2 Nephi 19:1. Second, it does not agree with the evidence presented above that Joseph was comfortable with the presence of "red" in the Book of Mormon.[22]

Oliver Making a Copyist Error

D. Charles Pyle suggested that "[i]t is possible that it is a scribal error on the part of Oliver Cowdery in copying the printer's manuscript from the original manuscript."[23] However, as noted by Pyle, "[t]he problem is that this cannot be proven or disproven because this portion of the original manuscript no longer is extant." In addition to this, Pyle's proposal does not account for the likely translation KJV translation error. Also, the solution does not easily accord with the textual evidence provided by Skousen that "red" was not an accidental insertion into the Book of Mormon text. Finally, it is not consistent with the evidence presented above that Joseph Smith was comfortable with the presence of "red" in the Book of Mormon.

Egyptian Translator Error

In the same source, Pyle suggests that "it also is possible that the Egyptian textual translation of the Hebrew is in error and that Joseph Smith translated it, error and all." Thus, Pyle suggests here that the addition of "red" is attributable to the ancient Egyptian translator-redactor of

22. A third problem might be, assuming that Tvedtnes sees this insertion as more accidental, is that it does not easily accord with the textual evidence provided by Skousen that this was a deliberate insertion into the Book of Mormon text.
23. Email from D. Charles Pyle to Jeff Lindsay, June 2004, quoted in Jeff Lindsay, "Feeling Blue About the Red Sea in the Book of Mormon?" *Arise from the Dust*, October 18, 2019, online at arisefromthedust.com. It is worth noting that, while Pyle offers multiple suggestions regarding this phrase, he notes at the end of his email that "[he is] not willing to state without good evidence that this passage is in error with any degree of certainty, for in [his] opinion there is no certainty either way. [He has] sifted through much contradictory 'evidence' and [has] formed no solid conclusion on this textual matter."

the brass plates upon which Isaiah was contained. It is unclear whether Pyle believes this was a more accidental or a deliberate translation. If deliberate, the theory does not offer a plausible explanation for why the translator of the brass plates thought it necessary to add "red" to "sea." What motive would they have had in doing such a thing? If accidental, it is a bizarre mistake for a translator to make. How does a translator accidentally translate the Hebrew *yam* as Red Sea? In either case, the theory does not account for the likely translation error in the KJV version of Isaiah and the Book of Mormon.

Joseph Smith Inserting a Word Where it was Missing

In an article in *Interpreter: A Journal of Latter-day Saint Faith and Scholarship*, Stan Spencer discusses the modification and deletion of KJV italics in the Book of Mormon. Spencer discusses the two most popular theories to explain the differences in italics between the KJV and the Book of Mormon. Namely, whether the Book of Mormon italics changes reflect a more ancient version of the biblical text being quoted (what Spencer calls the "Ancient Variants Hypothesis") or Joseph Smith being consciously aware of the meaning of italicized words in the King James Version and seeking to modify or delete them as he deemed necessary (what Spencer calls the "Italics Revision Hypothesis"). Spencer proposes a new theory that he terms the *Missing Words Hypothesis*. This theory suggests that the italics were missing from a translation that appeared on the seer stone when Joseph Smith translated. Joseph Smith and Oliver Cowdery then had the task of supplying or not supplying words (and specifically the *italicized* words) where they were missing and at their discretion.

Near the end of his paper and almost as an afterthought, Spencer states that "the Missing Words Hypothesis handily accounts for some of the more problematic variants in the Book of Mormon Isaiah chapters such as the addition of 'red' before 'sea' in 2 Nephi 19:1 (Isaiah 9:1)."[24] However, Spencer's theory does not account for this variant at all. Recall that Spencer's theory requires that italics (and, as far as Spencer stipulates, *only* italics) be missing from the translation that appeared to Joseph Smith. If it is only italics that were missing, then the addition of "red" still does not make sense given the fact that "red" is inserted next to no word placed in italics in the King James Bible. This variant, then, cannot

24. Spencer, "Missing Words," 106.

be explained by this hypothesis. Additionally, Spencer's theory does not account for the likely translation error in KJV Isaiah 9:1.

A "Restoration" of the Text

Book of Mormon scholar Brant Gardner offers another theory:

> Joseph Smith appears to have understood that the italicized words were added by the KJV translators to make sense of the Hebrew. Combined with the addition of the "Red Sea," these changes appear to suggest a modern interaction with the KJV text that intends to both "restore" by removing the italicized words that were not originally present, and by attempting to clarify which sea. Such changes warn us that we should be very cautious about suggesting a literal translation of the plates. The evidence suggests that Joseph's intellect participated in the project (also suggested by D&C 9:7–10).[25]

Thus, Gardner proposes that Joseph Smith is the one that is responsible for the addition of "red" and the deletion of the italicized *her*. Gardner does not seem to take a position on whether the addition is erroneous.

There are three broad problems with Gardner's argument.[26] First, Gardner does not offer any suggestion as to why Joseph Smith would have even wanted to add "red" in order to clarify which sea Isaiah was referring to. Why would Joseph Smith have seen that as warranted? Second, Gardner's argument does not account for the likely translation error in KJV Isaiah and the Book of Mormon. Third, Gardner's citation of Doctrine & Covenants 9:7–10 may not actually be referring to the translation process. As argued by Stan Spencer, "[a] close reading of the entire revelation…suggests that the Lord was not telling Oliver Cowdery how to translate but rather how to know whether it was right for him to translate and how to obtain the faith necessary to do so."[27]

---

25. Brant A. Gardner, *Second Witness: Analytical & Contextual Commentary on the Book of Mormon, Volume 2: Second Nephi through Jacob* (Salt Lake City: Greg Kofford Books, 2007), 267.
26. A fourth might be that Gardner's argument relies at least in part on an assumption that Joseph Smith knew the meaning of the italics and was deliberately interacting with them in his translation of biblical texts quoted in the Book of Mormon. However, that has not been definitively established. For a brief summary of the debate over that question and the lines of evidence used to support both sides of the question, see "KJV italicized text in the Book of Mormon," *FAIR*, accessed February 18, 2024, online at fairlatterdaysaints.org.
27. Stan Spencer, "The Faith to See: Burning in the Bosom and Translating in

The Way of the Red Sea

Another proposal to the problem of 2 Nephi 19:1 was given by D. Charles Pyle and expanded on by Sarah Allen.[28] Pyle proposed two potential solutions for the text. Both potential solutions view this verse as a reference to some specific event in the life of Jesus Christ. First, Pyle proposes that 2 Nephi 19:1 may have reference to Joseph and Mary taking the infant Jesus along the King's Highway when returning from Egypt into Jerusalem. Second, Pyle proposes that 2 Nephi 19:1 may have reference to Jesus' baptism on the other side of the Jordan in Bethabara and speculates that Jesus passed through the King's Highway to arrive at Bethabara.[29]

A problem with Pyle's proposals is that they both rely on a strictly Christo-messianic interpretation of Isaiah 9:1, fulfilled by a specific event in the mortal life of Christ. While we do not reject attempts to interpret the text of Isaiah messianically wholesale, messianic interpretation—and specifically a messianic interpretation that includes fulfillment in the form of specific events in the life of Jesus Christ—is not desirable given the debate over messianism.[30] Second, neither of Pyle's solutions account for the likely translation error in KJV Isaiah and the Book of Mormon; nor do they make sense even if assumed to be a correct translation. Certainly the Savior's presence while coming along a particular path like the Way of the Red Sea for His baptism or first arrival into Jerusalem would bring glory and light, not affliction, to the people of surrounding areas. The accounts of those two events in the Bible do not mention affliction.

The possibility that Nephi and his family took the Way of the Red Sea while leaving Jerusalem has been discussed and supported by various scholars of the Book of Mormon.[31] The Hebrew word *derek* (דרך)

Doctrine & Covenants 9," *Interpreter: A Journal of Latter-day Saint Faith and Scholarship* 18 (2016): 219.

28. Sarah Allen, "The CES Letter Rebuttal, Part 2: Book of Mormon Questions, Section A," *FAIR Blog*, August 26, 2021, online at fairlatterdaysaints.org.
29. D. Charles Pyle to Jeff Lindsay, June 2004.
30. An overview of the potentially messianic themes in this chapter is provided in Donald W. Parry, "Isaiah chap. review: 2 Nephi 19 // Isaiah 9 Background and synopsis," in *Book of Mormon Reference Companion*, ed. Dennis L. Largey (Salt Lake City, UT: Deseret Book), 373–374.
31. Sidney B. Sperry, *Book of Mormon Compendium* (Salt Lake City: Bookcraft, 1968), 97–98 notes this as one of two possibilities without coming to any concrete conclusions. Similarly, S. Kent Brown proposes four possible solutions of which

is ambiguous enough that the King's Highway could be the referent of this verse.[32] However, others have discussed the problems with such theories such as how Judahite travelers like the Lehites would have been violently hunted by Edomites as they passed through Edom via the King's Highway. Thus, these scholars favor a more direct route to the Red Sea or at least one that bypasses Edom.[33] The possibility that Nephi was referring to the King's Highway as the route for the Lehites' exit from Jerusalem and travel down the Arabian peninsula is not likely.[34] Thus, in accordance with our theory, we favor viewing the Hebrew *derek* as referring broadly to a unspecific kind of road or journey and, specifically, to travel *near* a particular location.

---

the King's Highway is one in S. Kent Brown, "New Light from Arabia on Lehi's Trail," in *Echoes and Evidences of the Book of Mormon*, ed. Donald W. Parry, Daniel C. Peterson and John W. Welch (Provo, UT: FARMS, 2002), 57–59 and S. Kent Brown, "Jerusalem Connections to Arabia in 600 BC," in *Glimpses of Lehi's Jerusalem*, ed. John W. Welch, David Rolph Seely and Jo Ann H. Seely (Provo, UT: FARMS, 2004), 628. It is likewise briefly considered in George Potter and Richard Wellington, *Lehi in the Wilderness: 81 New Documented Evidences That the Book of Mormon Is a True History* (Springville, Utah: Cedar Fort, 2003), 21–22. However, the authors of this volume favor a second highway slightly east of the King's Highway. The possibility was also discussed by Allen, "CES Letter Rebuttal, Part 2": "It's also likely the beginning route that Nephi's family took during the beginning of their own flight from Israel. Imagine being Nephi, with the Hebrew love of wordplay, puns, and symbolism as part of your ingrained culture, fleeing from Jerusalem along the same path that your ancestors fled to Jerusalem from Egypt centuries before."

32. See *HALOT*, s.v. דרך.
33. See, for example, Warren P. Aston, "Into Arabia: Lehi and Sariah's Escape from Jerusalem," *BYU Studies Quarterly* 58, no. 4 (2019): 99–126; Jeffrey R. Chadwick, "Dating the Departure of Lehi from Jerusalem," *BYU Studies Quarterly* 57 no. 2 (2018): 34–35; and Jeffrey R. Chadwick, "The Wrong Place for Lehi's Trail and the Valley of Lemuel," *Review of Books on the Book of Mormon* 17 no. 2 (2005): 197–215; D. Kelly Ogden, "Answering the Lord's Call (1 Nephi 1–7)," in *Studies in Scripture: 1 Nephi to Alma 29,* vol. 7 of 8, ed. Kent P. Jackson (Salt Lake City, UT: Deseret Book, 1987), 21–24; Lynn Hilton and Hope Hilton, *In Search of Lehi's Trail* (Salt Lake City, UT: Deseret Book, 1976), 38.
34. Of course, given the lack of details in the Book of Mormon regarding this portion of Lehi's journey, it is impossible to ascertain with any specificity regarding which route is most accurate. Chadwick's arguments against traveling via the King's Highway in Chadwick, "The Wrong Place," 201–206, however, effectively show that this is the least likely route for Lehi's family to have taken.

Nephi's Error

Book of Mormon scholar Grant Hardy put forth the theory that the addition of "red" might have been an error on the part of Nephi.[35] However, Hardy does not give any explanation as to why or how Nephi would have made this error. We could not imagine a plausible explanation. Thus, this theory does not amount to much.

Joseph Smith's Error

Critics of the Book of Mormon are surely sympathetic to the notion that this textual oddity in 2 Nephi 19:1 can be ascribed to an error on the part of Joseph Smith in his attempt to make the Book of Mormon appear more ancient. Similarly, Grant Hardy proposed that the data of 2 Nephi 19:1 may be ascribed to such an error on the part of Joseph.[36] But there are problems that must be overcome even with this "solution." Why does Joseph Smith put "red" into scripture in such a gratuitous, decontextualized way? Why would Joseph Smith have thought that that would be appropriate or even remotely convincing as evidence of the Book of Mormon's antiquity for his future readers? Would Joseph Smith not have corrected his error when he was reviewing Isaiah 9:1 in his new translation of the Bible or when he made edits to the Book of Mormon for its 1837 or 1840 editions? These questions remain unconvincingly answered by any proponent of this theory. Even if assuming that the Book of Mormon is not a product of divine revelation, a much more warranted explanation of the data would be that it is part of a larger and more integral device rather than merely a thoughtless blunder on the part of Joseph Smith alone or in tandem with his other supposed co-conspirators in the creation of the Book of Mormon.

Moses and the Exodus

Scholars Donald W. Parry, Jay A. Perry, and Tina M. Peterson write that "[t]his expression refers to events surrounding Moses and the Israelites as they fled across the Red Sea from Egyptian bondage."[37] Though,

---

35. Grant Hardy, ed., *The Annotated Book of Mormon* (New York: Oxford University Press, 2023), 133.
36. Hardy, *The Annotated Book of Mormon,* 133.
37. Donald W. Parry, Jay A. Perry, and Tina M. Peterson, *Understanding Isaiah* (Salt Lake City: Deseret Book, 2009), 90. This is most clearly commentary on the Bible and JST, but we found it likely that either the authors or those that read them

as we have documented above, both the original context of Isaiah and the most likely correct translation of this verse do not support the notion of the verse having reference to the Exodus. On the other hand, it may be of interest to note that interpreting the verse to refer to the Red Sea is not foreign to the Targumic tradition. Targum Jonathan creatively interprets this verse to refer to the Red Sea.[38] This, along with the presence of "red"

---

might think of this at least as a potential solution for 2 Nephi 19:1 and thus its inclusion in our paper. Allen, "CES Letter Rebuttal, Part 2" also sees Nephi as working in allusions to the Exodus in this passage.

38. The Targum of Isaiah engages in a similar kind of editing as Nephi and, just like Nephi, appropriates the "sea" of Isaiah 9:1 to refer to the Red Sea while also rendering the verb hikbîd in the same context as afflicting. Targum Jonathan validates Nephi's method for reimagining the text given a unique historical setting and set of theological concerns. Although generally believed to have been translated into Aramaic in at least the second century AD if not later, this Targumic expansion reflects the exact same nuances that Nephi appears to have had in mind. For a brief discussion on the dating of the text, see Bruce D. Chilton, ed., *The Isaiah Targum: Introduction, Translation, Apparatus, and Notes* (Edinburgh: T & T Clark, 1987), xxi–xxiii. See *Targum Jonathan*, Isaiah 8:23. The relevant passage has been translated by Spencer Kraus as follows: "For all who come to oppress them will not be weary, like at the first time the people of the land of Zebulon were exiled, and the people of the land of Naphtali; and a strong king will exile their remainder because they did not remember the power of the Sea, the miracles of the Jordan, the war of the people's walled cities." The Aramaic text of this Targum from which this translation was based is available online at sefaria.org. Although the Targum simply states "the power of the Sea," context clearly indicates that the Targumist has the Red Sea in mind as it is immediately followed by two allusions to the Israelites entering the Promised Land. This has been noted by Leivy Smolar and Moses Aberbach, *Studies in Targum Jonathan to the Prophets* (Baltimore, MD: KTAV Publishing House, 1983), 201 and 201n471. English translators of this Targum have long recognized this to be the case. C. W.H. Pauli, trans., *The Chaldee Paraphrase of the Prophet Isaiah* (London: London Society's House, 1871), 29–30, for example, added the word "red" to his translation, making the verse read "the power of the *Red* Sea" to clarify what sea was the referent in this verse (italics in original; available online at archive.org). Chilton, *The Isaiah Targum*, 21 does not (as Pauli does) include the word "Red," but notes that "Their 'distress' will be complete, as complete as long ago, when the exodus, the crossing of the Jordan, and the glorious possession of the promised land were forgotten." Robert S. Boylan has previously offered some brief thoughts on this translation at Robert S. Boylan, "'Red Sea' in Isaiah 9:1 of the Chaldee Paraphrase of the Prophet Isaiah," *Scriptural Mormonism*, April 15, 2017, online at scripturalmormonism.blogspot.com.

in the JST, may be the source of confusion for these authors' reading of the text.

Sufah *and the Arnon River*

Another interesting proposal to the issues presented in 2 Nephi 19:1 was given by E. Jan Wilson.[39] Wilson proposes "that the word *sufah* was replaced using the term *yam* by some scribe between Lehi's time and the time when the Great Isaiah Scroll was copied."[40] This would be significant as the passage in Isaiah 9:1 would be referring to a place near the Arnon River, also known as Wadi-al-Majib, on the east side of the Dead Sea. Joseph Smith then, according to Wilson, translated *sufah* on the brass plates version of Isaiah as "Red Sea." Why the translation as Red Sea? "[P]erhaps," Wilson suggests, "there were constraints such as limits to what people were able to accept during his day, or perhaps more significant changes to clarify the verse were not viewed as necessary at that time. Yet perhaps by changing 'sea' to 'Red Sea,' the translation leaves a hint concerning the original verbiage of that verse and what Isaiah was actually saying."[41]

There are, unfortunately, crucial problems with this proposal. First, it does not solve for the likely translation error from KJV Isaiah 9:1 in 2 Nephi 19:1 as documented above. Wilson (himself educated in Hebrew) translates the passage very similarly to Kraus above but does not explain why the erroneous translation survives in the Book of Mormon. Second, as noted by Wilson, the notion that the word "sufah" was present in Isaiah's original writing is, at best, "speculative,"[42] especially considering there being no manuscript evidence that such a reading has ever been present in Isaiah. Third, even if the word was present in the original writings of Isaiah, and considering the likely correct translation of the verses that we presented above (and that Wilson himself recognizes given his translation of the text), Wilson fails to satisfactorily explain how the Arnon River would have been situationally relevant to Isaiah, such that Isaiah would include mention of it in his writings to the kings of Syria, southern Israel, and Northern Israel. How would the Lord honor this

39. E. Jan Wilson, "Joseph Smith and the 'Red Sea' in 2 Nephi 19:1," *Interpreter: A Journal of Latter-day Saint Faith and Scholarship* 60 (2024): 183–95.
40. Wilson, 194.
41. Wilson, 194–95.
42. Wilson, 194.

place along the Arnon River? Why would He do that? These questions remain unanswered.

The Assyrians Invading via the Way of the Red Sea

Most Latter-day Saint authors that have commented on 2 Nephi 19:1 propose that it is referring to a route used by the Assyrians in a theoretical second military pass on Israel, Judah, and Syria, and that 2 Nephi 19:1 clarifies the route the Assyrians took in this second pass: the Way of the Red Sea or King's Highway.[43] Some seem to assume that "red" is thus a part of a more ancient version of Isaiah while others seem to believe that the addition was made by a later author or editor. Yet others seem to have no position. In any case, this proposal attempts to fit the "Red Sea variant" into Isaiah's original context. However, it is important to keep in mind the correct translation and interpretation of Isaiah 9:1 noted above: Isaiah is discussing a time of affliction and then a forthcoming state of peace, honor, and glory. He is not discussing a time of light affliction and then a time of equal or greater affliction. Thus, if Nephi is doing anything with Isaiah, he is not *clarifying* Isaiah's words (which Nephi would have understood in their original context) but *reappropriating* and *retooling* them. This is exactly what we now argue.

43. Allen, "CES Letter Rebuttal, Part 2"; Victor L. Ludlow, *Isaiah: Prophet, Seer, and Poet* (Salt Lake City, UT: Deseret Book, 1982), 152; Hoyt W. Brewster, Jr., *Isaiah Plain and Simple: The Message of Isaiah in the Book of Mormon* (Salt Lake City, UT: Deseret Book, 1995), 88–89; Robert L. Miller, *Isaiah: A Prophet's Prophet*, 2 vols. (Springville, UT: Cedar Fort, 2021), 1:122; Monte S. Nyman, *Great Are the Words of Isaiah* (Salt Lake City, UT: Bookcraft, 1980), 66–67; *I, Nephi, Wrote this Record: A Teaching Commentary on The First Book of Nephi and the Second Book of Nephi* (Orem, UT: Granite Publishing & Distribution, 2003), 587–588; W. Cleon Skousen, *Isaiah in Modern Times* (Salt Lake City: Ensign Publishing Company, 1984), 220–21; Parry, "2 Nephi 19 // Isaiah 9," 373–374. For reasons why this may not be referring to a highway, however, see Roberts, *First Isaiah*, 147; cf. Blenkinsopp, *Isaiah*, 247. Those that support this kind of solution might cite 1 Chronicles 5:25–6:3 where the King James version tells us that "the God of Israel stirred up the spirit of Pul king of Assyria, and the spirit of Tilgath-pilneser king of Assyria, and he carried them away[.]" The King James version is translated such that it makes it sound as if Pul and Tilgath-pilneser are two separate individuals. The problem is that they are one and the same individual.

A New Solution to the Problem of 2 Nephi 19:1

We now present what we believe is the better solution to the problem of 2 Nephi 19:1 given the various desiderata presented above.

Nephi's "Likening" of Isaiah

It is well-known by scholars that Nephi creatively "likens" (1 Nephi 19:23) Isaiah's words to his own historical context and theological concerns.[44] How this likening occurs may not be fully understood, but what all scholars recognize is that there is a conscious and deliberate selection of passages from Isaiah as well as textual differences between KJV Isaiah and the Book of Mormon's version of Isaiah.[45] It may be that at least some of the textual differences in Isaiah present in the Book of Mormon represent a more ancient version of Isaiah than that present in the Masoretic Text from which the King James Bible was translated. On the other hand, it is possible that Nephi is inserting his own, perhaps divinely inspired, emendations into Isaiah to explain Isaiah and make it relevant to his own historical context and unique set of theological concerns.[46] We find the evidence for this hypothesis strong for at least some of the variants between the KJV's Isaiah and the Book of Mormon's Isaiah. For example, the Isaiah of Isaiah 49:17 and 2 Nephi 6:17 (Jacob quoting Isaiah) is different from 1 Nephi 21:17, where Nephi is quoting Isaiah. We encourage interested readers to become familiar with the arguments that scholars have offered for this hypothesis. Their work is cited below.[47]

---

44. See, for example, John Gee and Matthew Roper, "'I Did Liken All Scriptures Unto Us': Early Nephite Understandings of Isaiah and Implication for 'Others' in the Land," in *The Fulness of the Gospel: Foundational Teachings from the Book of Mormon*, ed. Camille Fronk Olson, Brian M. Hauglid, Patty Smith, and Thomas A. Wayment (Provo, UT: Religious Studies Center, Brigham Young University; Salt Lake City, UT: Deseret Book, 2003), 51–65.
45. For chapter selection, see Joseph M. Spencer, *The Vision of All: 25 Lectures on Isaiah in Nephi's Record* (Salt Lake City: Greg Kofford Books, 2016). For a good summary, see Book of Mormon Central, "What Vision Guides Nephi's Choice of Isaiah Chapters? (2 Nephi 11:2)," *KnoWhy* 38 (February 22, 2016), online at Scripture Central. For changes in wording, see Dennis L. Largey, ed., *Book of Mormon Reference Companion* (Salt Lake City: Deseret Book, 2003), 347, 350, 353, 356, 359, 361, 367, 375, 378, 384, 387, 391.
46. It should be noted that these options are not mutually exclusive to explain differences between KJV Isaiah and the Book of Mormon version of Isaiah.
47. Ryan Sharp, "Except Some Man Should Guide Me," in *They Shall Grow Together:*

Seemingly under the assumption that Nephi was consciously shaping the text, one solution to the problem of 2 Nephi 19:1 was noted by BYU professor Kerry Muhlestein: "It is possible that as Nephi likened Isaiah's writings to the situation of his own people, and since they did travel by the way of the Red Sea, he altered it to fit his own situation."[48]

Under this proposed solution, Nephi, in 2 Nephi 19:1, reminds his audience through Isaiah about the captivity of Israel and then creatively shifts the intent of Isaiah from focusing on Naphtali's and Zebulon's afflictions to the afflictions imposed by God on Nephi's own family "by the way of the Red Sea." Thus the absence of the italicized *her* since – with the addition of *her* – the text refers to Naphtali and Zebulon and not Nephi's family. Muhlestein believes that "we cannot conclusively tell the reason for this difference" between KJV Isaiah and 2 Nephi.[49] However, we believe that the data firmly support his hypothesis.

Nephi's account of the Lehites' travels in the Arabian peninsula states that they traveled in a "south-southeast direction … in the most fertile parts of the wilderness, which were in the borders *near the Red Sea*" (1 Nephi 16:13–14; emphasis added). During this part of their journey lasting "many days," (1 Nephi 16:15, 17) Nephi recounts the incident of his broken bow, the family being chastened by the Lord for their murmuring, Ishmael's death and burial, and the plot of Laman and Lemuel

---

The Bible in the Book of Mormon, ed. Charles Swift and Nicholas J. Frederick (Provo, UT: Religious Studies Center, Brigham Young University; Salt Lake City: Deseret Book, 2022), 326–63. Sharp makes the good point that some of the emendations can be understood as clarifications by Joseph Smith. See also Daniel L. Belnap, "The Bible, the Book of Mormon, and the Concept of Scripture," in *No Weapon Shall Prosper: New Light on Sensitive Issues*, ed. Robert L. Millet (Provo, UT: Religious Studies Center, Brigham Young University; Salt Lake City: Deseret Book, 2011), 157–65; Hardy, *The Annotated Book of Mormon*, 66–77, 121–44; Spencer, *The Vision of All*, 95–117. Joseph Spencer reminds us that we need to decide on a case-by-case basis whether Nephi is making edits to Isaiah consciously. See Spencer, *The Vision of All*, 97.

48. Kerry Muhlestein, *Learning to Love Isaiah: A Guide and Commentary* (American Fork, UT: Covenant Communications, 2021), 80. Allen, "The CES Letter Rebuttal, Part 2" also favors Nephi being responsible for the changes and briefly indicates such. These authors did not present nearly this detailed critique nor did they detail and offer this much evidence for their replacement theory.
49. Muhlestein, 80. Allen, "The CES Letter Rebuttal, Part 2".

to kill Lehi before the family turned eastward (1 Nephi 16:15, 18–25, 34, 37).[50]

After arriving at Bountiful, Nephi reflected that the Lehites "had suffered many afflictions and much difficulty, yea, even so much that we cannot write them all" (1 Nephi 17:6). These mentions of affliction in 1 Nephi 16 and 17 are the first mention of such in a context that is neither visionary (as in 1 Nephi 11:31) nor part of a biblical quotation (as in 1 Nephi 21:13). While Nephi can be understood as reflecting on the Lehites' entire journey to Bountiful, it is clearly more likely, given the explicit text as well as informed estimates regarding how much time the Lehites' could have been traveling per day, that Nephi here has the afflictions experienced near the Red Sea in mind.[51] The events of 1 Nephi 16 and 17 can accurately fit into the Lord "grievously afflict[ing] by the way of the Red Sea" in 2 Nephi 19:1 and "Nephi can engage in his creative editing of Isaiah, including a play on Isaiah's *hikbîd* (הכביד), to reflect those afflictions imposed by God.[52]

---

50. See 1 Nephi 16:15, 18–25, 34, 37.
51. Nephi seems to refer to these same afflictions in 1 Nephi 18 as well as 2 Nephi 1–5. While it is impossible to tell exactly how long they spent traveling compared to how long they were camped at any location, Aston, "Into Arabia," 114 notes that loaded camels could travel at a speed of 20–25 miles per day. Should Lehi and his family have taken camels, we would not expect them to exceed this travel distance in a single day. Had no camels been employed, Chadwick, "The Wrong Place," 202 notes that Lehi and his family would have likely traveled no more than twenty miles a day, and camels would only have marginally sped their travel. Because the Book of Mormon does not mention camels, neither conclusion can be taken with any certainty; however, the general consensus regarding travel distance during these "many days" would be approximately the same in either scenario.
52. The reading of "grievously afflicting" may also be supported in the Peshiṭta, an early Syriac translation of the Bible. The verse in question reads: "For he will not harass the one who is distressed as in former time. The land of Zebulun has hastened, (so has) the land of Naphtali, and the possession has prevailed: the way of the sea, the other side of the river Jordan, Galilee of the nations." Translation from Gillian Greenberg and Donald M. Walter, *The Syriac Peshiṭta Bible with English Translation: Isaiah* in *The Antioch Bible*, ed. George A. Kiraz and Joseph Bali (Piscataway, NJ: Gorgias Press, 2012), 41–43, spelling in context. Note that this verse has been split between Isaiah 8:22 and Isaiah 9:1 in the Syriac. The "possession" mentioned here may refer to the Assyrian conquest; however, it is also possible that this is a corruption of the text based on similar letters. See Greenberg and Walter, *Isaiah*, xxiv.

Nephi specifically mentions how his father Lehi "began to murmur against the Lord his God" (1 Nephi 16:20) because of their afflictions, which may provide evidence of God imposing these afflictions on the family. 2 Nephi 19:1, on this theory, would represent the only explicit claim in the Book of Mormon text that God specifically was responsible for the Lehites' afflictions. God imposing the afflictions would fit into the original context of Isaiah where God brought afflictions upon Israel by Assyria. God and Joseph Smith as translator-revelator tandem can keep the language of KJV Isaiah 9:1 to reflect Nephi's emendations as well as delete the italicized *her* in the Book of Mormon text to emphasize more strongly that Naphtali and Zebulon were not the ones being afflicted but rather Nephi's family.

It may be that Nephi has another part of the journey down the Arabian peninsula in mind when making the revisions in Isaiah 9:1. We simply believe that the textual evidence from the Book of Mormon more strongly suggests that Nephi had the afflictions experienced while traveling near the Red Sea in mind.

Accounting for the Data With Our Proposal

How does this solution account for the desiderata presented above? First, our solution proposes that the inclusion of "red," per the evidence presented by Skousen, is original to the plates of the Book of Mormon and not an accidental insertion on the part of either Joseph Smith or Oliver Cowdery. Second, our theory proposes that the addition of "red" is not an error, but an illuminating and integral part of the text of the Book of Mormon. Third, our solution easily accounts for the likely translation error on the part of the King James translators of the Bible. Fourth, our solution avoids debates over messianism in Isaiah 9, which is attractive for both those that support and argue against messianism in Isaiah 9.[53] Fifth, our proposal allows for Isaiah to be understood in his context correctly and Nephi to be understood in his context correctly, thus not driving us into the wall of any of the historical problems faced by other proposals mentioned above. Sixth, the data is congruent with the data of the JST. One of the kinds of changes which Joseph Smith introduced

53. Indeed, while Isaiah 9 is often read as a prophecy of the birth of Christ, the context appears to rather be a prophecy regarding His millennial reign, using language of enthronement. Parry, Parry, and Peterson, *Understanding Isaiah*, 91–92 note many of the connections to the eschatological rule of the Messiah.

in his new translation was "[e]diting to bring biblical wording into harmony with truth found in other revelations or elsewhere in the Bible."[54] It is at least just as likely, if not more likely, that Joseph Smith was simply trying to bring the JST into conformity with the teaching of the Book of Mormon as it is that the JST is restoring a genuine and perhaps more ancient version of Isaiah.

Potential Limitations

Engagement with potential criticisms of our proposal is now appropriate. The first of these is that it relies on a specific translation and interpretation of the Hebrew *derek*. Most uses of the Hebrew *derek* in the Hebrew Bible would fit in with our proposal, of seeing it as a broad reference to any road through, by, or near a given place, and the translation of the Book of Mormon tends to reflect the King James idiom when it is sufficient to communicate the essential message of the translation (See also Doctrine & Covenants 128:18). Thus, if a limitation, it is a weak one.

Another potential criticism is that it is too convenient to allow Joseph Smith to get away with the preservation of supposedly erroneous King James translations in the Book of Mormon. However, the addition of "red" as well as the deletion of *her* from KJV Isaiah are the jarring data that led to the investigation of this issue and provide this solution to the King James translation errors "perpetuated" in the Book of Mormon. Thus, it may be argued that God, Joseph Smith, and Nephi provided the "escape hatch" of adding "red" and deleting *her* in the Book of Mormon. In other words, they did their job in leaving breadcrumbs towards the path of resolution to this issue and, correlatively, a coherent justification for retaining the "erroneous" King James language. Whatever supposed excess of "convenience" found in this solution is only due to the correlative level of "inconvenience" left in the text of the Book of Mormon.

A final criticism may be that the solution does not deal with how the verse in both KJV Isaiah 9:1 and 2 Nephi 19:1 ends with "beyond Jordan in Galilee of the nations." Certainly, the Red Sea is not located there. Our rejoinder may be similar to the one just given: the addition of "red" and the dropping of *her* in this verse are already so jarring. Leaving "beyond Jordan in Galilee of the Nations" makes sense when supposing that Nephi is responsible for the addition of Red. Nephi may have wanted to

54. Faulring, Jackson, and Matthews, *New Translation*, 9–10.

make it so obvious that the change was being made that he left the last line as it was written.

Conclusion

Nephi saw great value in Isaiah's words and introduced his lengthy citations by declaring "[a]nd now I, Nephi, write more of the words of Isaiah, for my soul delighteth in his words. For I will liken his words unto my people, and I will send them forth unto all my children, for he verily saw my Redeemer, even as I have seen him" (2 Nephi 11:2). With Nephi's own explicit remarks that his selected passages would include his own "likening" of the scriptures, would it be any surprise that he could view this verse in regards to his own sufferings by the way of the Red Sea? We believe that it would not.

Barring an inability to appropriately adjust assumptions regarding the nature of scripture on the part of the reader, we believe that the data clearly support this solution as the strongest to date for the puzzling 2 Nephi 19:1. It is the solution that is most promising in bolstering faith in the Book of Mormon's authenticity as a divinely crafted and ancient work.

8

Observations on Jaredite Ships and Travel to the Promised Land

A Peculiar Journey

Charles Dike

There are a total of forty-two verses in the Book of Ether which apply to this discussion. Because of the limited information provided there must be some speculation. The Jaredites collected seeds, swarms of bees, fowl, and live fish: this article discusses why they might do that and where they might do that. That 'quarter where there never had man been' is potentially identified (Ether 2:5). The fowl that made the ocean journey were likely descendants of the red jungle fowl (chickens). The Jaredites were early travelers on the Silk Road. The brother of Jared cut a hole in the bottom of an ocean-going boat, that hole being necessary to ensure a safe and healthy ocean passage. An MIT experiment demonstrates the viability of the proposed ventilation system for the boats. The psychological effect on the crews is taken into consideration and the conclusion is that the journey was made in two legs.

Introduction

This article focuses on mundane issues involving the Jaredite travels beginning in the area generally around Babylon (Ether 1:33). We are told that the Jaredites collected live fish, live fowl, and swarms of bees while building barges and then departing temporarily to a 'quarter where there never had man been' (Ether 2:5). This peculiar behavior potentially indicates the location of that quarter, and that the Jaredites ultimately went toward the Chinese coast. Following that, the paper discusses some of the challenges the ocean-going Jaredites faced. These may be considered hypothetical. After all, there are only three chapters detailing the travels and, of those, only forty-two verses that apply to this article.[1] Nevertheless, recognizing that the Jaredites are highly competent allows us to potentially glean a great deal of information. The reasoning about the live wild cargo and the approach to the issues with the ocean-going boats are unique. Hugh Nibley's *Lehi in the Desert and the World of the Jaredites* will be referred to often, with his work serving as a quasi-outline on my topics.[2]

The Jaredites

The Jaredite band is comprised of twenty-four multigenerational families (Ether 6:16). As a body, they are wealthy. We are told that they have flocks and herds of every kind, which would include camels and horses (Ether 2:1). Many of them appear to be well travelled and are not intimidated by the prospect of a multi-year journey. We will see that they know what to take with them based on their destination. They are aware from the beginning of their journey that they are to establish a civilization in a new land (Ether 1:42-43).

The Journey Setup

The Jaredites first moved northward from the great tower. Nibley has them moving into the valley of Nimrod (Ether 2:1), which he locates somewhere in the Tigris/Euphrates valley headwaters north of Babylon.[3] This is in present-day northern Iraq. It is due west of the southern tip of the Caspian Sea and southeast of the Black Sea. This land, bearing the name of a hunter of legend, would seem to be an excellent place to gather animals like fish, bees, and wild fowl (Ether 2:2-3). Nibley suggests that as more people fled the locale of the tower, resources here would come under pressure, so this area would serve only as a temporary respite. I somewhat differ with him on this point; this paper argues that the Jaredites went into what is now Azerbaijan, and into the valley formed by the Mtkvari (Kura) and Aras rivers. I propose that the Jaredites found a site in that valley and on the shore of the Caspian Sea to build barges

1. Ether 1:33, 40-43; Ether 2; Ether 3:3, and Ether 6:1-12.
2. Hugh Nibley, *Lehi in the Desert; The World of the Jaredites; There Were Jaredites*, vol. 5 of *The Collected Works of Hugh Nibley* (Salt Lake City: Deseret Book; Provo, UT: Foundation for Ancient Research and Mormon Studies, 1988), 185–189.
3. Nibley, *Lehi in the Desert*, 181.

prior to moving across the sea to the quarter "where there had never man been" (Ether 2:5).

Nibley makes the following statement, "Whether the party moved east or west from the valley of Nimrod is not a major issue though a number of things favor an eastern course."[4] I place more significance on the direction of travel, but I enumerate his points:

1. There is the great length of the journey (Ether 3:3)
2. A terrain favorable to cattle raising
3. A region "in which there never had man been" (Ether 2:5)
4. Prevailing westerly winds prefer a Pacific crossing
5. The assumed northern latitude sea voyage "between the thirtieth and sixtieth parallels north" favors a trek to the China coast as opposed to a more southern route
6. The mountain of "exceeding height" near the point of the Jaredite embarkation (Ether 3:1) does not exist on the Atlantic seaboard of Europe.[5]

To this list, I add three others: First; collecting bees, fowl, and fish implies moving to a quarter where the Jaredites would have an opportunity to manage them. One would expect the collection point to be west of the quarter if the Jaredites were heading east. Second, the major trade goods that moved along the Silk routes toward China were horses, camels, wine, gold, and honey. The Jaredites appear to have at least four of these when they leave the quarter. Third, the fowl that crossed the Pacific Ocean were likely chickens.

Beginning Their Journey

The brother of Jared, after petitioning the Lord, received the following instructions:

> Go to and gather together thy flocks, both male and female, of every kind; and also of the seed of the earth of every kind; and thy families; and also Jared thy brother and his family; and also thy friends and their families, and the friends of Jared and their families. And when thou hast done this thou shalt go at the head of them down into the valley which is northward. And there will I meet thee, and I will go before thee into a land which is choice above all the lands of the earth. And there will I bless thee and

4. Nibley, *Lehi in the Desert*, 181.
5. Nibley, *Lehi in the Desert*, 182.

> thy seed, and raise up unto me of thy seed, and of the seed of thy brother, and they who shall go with thee, a great nation. And there shall be none greater than the nation which I will raise up unto me of thy seed, upon all the face of the earth. And thus I will do unto thee because this long time ye have cried unto me. (Ether 1:41-43)

> And it came to pass that Jared and his brother, and their families, and also the friends of Jared and his brother and their families, went down into the valley which was northward, (and the name of the valley was Nimrod, being called after the mighty hunter) with their flocks which they had gathered together, male and female, of every kind. And they did also lay snares and catch fowls of the air; and they did also prepare a vessel, in which they did carry with them the fish of the waters. And they did also carry with them deseret, which, by interpretation, is a honey bee; and thus they did carry with them swarms of bees, and all manner of that which was upon the face of the land, seeds of every kind. And it came to pass that when they had come down into the valley of Nimrod the Lord came down and talked with the brother of Jared; and he was in a cloud, and the brother of Jared saw him not. And it came to pass that the Lord commanded them that they should go forth into the wilderness, yea, into that quarter where there never had man been. And it came to pass that the Lord did go before them, and did talk with them as he stood in a cloud, and gave directions whither they should travel. And it came to pass that they did travel in the wilderness, and did build barges, in which they did cross many waters, being directed continually by the hand of the Lord.[6] And the Lord would not suffer that they should stop beyond the sea in the wilderness, but he would that they should come forth even unto the land of promise, which was choice above all other lands, which the Lord God had preserved for a righteous people. (Ether 2:1-7)

> And the friends of Jared and his brother were in number about twenty and two souls; and they also begat sons and daughters before they came to the promised land; and therefore, they began to be many. (Ether 6:16)

The Jaredites were dealing with flocks of animals, having collected multiple swarms of honeybees, many fowl (likely game birds and/or ducks because snares were laid per Ether 2:2), and fish in a vessel. The

6. Nibley, *Lehi in the Desert*, 183-184. "The crossing of many waters under continual direction comes as a surprise."

text does not tell us if the Lord specifically told the Jaredites to collect these animals. That potentially means that some of the Jaredites were experienced long-distance travelers and knew how to prepare for the journey. Collecting the live fish does tell us that the Jaredites knew that they would be moving to a quarter where there was fresh water, but either no fish of a preferred species or a limited number of those fish – there is no other reasonable explanation for that behavior.

The Landscape

The Caspian and the Aral Seas are, among several others, remnants of the Paratethys Sea. These are both brackish seas and both are endorheic – meaning that neither has an outlet to the ocean. Once the weight of the sea water dissipated and Ice Age glaciers retreated, crustal rebound reshaped the landscape.[7] Eventually, rain leached the salt from the lands. Because these waterways flowed into salty or brackish waters, no freshwater fish were able to swim upstream into them. New and reshaped rivers could be barren or have only a limited number of species. If the Jaredites went east they could be moving into areas that had been wetlands, which due to climate change after the ice age would have developed into grasslands.

There is almost no current in the Caspian Sea, and it can be crossed in a day under sail.[8] For that matter, the Caspian could have been crossed and recrossed several times as the Jaredites temporarily settled and improved the quarter into which they had moved. I suspect they had more than one barge, with each being used multiple times (Ether 2:6). The Jaredites would have had an opportunity to improve the habitability of the lands that they crossed by stocking the streams and lakes, by growing clovers, fruits, and so forth for the bees that they brought with

7. Sifan A. Koriche et al., "What Are the Drivers of Caspian Sea Level Variation During the Late Quaternary?" *Quaternary Science Reviews* 283 (May 2022): 107457, online at sciencedirect.com. The Holocene period is from the retreat of the glaciers 11,700 years ago to the present. One impact of the crustal rebound is that it is believed that the Amu Darya's course across the Karakum Desert has gone through several major shifts in the past few thousand years. See "Amu Darya," *Wikipedia*, last modified April 1, 2025, accessed May 20, 2025.
8. Assuming a sailing speed of 10 miles per hour (8.8 knots) and a distance of 200 miles, travel would take 20 hours. This is quite reasonable but dependent on many factors.

them (and placed in manmade hives), and by growing "all manner of that which was upon the face of the land, seeds of every kind" (Ether 2:3).

This would have been of great value to them in preparing for their longer journey. A few swarms of bees, a single vessel of fish, and a few game birds is not enough to provision such an enterprise. There must be time to produce more honey and grow stocks of fish and fowl. Stocking streams or a fish farm, colonizing bees, and husbanding fowl implies a slow journey across Asia. An alternative for the fish would be for the Jaredites to capture fry and fingerlings. Producing a useful mature fish (10 to 12 inches) would take about three years. Certain birds like the grey partridge and the wood duck produce large clutches – in the vicinity of 7 to 15 eggs. After three years, the Jaredites could have a significant population of fowl. Eventually, on the way across Asia, the Jaredites would need to pass through deserts. For that reason, I think the Jaredites would favor partridges over waterfowl. The Jaredites would want a large flock of a single species of highly prolific fowl to travel with them. The fresh protein from the fowl eggs and meat would be especially of value to the growing population.

My Proposed Quarter

On the northwestern corner of the Karakum desert, the Uzboy River – until the 17th century – flowed into the Caspian's Türkmenbaşy Gulf – the relatively small body of water to the south of the Türkmenbaşy peninsula. The river produced a thriving agricultural community. Unfortunately, the river dried up and the community collapsed. What was the mouth of the river has now become salt marshes. I propose that the quarter was near the mouth of the Uzboy.[9] This seems an ideal place for the Jaredite encampment.

The arrow in Figure 1 marks the quarter. Immediately to the north lies the Garabogazköl, a shallow, highly saline lagoon which extends about 50 miles east from the Caspian Sea. Anyone traveling down the east side of the Caspian would meet up with the lagoon blocking their way. After going around the lagoon, they might find the Uzboy but would have little incentive to turn toward the Caspian through the desert. Travelling north, one would first need to cross the Kopet Dagh mountains and then be faced with 300 miles of the Karakum desert.

9. The quarter would be at latitude 39°35' north, longitude 54°00' east.

Figure 1: The Caspian Sea and its immediate geography.

Looking west from the Amu Darya, the desert extended for 700 miles of nearly featureless terrain. The only direction from which to appreciate the promise of this quarter at the mouth of a river may have been from the sea. Curiously, the Amu Darya earlier flowed into the Caspian Sea, but crustal rebound changed its direction into the Aral Sea, leaving the remnant Uzboy River. The city of Türkmenbaşy now sits on the south-eastern edge of the Türkmenbaşy Peninsula.

The Hypothesis

In my hypothesis, the quarter where there "never had man been" must have certain characteristics. It must possess good water – enough to supply a population of perhaps two hundred people, plus flocks and herds of all kinds, and water sufficient for fields of grains and grasses. In addition, it needs to supply water for a fish farm, pollen for many beehives, and grain for fowl. It must be within a day or two's journey from where the Jaredites collected swarms of bees and live fish. A swarm is viable for only about three days without a pollen source. The bees would have been put in manufactured beehives and placed into the fields immediately upon crossing the Caspian Sea.[10] The fowl would likely have been in pens of some sort. This would be valuable land – for it not to have been settled already, it must be hidden away. There is another requirement for the quarter – there must be a site on the west side of the Caspian that can supply the needed bees, fish, and fowl.

I suggest that the launch point on the west side of the Caspian was in the general area of Lankaran, Azerbaijan. Lankaran is known for its beekeeping, fishing, grain farming, and cattle-breeding. It is 240 miles by sea to their destination. It is not the shortest route, but one must launch from where the bees and fish are located. It is also at the end of what could properly be called a great valley – if the hypothesis is correct, then this is the valley of Nimrod.

The Crossing

If sailing with the prevailing winds, travel time from Lankaran to the mouth of the Uzboy would be roughly twenty-four hours. Fortunately, the bees are within a short distance of the shore and beekeepers have some control over when bees swarm (or minimally, some warning as to when the swarming will occur). They would be the most time-critical passengers. Per this hypothesis, the transport is doable within the necessary timeframe. For the sailors, the run would be a straight shot, with minimal tacking to cost them time, they would simply make a beeline to the Uzboy. Mount Arlan rises 6,100 feet above the Uzboy River and would serve as a convenient and excellent landmark (see Figure 1). Sailing against the headwinds, the return trip would take considerably longer.

The Silk Routes

As the crow flies, an 8,000 mile journey at a rough speed of eight miles per day – and no lengthy stops – would take three years. However,

10. "The Progression of the Hive: Ancient Times," *Planet Bee Foundation*, March 10, 2022, online atplanetbee.org. "Beehives have been around for millennia, protecting bee colonies from the weather and other natural adversities. They have also acted as a space where bees can safely produce honeycomb. While there is no record of humans building beehives until 2500 B.C. in Ancient Egypt, humans have been interacting with bees for at least 10,000 years." See also Mark Patterson "Tears of Re: Beekeeping in Ancient Egypt", Api: Cultural, January 23, 2016. "The first actual evidence of beekeeping whereby man captured or lured honey bees to nest inside artificially made cavities/hives comes from Bronze age ancient Egypt during the 1st Dynasty around 3100bc." Online at apicultural.co.uk.

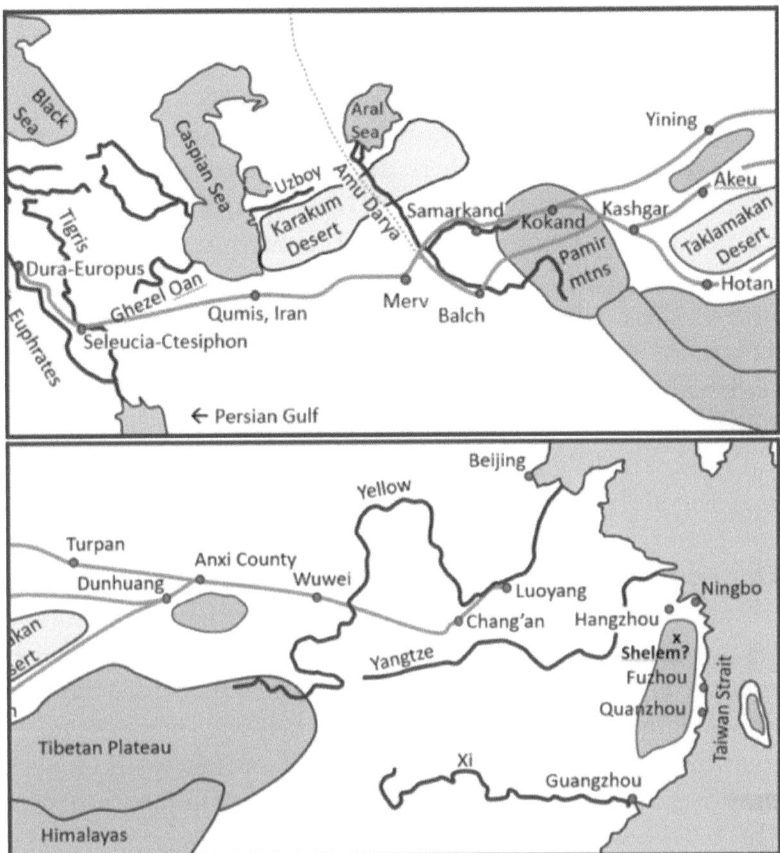

Figure 2: The Silk Road (Routes) in the first century. The light grey lines indicate available routes.

flocks need time to graze, and the Jaredites would want to replenish their foodstuffs during the growing seasons. Further, their path would be meandering; they would probably walk approximately 20,000 miles while covering the 8,000 mile distance.[11] This trip from Babylon to the Chinese coast may have taken more than ten years. The Book of Mormon only tells us that the trip to the great sea took "many" years (Ether 3:3). Over three millennia later (1271 AD), Marco Polo took 3 ½ years to make the journey from Acre in Israel to Beijing.[12] (See bottom diagram in Figure 2)

11. The Great Wall of China is over 13,100 miles long but only covers 5,500 miles of latitude. This trip would have been arduous, but they could have been some of the first to traverse what later came to be known as the 'Silk Road.' Marco Polo followed the Silk Road to China (then Cathay) some 3,500 years later.
12. He actually took 2½ years, but for an uncertain reason he chose to spend a year

The Silk Road served as a trade route to connect Asia with Europe. With the expansion of the Han dynasty into Central Asia, it is claimed to have been active beginning in the second century BC. There are written dynastic records that acknowledge this information.[13] These rulers improved the routes to facilitate trade, but they existed long before that occurred. Near the center of the upper diagram in Figure 2 is Balch, the capital city of a region known as Bactria. This region is the home of the two-humped Bactrian camel; an essential beast for moving trade goods over the northern Silk Routes through the Pamir Mountains range.

Also in the upper diagram of Figure 2 is the city of Hotan (Khotan). This city had two rivers, the Black Jade River and the White Jade River. From their banks, the city's residents pulled jade and were trading it in what is now called Beijing two millennia before the Jaredites headed across Asia.[14] If the Jaredites took the southern route around the Taklamakan desert, then more than half of their journey would have already been travelled by others many times. The Yining and Akeu routes probably served travelers at the same time and might have been somewhat easier routes for those passing through the Pamir mountains. The Book of Ether serves as additional potential evidence that trade along these routes began much earlier, but on an informal and smaller scale. If the Jaredites went east, as hypothesized here, then they would have been traveling over known routes at least most of the way to the Chinese coast.

The Jaredites would have needed considerable wealth to make the trip. Some of the twenty-two friends who joined Jared and his brother could have been merchants or skilled craftsmen. Based on the text, part of their wealth may have been in honey. Since the primary Western exports were horses, camels, honey, wine, and gold, these are also pos-

---

in Ganzhou, a city near Wuwei. Marco Polo, *The Travels of Marco Polo*, trans. William Marsden, rev. Peter Harris, intro. Colin Thubron (New York: Alfred A. Knopf, 2008), 79.

13. "Silk Road," *History*, updated June 6, 2023, online at history.com; see also "Silk Road," *Wikipedia*, last modified May 18, 2025, accessed May 20, 2025.

14. See Frances Wood, *The Silk Road: Two Thousand Years in the Heart of Asia* (Berkeley: University of California Press, 2002), 26. "Some seven thousand years before the Silk Roads were first given that name, goods were traded between the oasis towns (e.g., Hotan in Figure 2) surrounding the Central Asian deserts and China. One of the earliest materials to have been transported from the Khotan area on the southern Silk Road was jade." See also "Chinese Jade," *Wikipedia*, last modified May 18, 2025, accessed May 20, 2025.

sible.[15] All of these again suggest that the Jaredites went east. Once the group was provisioned, they could have moved east to the Amu Darya and followed it upstream (along the lower part of the line in Figure 2 representing a caravan route to the silk road) into the Pamir mountains.

Once out of the wet areas and into the steppes, the Jaredites could have built wagons, as described by Nibley.[16] They would be traveling with the tools of their trades, and all things necessary to re-establish their livelihoods. After much travelling, the Jaredites arrived at the great sea where they pitched their tents and dwelt for four years.

> And now I proceed with my record; for behold, it came to pass that the Lord did bring Jared and his brethren forth even to that great sea which divideth the lands. And as they came to the sea they pitched their tents; and they called the name of the place Moriancumer; and they dwelt in tents, and dwelt in tents upon the seashore for the space of four years. (Ether 2:13)

We know that the Jaredites took many years to arrive at the seashore, and they then settled there for four years prior to being instructed by the Lord to build the ocean-going boats (Ether 2:14). The brother of Jared went up (Ether 3:1) on mount Shelem (a mountain of exceeding height) and conversed with the Lord about making sixteen small stones glow. At 7,080 feet, Mount Huanggang is the dominant mountain in the region, and my proposed site for the location where the Jaredites pitched their tents and which they called Moriancumer (Ether 2:13).[17] (See the bottom diagram of Figure 2.) There are other smaller mountains much closer to the shore than Mount Huanggang, but the height best suits Shelem's description. It sits south of Hangzhou. Further, the coast between Quanzhou north to the mouth of the Yangtze River contains many natural harbors. My hypothesized oceangoing departure point is on about the 30th parallel north near Ningbo, to allow the Jaredite boats to pass north of Taiwan and through the Ryukyu islands chain.

---

15. National Geographic Society, "The Silk Road," July 26, 2019, online at education.nationalgeographic.org. The Jaredites had flocks of every kind (Ether 1:41). Nibley suggests these could include horses and camels. See Nibley, *Lehi in the Desert*, 180.
16. Nibley, *Lehi in the Desert*, 185–189. The Jaredites had flocks of every kind (Ether 1:41). Nibley suggests these could include horses and camels.
17. Mount Huanggang, marked by the X in figure 2, is in Fujian province and is the largest mountain (8070 ft) in either province but is some distance from the coast.

Fowl Onboard

There were birds onboard the ocean-going boats. The best candidate for these would be domesticated red jungle fowl – the chicken.[18] Chickens are far more productive egg-layers than partridges and ducks, and could likely be obtained from the indigenous people on the coast of China. The chicken had reached Taiwan and the Philippines between 5,500 to 4,500 years ago via southeast Asia, but had not arrived in Mesopotamia by Jaredite times. If the fowl on board were chickens, then the Jaredites would most likely have passed through China. In this regard in *Mormon's Codex*, John Sorenson suggests that the Olmecs had a word for chicken and chicken bones have been found in Classic Mayan sites.[19] That these bones were found is strong evidence that a population of chickens were purposely brought across the Pacific to establish them in Mesoamerica. This could only be done by a large ship of the nature of some later Chinese vessels or perhaps at a much earlier date, possibly by the eight Jaredite ocean-going boats.

What the nature of the flocks and herds mentioned in Ether 6:4 were is not known. Pigs would be a candidate – they were available in China at that time. Whatever the Jaredites took with them would need to be prolific reproducers, but apparently the Jaredites did not move a suffi-

---

18. See "The Wild Species Genome Ancestry of Domestic Chickens," *National Library of Medicine*, February 12, 2020. See also Anne Gibbons, "How the Wild Jungle Fowl Became the Chicken," *Science*, June 6, 2022, online at science.org. Chickens first appeared in Taiwan and the Philippines no later than 4,500 BP, just in time for the Jaredites to learn of them. The Hawaiian Islands are a potential intermediate stop for the Jaredites on their way to the Americas according to my hypothesis. Some of the earlier feral chickens of Kauai are believed to have reached the island in about 1200 AD. But these chickens are much more closely related to the Red Junglefowl than modern chickens. I speculate that, since we know that the chicken reached the Americas long before 1200 AD, those primitive chickens could have arrived there 3,500 years earlier as the Jaredites passed through. See Maria Luisa Martin Cerezo, Saioa López, Lucy van Dorp, Garrett Hellenthal, Martin Johnsson, Eben Gering, Rie Henriksen, and Dominic Wright, "Population Structure and Hybridisation in a Population of Hawaiian Feral Chickens," *Heredity* 130, no. 3 (March 2023): 154–162
19. John L. Sorenson, *Mormon's Codex: An Ancient American Book* (Salt Lake City: Deseret Book; Provo, UT: Neal A. Maxwell Institute for Religious Scholarship, 2013), 154–155.

ciently large body of these animals to produce a sustainable population apart from chickens.

As stated, the path for the boats would be through the East China Sea and then the Ryukyu islands before reaching the open ocean. North of the Yangtze, the boats (driven by a furious wind – Ether 6:5) would have to deal with the large Japanese islands. This is about precisely what Hugh Nibley suggested in regard to the thirtieth parallel.

To this point, I have been following Hugh Nibley's lead in most of these things, but with some minor additions. His interest lies primarily in the culture. I have some interest in the practicality of oceangoing vessels.

The Hole in the Bottom of the Ocean-going Barge

> And the Lord said: Go to work and build, after the manner of barges which ye have hitherto built. And it came to pass that the brother of Jared did go to work, and also his brethren, and built barges after the manner which they had built, according to the instructions of the Lord. And they were small, and they were light upon the water, even like unto the lightness of a fowl upon the water. And they were built after a manner that they were exceedingly tight, even that they would hold water like unto a dish; and the bottom thereof was tight like unto a dish; and the sides thereof were tight like unto a dish; and the ends thereof were peaked; and the top thereof was tight like unto a dish; and the length thereof was the length of a tree; and the door thereof, when it was shut, was tight like unto a dish. And it came to pass that the brother of Jared cried unto the Lord, saying: O Lord, I have performed the work which thou hast commanded me, and I have made the barges according as thou hast directed me. And without behold, O Lord, in them there is no light; whither shall we steer? And also we shall perish, for in them we cannot breathe, save it is the air which is in them; therefore we shall perish. And the Lord said unto the brother of Jared: Behold, thou shalt make a hole in the top, and also in the bottom; and when thou shalt suffer for air thou shalt unstop the hole and receive air. And if it be so that the water come in upon thee, behold, ye shall stop the hole, that ye may not perish in the flood. (Ether 2:16-20)

The above describes a strange vessel. It is the length of a tree. This implies a barge that has no unnecessary joints, thus producing a strong hull. The design as given is a sealed space when the door is shut. There is no light or ventilation, and it is watertight. The ends are peaked, as many boats are that would need to cut through waves.

The brother of Jared was concerned about three issues: light, steering, and breathing. He and the Lord resolved the light issue with glowing stones (Ether 3:1-4). I am interested in the steering and the breathing portion of the problems. These both seem to be addressed by cutting a hole in the top and in the bottom of the boat. I believe that a person could steer using a demountable sail to navigate in and around harbors.[20] This would require a fairly large opening topside for loading and to allow the passengers to breathe. It could then be sealed as the boat hit the open sea. However, there needed to be a smaller hole in the top of the boat, perhaps less than four inches in diameter that would work in conjunction with the hole in the bottom of the boat when at sea."[21]

The brother of Jared was told "when thou shalt suffer for air thou shalt unstop the hole and receive air" (Ether 2:20). The text is the beginning of describing a self-bailer or an automatic bailer. An automatic bailer, in its simplest form, is a hole in the bottom of a boat with a plug. When the boat is moving fast enough across the water the hole can be unplugged. The water flowing past the hole creates differential pressure and pulls any water in the boat into the sea.[22] If the boat is not moving fast enough, seawater will pour into the boat. Figure 3 shows a schematic representation of a sailboat compared to a liquid fertilizer canister that is often used for lawn maintenance. The difference is that the sailboat is being driven right to left by the wind while the water from the hose is moving left to right. The Jaredite boats need the top hole because otherwise they are airtight. If the bottom hole were unplugged and the top hole was blocked while the boat was being driven fast enough across the water to drain the bilges, then the differential pressure would create a partial vacuum inside of the boat.[23]

---

20. The demountable sail idea comes from Captain Richard Rothery. See Captain Richard Rothery, "Jaredite Journey by Sea," updated January 2012. [Hard copy on file.]
21. The Book of Ether never mentions plugging the top hole. It is possible that the top hole was designed to be self-sealing when water is over top of the boats.
22. This is called the Bernoulli effect and plays a role in carburetors, airfoils, and many other applications. The first patent of a bailer using this effect was U.S. Patent 2,772,648, granted to J. L. De Persia on December 4, 1956.
23. The largest self-bailer commercially available today has the equivalent of a one-inch diameter hole. See "Andersen Automatic Bailers," online at westmarine.com.

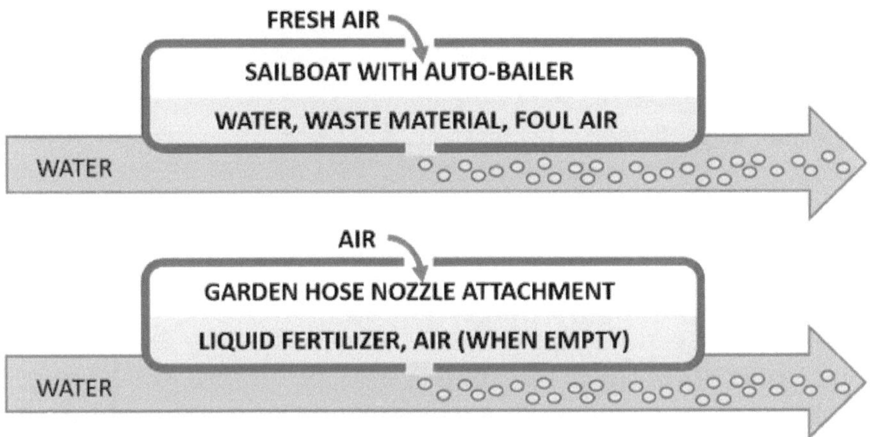

Figure 3: Schematics of a sailboat with an auto-bailer compared to a garden hose with a fertilizer attachment

There are three modes of operation for a self-bailer. The first mode is when the boat is travelling too slowly over the water to produce a differential pressure. This causes the boat to take on water if the bailer isn't plugged. The second mode occurs when a boat hits about 7.5 mph (11 ft/sec – 6.6 knots). By that point the differential pressure causes water inside the boat to be expelled through the bailer. The third mode is the "ventilation" condition. By 9.5 mph (14 feet/sec – 8.4 knots) the differential pressure is sufficient to pull significant air out of the bailer and into the sea.[24] The numbers presented here are for a small commercially available production bailer, improved bailers operate at much lower speeds.

> 5 And it came to pass that the Lord God caused that there should be a furious wind blow upon the face of the waters, towards the promised land; and thus they were tossed upon the waves of the sea before the wind.
>
> 8 And it came to pass that the wind did never cease to blow towards the promised land while they were upon the waters; and thus they were driven forth before the wind. (Ether 6:5, 8)

The Jaredites are in vessels which are airtight, excepting the holes in the top and bottom. The scripture makes it clear that the boats are

It is certain that those holes could be made larger. See the appendices at the end of this paper.

24. The conclusions on the bailing mechanism are derived from Britton Reynolds Ward. See Britton Reynolds Ward, *The Hydrodynamics of Sailboat Bailing Devices* (master's thesis, Massachusetts Institute of Technology, 1996), online at dspace.mit.edu. This was a study on self-bailers of the Andersen-Elvstrom type.

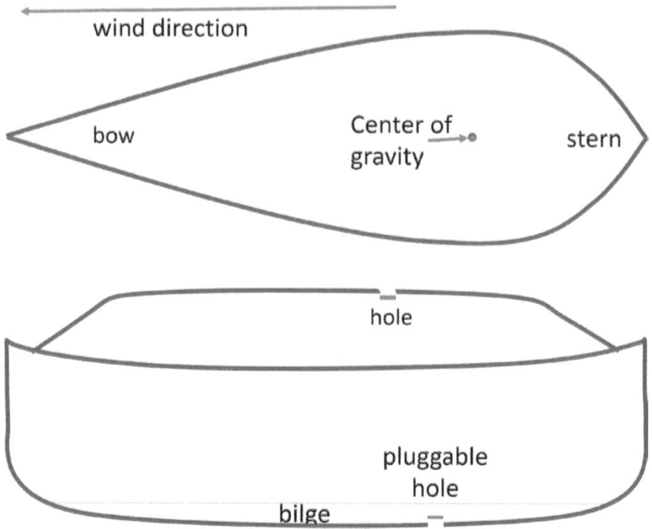

Figure 4: Boat being oriented to the wind

moving, not by currents, but by a never-ceasing *furious* wind. If that wind stopped for any significant amount of time, the lives of the Jaredites would be in jeopardy because a build-up of carbon dioxide and a reduction of oxygen would begin to poison them.

Two appendices follow this article. They are entitled "Appendix 1: The Hydrodynamics of Sailboat Bailing Devices" and "Appendix 2: Orifice Flow Formula applied to Jaredite Boats". The first appendix shows the simplicity of the bailer that one would expect the Jaredites to use. The second discusses air flow. In combination, they demonstrate that a boat similar to the Jaredite barges can receive sufficient ventilation for the personnel to survive if the boat can maintain a speed across the water of six or seven knots.

Characteristics of the Boats

The boats' main propulsion is wind; they need to be able to move fast across the water. The freeboard on the Jaredite boats would act as the sails. In this proposed design, the boats would respond to the wind by orienting themselves in a manner to reduce their exposure to the wind, that is, they would turn bow away from the wind. The hull essentially acts as an air foil, with the boat turning about the center of gravity. Because the boats would turn downwind, there is no significant crosswind and leeward is always toward the bow (Figure 4).

Being without an extended keel would allow the boat to sit higher in the water, similar to Ether 2:16's description of the vessels being "unto the lightness of a fowl", and minimize drag so that the boat could travel over the water faster. This faster speed would allow the hole in the bottom of the boat to be unstopped for longer, which in turn would mean more fresh air could be pulled into the boat through the top hole, and more foul air would be expelled into the water through the bottom.

The shape of the hull would be termed as a planing hull.[25] From fore to aft, the bottom of the boat would have a slight convex curve. From side to side, the bottom would be essentially flat. At speed, the front of the boat would tend to rise. This in turn would reduce drag and allow the boat to perform better. A term for this is hydroplaning. This is similar to how a 470-class racing dinghy works. The dinghy with its two-member crew, responds to a light breeze. A Jaredite boat, because of its size and weight – which I suspect to be in the range of 100 tons – would require a furious wind. As a reference, that is approximately the size of Christopher Columbus's Santa Maria.

With animals on board, not only was feed required, but also bedding and nesting materials. These are bulk items eating up precious storage space. Furthermore, the used bedding must be disposed of along with other waste materials. Again, we turn to the hole in the bottom of the boat. That hole is, in effect, a continuously operating wet/dry vacuum cleaner. Once any residual water in the bilge is purged to sea, solids can be passed through the hole (see Figure 3). When neither are available, the differential pressure at the hole will pull air out of the boat into the sea. When the hole is unplugged, the fresh air replaces the fouled air in the boat and helps to dry out the interior. A continually damp environment could create pulmonary issues for the crew.

On Setting Sail

The Jaredites must travel at the edge of tropical depressions, storms, or typhoons because they must be continuously in those furious winds to survive.[26] Ether 6:5-8 can only describe something like a typhoon.

25. A displacement hull generally has a heavy keel and is designed to plow through water. The displacement hull designs are slower than the planing hull but give a more comfortable ride. The Jaredites' boats were planing hull design.
26. See "Beaufort Scale," online at metoffice.gov.uk. Strong winds at 24 knots might give the crew a rest. Probably a near gale with winds of 30 knots would make the ride rougher. The boats would not be moving at the same speed as the winds.

Nibley also mentions "that at the time of the dispersion the world was swept by winds of colossal violence."[27] The Jaredite ships were designed for the violence they would face at sea. Without the winds and the self-bailer, the boats would fill with carbon dioxide and methane. Moreover, they must enter these winds within a day of casting off from the shore to control the build-up of carbon dioxide.[28] The hole in the bottom of the boat would require a 24-hour watch while at sea. The individual standing watch would be obliged to muck the waste into the hole as the opportunity presented itself.

Ether 6:10 states: "And thus they were driven forth: and no monster of the sea could break them, neither whale that could mar them; . .." This was a danger for wooden ships. Marco Polo discusses the danger of a ship having an accident causing a leak, "such as striking on a rock or receiving a stroke from a whale, a circumstance that not infrequently occurs." He explained that the larger merchant ships were compartmentalized and double hulled so that one part of the ship could be damaged without putting the ship at risk of sinking. The Jaredites recognized the precise hazard that the Chinese designed their ships around 3,500 years later.[29]

Ether 6:11 creates a problem which must be addressed. It states, "And they were driven forth, three hundred and forty and four days upon the water." I do not believe they were continually at sea for that amount of time. It is my opinion that they travelled in two different typhoon seasons, with the intermediate time spent on an island in the Hawaiian archipelago. Captain Richard Rothery, who has far more sea experience than myself, concurs that they would have likely completed the journey in two legs.[30]

Rothery specifically cites storage space issues for that long of a time. I also suggest that the weight of those materials, especially the fresh water,

27. Nibley, *Lehi in the Desert*, 180.
28. Mathew Eng, "Carbon Dioxide Poisoning and Causes of High CO_2 in the Blood," *SelfDecode*, January 15, 2021, online at labs.selfdecode.com. See also "Long-term Health Effects of High CO_2 Levels," online at labs.selfdecode.com.
29. Polo, book 3, chapter 1, 235–236. Modern metal hulls aren't at the same risk. The risk is now primarily on the whales' (and other large sea creatures') side. See, for example, National Oceanic and Atmospheric Administration, "Understanding Vessel Strikes," accessed July 31, 2023, online at fisheries.noaa.gov.
30. Rothery, 2. Sea Captain Rothery who claims mastery of cargo storage, among many other sea-going skills, understands the need to refurbish the stocks and provide rest for the crew and flocks.

would cause the boats to ride low in the ocean, decreasing their sail area and increasing the drag of the water to the point where the boats would be in jeopardy of not being able to travel fast enough. To be clear, the freeboard was the sail area. These boats did not have physical sails (except possibly for navigating harbors).

There is also the serious challenge to both the mental and physical health of the crew and animals over such a long deployment in damp conditions and rough seas. As an aside, the longest deployment of a nuclear submarine, the HMS Warspite, was 111 days submerged – a ship that produces its own air and water. The submarine could also dive to escape the rough seas: an option not available to the Jaredites.

The Toll on the Travelers

Typically, on oceangoing vessels much larger and more stable than the Jaredite barges, sea sickness in rough seas becomes a crew issue. I was a crew member on board a 560-foot surface vessel in near gale conditions for two weeks. I would not have wanted to be on the surface in a boat perhaps sixty-feet long riding those waves and wind. Based on my experience, riding on a small surface craft in rough seas can be exhausting for only two weeks, much less in 344 days. There are other problems for the crew. Fresh water and space would be at a premium.[31] The livestock would need to be maintained during these times. That is not to say the passengers could not endure more, they surely could, but this would be a most unpleasant journey. The occupants of the boat would not get the opportunity to fully dry out once they got wet in the enclosed damp environment. They would only rarely catch glimpses of daylight through the top hole in the boat, and they most likely would only see an overcast sky.

Hurricanes typically move across the ocean at a speed of about 15-20 miles per hour but have been known to accelerate to over 60 mph.[32] Assuming the distance travelled across the Pacific was 10,000 miles,

31. "Life Aboard a U-Boat," *U-Boat Aces*, accessed May 20, 2025, online at uboataces.com. "No other vessel of war presented poorer living conditions than that of a U-boat. Each war patrol could take anywhere between three weeks to six months. During this time, U-boat crews were not able to bathe, shave or change their clothes. It's not difficult to imagine how unpleasant life would be for someone who had not taken a bath or had a change of clothing for six months." Life on board the Jaredite vessels would not be much different.
32. National Oceanic and Atmospheric Administration, *Hurricane Basics* (May 1999), accessed December 24, 2022.

the Jaredites could cover that distance in six weeks (at 10 knots average speed) or less with each of two legs of the journey about three weeks long. That might be uncomfortable, but it is doable.

Alternate Views

Captain Richard Rothery, Jerry Grover, and John Tvedtnes have chosen ocean currents as the primary source of propulsion for the Jaredite boats.[33] The Book of Ether never mentions currents. If the boats rode on currents, the hole in the bottom of the boat would have no purpose, because whenever the hole was unplugged, water would enter the boat. Hugh Nibley favored winds. The Book of Ether insists on a continual furious wind as the mode of propulsion and a violent sea. Because the boats sat high in the water, they would be especially susceptible to winds and less influenced by currents. Their texts do not deal with the problem of the damp environment, waste disposal, and the carbon dioxide issue. Waste disposal for a crew of fifty would be a particularly onerous task without a hole in the bottom as hypothesized here. The alternative suggestions by others tend to require the waste to be lifted up and dumped into a tube.

Conclusion

The Jaredites collected seeds, birds, bees, and fish in anticipation of moving temporarily into a land where never had man been and making

33. Rothery, 2. See Jerry D. Grover Jr., "Travel Path of the Jaredites," in *The Swords of Shule: Jaredite Land Northward Chronology, Geology, and Culture in Mesoamerica* (Provo, UT: Challex Scientific Publishing, 2018), 79–91. Grover argues for an Atlantic crossing. Also see John A. Tvedtnes, "The Jaredite Ocean Voyage," in *The Most Correct Book: Insights from a Book of Mormon Scholar* (Salt Lake City: Cornerstone Publishing, 1999), 285–290. Typhoons in the northern hemisphere rotate counterclockwise. There are two general typhoon areas in the northern Pacific – between the coast of Asia to the Hawaiian chain and from the Hawaiian chain to Central America. The Japan current flows down the west coast of the United States and cools its ocean waters. This prevents most typhoons from reaching California. If the Jaredites travelled using the furious winds of the typhoons, they would be driven through the warmer southern waters north of the equator, with the high likelihood that their intermediate stop would be somewhere in the Hawaiian chain and their second leg would again pass through the more southern waters toward Central America. For more, see NASA Earth Observatory, "Historic Tropical Cyclone Tracks," Earth Observatory, NASA, November 2, 2006, accessed June 18, 2025, online at earthobservatory.nasa.gov.

that quarter habitable, thus began their journey across Asia. Those bees would have been left in that quarter. Dried fish would have been part of the diet on the trek. Fowl provided eggs and meat. The Jaredites were some of the early travelers along the Silk Road. They knew what commerce to take on their trip and what provisions would be valuable to them. Having arrived at the coast, ocean-going barges were built. Those fowl that travelled across the ocean were most likely not the fowl snared on the west side of the Caspian Sea, but chickens because they produce significantly more eggs than the fowl captured in Mesopotamia. This leads to speculation that the chickens found in Mesoamerica may possibly be the descendants of the Jaredite fowl. The peculiar design of these boats was discussed, and a technical explanation was made explaining the absolute necessity of the holes in the top and bottom of the boat to provide air to the crew. This obligated the boats to be driven by a furious wind essentially for the entirety of their time at sea, in order to purge the poisonous gasses and waste materials that the crew and livestock would have produced. Consideration was given to the psychological state of the people and animals aboard the Jaredite vessels, and this resulted in deciding that while the people were with the boats for 344 days, they were not at sea in high winds for all that time.

Finally, the Book of Ether was published 126 years before the first primitive self-bailer was patented by J. L. De Persia.[34] The self-bailer technology was used 4,300 years before it was re-invented in the modern age. We can be sure of that because the Jaredites would not have survived without that technology as described in the Book of Ether.

34. John L. De Persia, "Bailer Device," U.S. Patent 2,772,648, granted December 12, 1956, online at patents.google.com.

Appendix 1: The Hydrodynamics of Sailboat Bailing Devices

In 1996 Britton Reynolds Ward submitted a study of a hole in the bottom of a boat to the Department of Ocean Engineering at the Massachusetts Institute of Technology. His goal was to optimize the hole to improve racing speeds of sailboats. In order to improve those speeds, the sailboat would need to be able to bail water out of the boat. Commercial bailers were in use for this purpose but Ward wanted to improve the bailers. Ward's constraints were as follows: "The ideal bailer would have the greatest flow rate, lowest drag when deployed, be able to operate at the lowest possible speed, be largely self-operated, prevent any back flow and would seal completely when closed."[35] The Jaredites were not constrained by drag and their bailer/hole was constantly monitored by a watch stander. Their concern would be to have the greatest flow rate at the lowest possible speed.

Ward writes: "[T]he bailer has three distinct modes of operation; the condition when bailing occurs, the condition when the bailer is deployed but speed is insufficient to cause bailing and when suction is sufficient to drain the boat entirely and to proceed to draw out air. This last condition will subsequently be called the "ventilation" condition. These three regimes of operation have respectively greater amounts of drag associated with them and thus any optimum drag condition must consider all three modes of operation."[36] We're warned in Ether of the state where speed is insufficient to cause bailing – water flows back into the boat (Ether 2:20). Ward would want to operate when suction is sufficient to drain the boat entirely and then he would want to secure his bailer to minimize drag - this is after all, a racing hull. The Jaredites want to both drain the bilges and then proceed to draw out air.

The ubiquitous self-bailers for racing yachts are the Andersen-Elvstrom bailers. These are produced in five different sizes from the Super Mini to the Super Max. Ward states: "To systematically consider the effects of the major design features on the performance of production bailers a Super Mini Andersen production bailer was chosen as a control and a series of modifications made to identical bailers."[37] He chose the

35. Ward, *Hydrodynamics of Sailboat Bailing Devices*, 19.
36. Ward, 19–20.
37 Ward, 65.

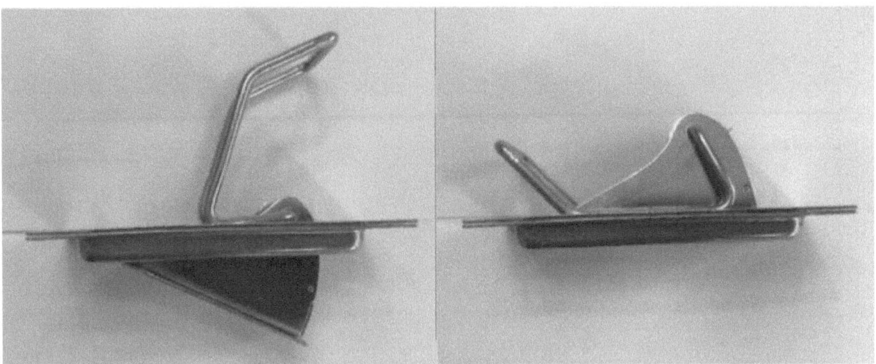

Figure 5: Super Mini Bailer deployed and retracted.

smallest bailer because it naturally has the lowest drag when deployed. His goal was to increase the flow rate and lower the speed at which bailing would occur. This would allow bailers to be deployed less, thus improving yacht performance.

Figure 5 shows the Super Mini bailer. The bottom of the retracted bailer will be flush with the bottom of the hull. This bailer is designed for a one-fourth inch fiberglass hull thickness. The deployed bailer can be retracted with a push on the bailer handle by a hand or foot.

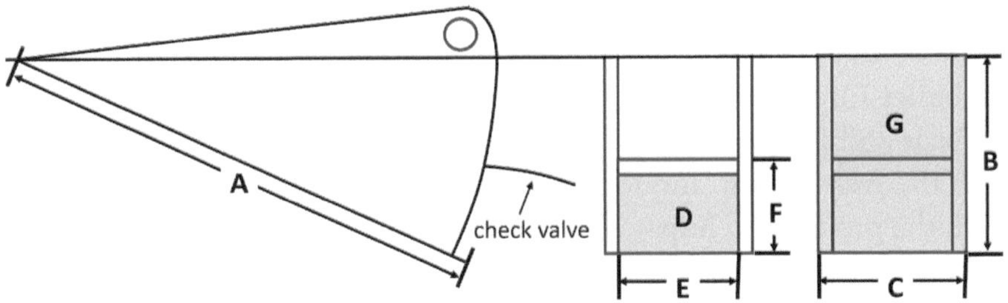

Figure 6: Critical Bailer Dimensions

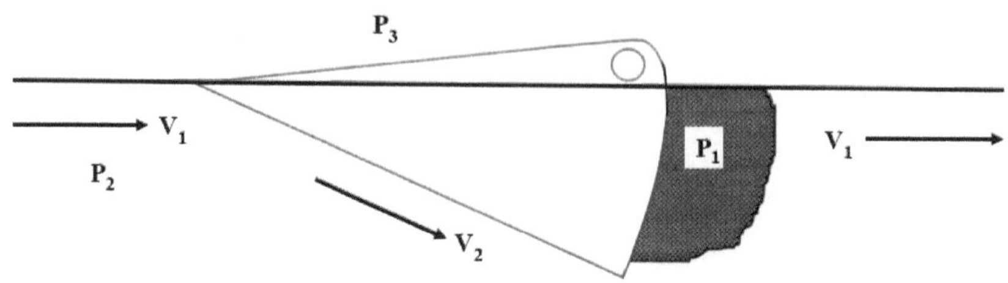

Figure 7: different pressures around the bailer

Table 1: Production Bailer Dimensions - A,B,C,E,F in cm; D,G in cm².
From Ward's table 5.1.

Bailer	*A*	*B*	*C*	*D*	*E*	*F*	*G*
Super Mini[38]	6.168	2.780	2.490	2.797	1.940	1.442	6.922
Super Max	8.766	4.104	3.582	5.407	3.162	1.710	14.70
New Large	9.932	4.792	3.902	4.625	2.500	1.850	18.70

The basic operation of a bailer is based on Bernoulli principles. The three pressures (P_1, P_2, and P_3) in Figure 7 are as follows: P_3 is the hydrostatic pressure inside the boat, P_2 is the pressure caused by the stream, and P_1 is the pressure at the output of the bailer. P_2 is always larger than P_3 in a floating boat. If the bailer is deployed and the boat is stopped P_1 equals P_2 and water will attempt to enter the boat through the bailer. As the boat picks up speed, P_1 begins to drop. When the speed is sufficient so that P_1 is slightly less than P_3, water will begin to flow out of the bailer into the stream. At a point where the water is no longer in the boat and P_1 is less than P_3 (now barometric pressure), the bailer will enter the "ventilation" mode. Air will be pulled into the stream of water. With the production Super Mini water bailing begins at 11.91 ft/sec, air bailing begins somewhere before 14 ft/sec.[39] Ward did not specify any more accurate data for this mode because he was concerned with racing yachts, not Jaredite breathing.

38. Ward made an error by reversing dimensions D, E, F and G in his table 5.1. I corrected this in my table based on personal measurements of the Super Mini bailer.
39. Ward, 99. He took a picture of a production bailer wake showing the ventilation.

As one of his experiments, Ward removed the walls and check valve from the Super Mini. The face plate (measured by dimensions A and C in Figure 6) was the only component left (except for the frame). Ward welded the face plate into place as all support was removed. The C_p (non-dimensional pressure coefficient) magnitude of the now Sideless Super Mini increased to -0.374 and the new design allowed bailing to begin at 9.20 ft/sec. Extrapolating, the ventilation mode would likely start at around 11 ft/sec.

Table 2: Bailing Inception Results. From Ward's Table 6.1.

Bailer	C_p	*Bailer Inception Speed*		
		m/s	*ft/s*	*knots*
Sideless Super Mini	-0.374	2.81	9.20	5.45
Super Mini	-0.255	3.63	11.91	7.06
Super Max	-0.255	3.40	11.15	6.60
New Large	-0.327	3.00	9.84	5.83

$-C_p = 1 - V_2^2/V_1^2$ where V_2 = the perturbed velocity and V_1 = the free stream velocity.[40] The goal is to make C_p absolute magnitude as large as possible. From Table 2 the Sideless Super Mini bailer is superior to the Super Mini bailer. The Sideless bailer begins bailing at a much lower speed. The orifice area increased from 2.797 cm^2 to 2.490 cm x 2.780 cm = 6.922 cm^2 when the sides were removed.

The largest of the bailers, the New Large, evidently never went into production. Its C_p is surprisingly larger than the Super Max. That raises some design questions: could a wider-still bailer or generally larger bailer perform better for the Jaredites? What would happen if the sides were removed from the New Large bailer? I believe that a design could easily be reached where the width of the hole in the bottom of the Jaredite boat could be much larger. And bailer inception speed could drop to five knots with a point near six knots where P_3 is greater than P_1 and ventilation could start. Even this requires a little more information: the six-knot number is for ventilation of air, not carbon dioxide. Carbon dioxide and methane have a specific gravity 1.5 times air. The beginning ventilation point for these gases is lower than air. With the larger Jaredite bailer, ventilation of the poisonous gases might begin as low as 7.5 ft/sec (~ five miles per hour).

40. Ward, 58–59.

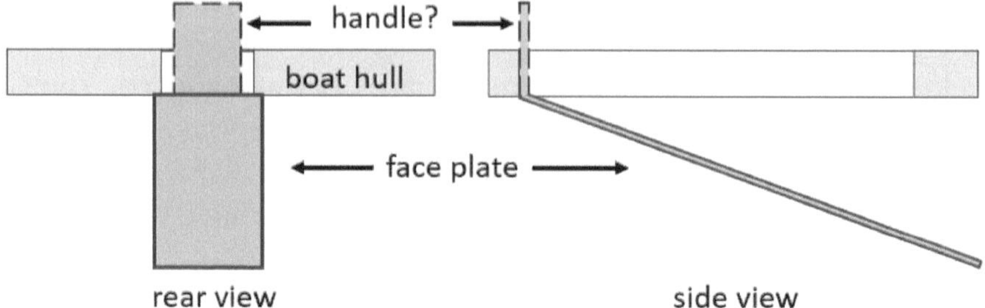

Figure 8: Proposed Jaredite bailer

The faster the boat moves, the more air will be pulled through the bailer. The boat moving at ten knots will pull much more air than when moving at 8 knots. Under typical circumstances as soon as the last of the water is bailed from a boat, P_3 is already greater than P_1 so ventilation begins immediately.

Figure 8 shows the simplicity of a highly efficient bailer. This is a similar conclusion arrived at by Ward.[41] I propose that the Jaredite face plate was likely made of iron and could be removed when the hole was plugged. The handle would have to be securely anchored while in use. There may be many other designs that would work, possibly without a separate face plate, but this one will work well.

41. Ward, 104.

Appendix 2: Orifice Flow Formula applied to Jaredite Boats

The following is derived from the website "Engineers for Engineers" and the exciting "Orifices and Flows" section.[42]

The flow of air or gas through an orifice can be determined by the formula:

$Q = 1658.5 \times A \times C_d \,(h/g)^{0.5}$

where:

Q =flow, cubic feet per hour
A =area of the orifice, square in
C_d =discharge coefficient of the orifice
h =pressure drop across the orifice, in w.c. (water column)
g =specific gravity of the gas, based on standard air at 1.0

This appendix will be only able to provide a rough estimate to this problem because many assumptions need to be made. The size of the Jaredite boat will be on average eight feet tall, 25 feet wide, and 60 feet long. This produces a space of 12,000 ft^3.

Example:
The area of the bailer orifice will be 2 inches square.
The assumption of a round edge means the C_d approaches 1.

The gas which first passes through the bailer will be CO_2 which has a specific gravity of 1.5. This equation will only assume air is passing through the bailer.

A w.c. of ~7 inches equates to a ¼ psi differential.
Q=1658.5 x 2 x $1(7)^{0.5}$ ~= 8,800 cubic feet per hour. (27.7 inches = 1 psi)
Doubling the area almost precisely doubles the air flow.
Doubling the pressure differential to ½ psi (14 w.c.) for the 2 in^2 hole increases the air flow by 1.414 times; to 12,400 cubic feet per hour.

If the bailer hole were 6 in^2 the flow rate would be nearly 37,000 cubic feet per hour at ½ psi. This establishes the ventilation as viable if

42. See "Orifices & Flows," *Engineers For Engineers*, last modified October 11, 2021, online at engineersforengineers.wordpress.com.

the Jaredite boats can maintain a speed of roughly 11 ft/sec or 7 knots. As a comparison, the Sideless Super Mini bailer has a hole of 1.813 in^2.

At ¼ psi the 2 in^2 bailer moves about twice the air volume as an average vacuum cleaner. An average airflow rating for a vacuum cleaner is between 50 – 100 cfm.[43]

Table 3: Air flow per hour with different sized orifices

Orifice size	*2 in^2*	*4 in^2*	*6 in^2*
¼ psi	8,800 ft^3/hr	17,600 ft^3/hr	26,400 ft^3/hr
½ psi	12,400 ft^3/hr	25,800 ft^3/hr	37,000 ft^3/hr

43. See "What Is the Best Suction Power for a Vacuum Cleaner?" *Home Vacuum Zone*, online at homevacuumzone.com.

9

"All things denote there is a God"

Lehi's Discourse on Natural Theology in 2 Nephi 2

Jacob Billings

A common critique of religion is that there is no evidence to support religious claims, a stance often used to question the rationality of faith. However, in the Latter-day Saint tradition, the prophet Lehi's discourse in 2 Nephi 2 counters this skepticism through natural theology. Lehi draws on causality, motion, and cause-and-effect relationships in the universe to establish a rational basis for belief. This approach contrasts revealed truth with truths derived from philosophical reflection on observed phenomena. Lehi introduces the cosmological argument of contingency, asserting that all contingent things depend on something else, ultimately requiring a necessary being—God—to explain existence.

In his book, *god Is Not Great: How Religion Poisons Everything*, the noted atheist Christopher Hitchens proposed that "What can be asserted without evidence can also be dismissed without evidence[1]." This phrase —commonly referred to as Hitchens's Razor —has become a common anti-religious trope to dismiss religious arguments as if there is no evidence or reason for their belief. This line of reasoning has led many to conclude that religion is nothing more than an irrational belief in a fabricated reality. When evaluating the existence of God and religion in the Latter-day Saint tradition, the prophet Lehi, in 2 Nephi 2 advances a basis for belief based on the natural theology of causality. A careful analysis of this chapter gives a solid rationale for religious belief based on natural theology and observation.

The core tenet of "Hitchens's Razor" is a contrast between revealed truth, which is obtained through seemingly supernatural channels, and

1. Christopher Hitchens, *god Is Not Great: How Religion Poisons Everything* (New York: Twelve Books, 2007), 89.

truth derived from philosophical reflection on observed phenomena of the natural world. This dichotomy serves as the foundation for the discipline of natural theology. Natural theology, as a theological branch, aims to comprehend God and religious truths through the application of reason and the scrutiny of the natural world, rather than exclusively relying on revealed religious texts or authoritative sources. In addressing this subject, the theologian St. Augustine of Hippo expounded upon it in the following manner:

> From this time on, however, I gave my preference to the Catholic faith. I thought it more modest and not in the least misleading to be told by the Church to believe what could not be demonstrated – whether that was because a demonstration existed but could not be understood by all or whether the matter was not one open to rational proof...You [God] persuaded me that the defect lay not with those who believed your books, which you have established with such great authority amongst almost all nations, but with those who did not believe them.[2]

Augustine presents the concept of accepting certain beliefs on authority, acknowledging their lack of demonstrability. Within the framework of natural theology, it is posited that the natural world offers evidence supporting the existence and attributes of God. This argument asserts that through the process of observation and logical inquiry, humans can attain knowledge and comprehension of divine aspects and the nature of the universe.

The origin of natural theology can be traced back to ancient Greece, where philosophers such as Plato and Aristotle laid the foundations for this field of study. Plato, in his dialogues, explored the existence of a transcendent reality beyond the material world and emphasized the role of reason and philosophical inquiry in understanding the nature of the divine. His famous "Allegory of the Cave" in *The Republic* exemplifies the search for knowledge and the ascent from the shadows of ignorance towards the realm of true understanding.

Aristotle, a student of Plato, significantly advanced the concept of natural theology by examining the natural world and the principles that govern it. He introduced the idea of a "prime mover"—an uncaused cause that initiates and sustains motion and order in the universe. Cen-

2. Saint Augustine, *Confessions*, trans. Henry Chadwick (Oxford: Oxford University Press, 1991), Book VI, v (7).

tral to his philosophy was the theory of causality, which explains phenomena through four types of causes: material, formal, efficient, and final. For example, when explaining why water boils, Aristotle would note the material (water), efficient (heat), formal (boiling process), and final causes (the purpose—e.g., making tea). Understanding all four causes, especially the final cause or purpose, was essential to comprehending the natural order. This teleological perspective, which emphasized purpose and design, laid a philosophical foundation for later theological developments.

During the medieval period, Christian thinkers integrated Aristotelian insights with religious doctrine. St. Augustine, drawing more on Neoplatonic philosophy than on Aristotle, emphasized the use of reason and philosophical inquiry in understanding God and creation. For Augustine, the created world offered glimpses of God's wisdom and goodness. Although divine revelation remained paramount, he believed rational exploration could aid in discerning divine truths embedded in nature.

St. Thomas Aquinas later synthesized the philosophical legacy of both Aristotle and Christian theology more directly. Deeply influenced by Aristotelian thought, Aquinas incorporated natural theology into his theological framework, arguing that reason and observation of the natural world could provide compelling evidence for God's existence. His "Five Ways" are philosophical arguments grounded in causality, motion, contingency, degrees of perfection, and teleology—each drawing on Aristotelian principles to demonstrate the rational basis for belief in God.

Thus, from Aristotle's foundational insights into causality and purpose, through Augustine's emphasis on reason and divine order, to Aquinas's systematic theological synthesis, natural theology evolved into a central pillar of medieval Christian thought.

This philosophical tradition, rooted in cause and effect as the basis of rational inquiry into existence, finds a striking parallel in the teachings of the Book of Mormon prophet Lehi. In 2 Nephi 2:11, Lehi introduces a metaphysical argument that mirrors the structure of Aristotle's argument from motion:

> For it must needs be, that there is an opposition in all things. If not so, my firstborn in the wilderness, righteousness could not be brought to pass, neither wickedness, neither holiness nor misery, neither good nor bad. Wherefore, all things must needs

> be a compound in one; wherefore, if it should be one body it must needs remain as dead, having no life neither death, nor corruption nor incorruption, happiness nor misery, neither sense nor insensibility.

Lehi presents a form of the argument from motion—described in his terms as "opposition"—by asserting that the presence of movement and interaction among entities is essential to existence. This interplay gives rise to causal relationships, where actions produce effects and entities influence one another. Lehi reasons that without such motion or opposition, interaction would cease, disrupting the entire chain of cause and effect. In the absence of causality, existence itself would unravel. He reinforces this conclusion in 2 Nephi 2:13, where he argues that without law there can be no sin, no righteousness, and ultimately no happiness or purpose—affirming the internal coherence and philosophical depth of his position.

> And if ye shall say there is no law, ye shall also say there is no sin. If ye shall say there is no sin, ye shall also say there is no righteousness. And if there be no righteousness there be no happiness. And if there be no righteousness nor happiness there be no punishment nor misery...for there could have been no creation of things, neither to act nor to be acted upon; wherefore, all things must have vanished away. .

Lehi identifies three essential components of existence: motion, causation, and response. Without these, existence itself would be impossible. Observing that elements within the universe are in motion naturally raises a fundamental question: What initiated that motion? For Lehi, such movement cannot begin without a cause—there must be an initial force to set things in motion. The notion of a "first change" becomes problematic, as any change would logically require a prior cause, leading to an infinite regress. This endless chain of causes ultimately points to the necessity of a true prime mover—an uncaused cause. According to Lehi, this initiating force is God. He affirms this in 2 Nephi 2:14:

> And now, my sons, I speak unto you these things for your profit and learning; for there is a God, and he hath created all things, both the heavens and the earth, and all things that in them are, both things to act and things to be acted upon.

In contrast to the argument from opposition in verse 11, verse 14 introduces a distinct philosophical approach: the argument from efficient cause. While both lines of reasoning address the conditions necessary for existence, they do so from different vantage points. The argument from motion considers the necessity of opposition and interaction to sustain being, whereas the argument from efficient cause asserts that all things must ultimately trace their origin to a first cause—God—who initiates all action and existence.

Lehi also develops a nuanced distinction between the actual and the potential nature of created beings. In verse 14, he classifies entities as either "things to act" (agents) or "things to be acted upon" (objects). However, he deepens this distinction in verse 26:

> And the Messiah cometh in the fulness of time, that he may redeem the children of men from the fall. And because that they are redeemed from the fall they have become free forever, knowing good from evil; to act for themselves and not to be acted upon.

In this verse, Lehi affirms that through the Atonement of Jesus Christ, humanity is liberated from a purely passive condition. Prior to redemption, human beings were primarily "acted upon"—subject to external forces and bound by the fallen state of the world. The Atonement, however, restores their capacity to choose, transforming them from passive recipients of causality into moral agents.

To understand Lehi's distinction between actuality and potentiality, one might consider the example of a seed and a tree. A seed is not yet a tree, but it contains within it the potential to become one. That potential can only be realized under the right conditions—sunlight, soil, and water. Similarly, Lehi suggests that the Fall left humanity in a fixed, limited state—comparable to a seed left unplanted. But through Christ's redemptive act, individuals are given the spiritual conditions necessary for growth. They are no longer confined to a static, actualized condition; rather, they are empowered to become something more. In this framework, human beings are not merely objects acted upon by the world—they are agents of their own, becoming capable of progress, transformation, and the realization of divine potential.

Lehi's argument from motion is rooted in the empirical reality that objects in the physical world are in motion. He reasons that each motion must be caused by a prior force, and that this chain of motion cannot regress infinitely without explanation. Such an infinite regress would make the existence of motion ultimately unintelligible. Therefore,

Lehi posits the necessity of a prime mover—an uncaused initiator of motion—who both begins and sustains the activity of all things. For Lehi, this prime mover is God, the foundational source from which all motion and change originate.

In contrast, Lehi's argument from efficient cause focuses not merely on motion but on the broader structure of causality. Every effect, he argues, must have a sufficient cause that brings it into being. This chain of causes must ultimately lead to a first efficient cause—one that is itself uncaused and exists necessarily. Without such a cause, the entire framework of dependent causality would collapse. Lehi identifies this necessary being as God, the ultimate efficient cause who grounds the existence of all subsequent causes and effects within the universe.

Lehi's conception of causality extends beyond the realm of physical interactions between objects and events. He engages with the metaphysical implications of causality, particularly as they pertain to ultimate origins. For Lehi, the existence of a first cause—an uncaused cause—is essential to account for the entire chain of dependent causes that structure reality. This first cause, which he identifies as God, functions as the foundational explanation for the existence and operation of the universe. In this way, Lehi constructs a metaphysical framework in which God is the necessary ground of all causal relations, providing coherence to the order, motion, and contingency observed in the world.

This emphasis on contingency leads naturally to a deeper philosophical paradox concerning existence itself. If everything is contingent—dependent upon something else for its existence—and if no entity can initiate its own motion or being, then an infinite regress of causes would leave the existence of anything ultimately unexplained. This is precisely the concern Lehi addresses in 2 Nephi 2:13, which can be read as an argument for the existence of a necessary being:

> And if there is no God we are not, neither the earth; for there could have been no creation of things, neither to act nor to be acted upon; wherefore, all things must have vanished away.

Lehi's argument affirms the necessity of a being whose existence is not contingent but necessary—one that exists by its very nature and does not depend on anything else. This reasoning aligns closely with the classical argument from contingency, as articulated by thinkers like Thomas Aquinas. According to this view, everything in the observable world is contingent—that is, it could have failed to exist and depends on external causes for its being. If all things were contingent, however, there would be no sufficient explanation for why anything exists at all.

Aquinas addresses this problem by asserting that the existence of contingent beings requires a necessary being—one that is not caused or dependent—capable of grounding and sustaining all contingent reality. At the heart of this argument is the Principle of Sufficient Reason, which holds that everything that exists must have an explanation, either in the necessity of its own nature or in something external.

The world we observe, including objects, events, and even the laws of nature—could conceivably have been otherwise or might not have existed at all. Their contingent nature points beyond themselves to an ultimate source. It concludes that a necessary being must exist to ground all contingent reality.

By grounding his reasoning in the metaphysical structure of causality and contingency, Lehi contributes to this enduring philosophical tradition. His teachings affirm that the universe is intelligible only if there exists a necessary being—identified as God—who is the ultimate cause and explanation for everything that exists.

Lehi's assertion that the existence of the universe implies a creator reflects a sophisticated engagement with the principles of natural theology, particularly those concerning causality and design. Recognizing motion, causation, and the ordered structure of the cosmos, Lehi deduces the necessity of an intelligent being who initiated and sustains these processes. His reasoning aligns with the classical conception of a creator God—one whose intentionality and intelligence are evident through the observable patterns of the natural world.

In 2 Nephi 2, Lehi offers a robust theological and philosophical foundation for belief in God grounded in philosophical reflection on observed phenomena and rational reflection. Contrary to the skepticism encapsulated by Hitchens's Razor—which dismisses religious claims that lack empirical evidence—Lehi's discourse demonstrates a reasoned and logically rigorous approach. By employing the tools of natural theology, Lehi makes a strong argument for divine existence, appealing to reason, experience, and metaphysical necessity.

Central to natural theology is the distinction between revealed truth and truth discernible through reason and observation. Lehi's discourse operates within this framework, drawing from the natural world to support theological conclusions. He affirms that the universe, in its order, motion, and contingency, bears witness to divine reality. This approach situates Lehi within a philosophical tradition reaching back to Plato. While Plato stopped short of equating the Form of the Good with a personal deity, his student Aristotle would later introduce a more systematic approach to metaphysics, grounding reality in a prime mover.

Aristotle's theory of causality—comprising material, formal, efficient, and final causes—offers a philosophical scaffolding for understanding Lehi's reasoning. Observing that all things in motion require a cause, Lehi echoes Aristotle's conclusion that an infinite regress of causes is untenable. Motion and change point to the necessity of a prime mover—an uncaused cause—who initiates and sustains all activity in the universe. For Lehi, this being is God.

Beyond physical motion, Lehi also explores the metaphysical dimensions of causality. He argues that the entire network of contingent beings requires a first cause that exists necessarily and independently. This conception of God as the ground of all existence is not only consistent with Aristotelian thought but also anticipates Aquinas's argument from contingency: if all beings are contingent, there must be a non-contingent being from whom all else derives. Lehi affirms this in 2 Nephi 2:13, reasoning that without God, "we are not," for without a necessary being, existence itself would vanish.

Thus, Lehi's discourse supports the cosmological argument from contingency, asserting that the dependent nature of the universe demands a necessary foundation. While philosophical objections persist, Lehi's line of reasoning remains logically coherent and theologically substantive. His engagement with natural theology provides an intellectual framework that unites faith and reason, demonstrating that belief in God need not be blind or irrational.

In conclusion, Lehi's teachings in 2 Nephi 2 exemplify a profound synthesis of theological insight and philosophical argument. By integrating philosophical reflection on observed phenomena, logical analysis, and metaphysical reasoning, he articulates a clear and strong argument for the existence of God. Far from dismissing evidence, Lehi appeals directly to it—affirming the compatibility of reasoned inquiry and spiritual conviction. His discourse offers a model of faithful reasoning within the Latter-day Saint tradition and contributes meaningfully to the broader philosophical conversation on the existence of God.

10

Is the Book of Mormon a "Translation" or a "Revelation"?

Stephen O. Smoot

Joseph Smith maintained throughout his life that he translated the Book of Mormon from ancient golden plates by "the gift and power of God." Exactly what kind of a translation the Book of Mormon is, however, and the precise method of its production has long been debated in both academic and polemical literature. One of the questions still debated is what terminology best describes a text like the Book of Mormon. Is the book best understood as a "translation," or should it perhaps instead be called a "revelation" given the peculiar method of its production? This paper will discuss how early Latter-day Saints understood the terms revelation and translation to be synonymous or nearly synonymous categories that fell under the broader umbrella of seership. It will situate the language used by early Saints to describe the Book of Mormon in its historical context in order to address the question posed in this abstract. It will also thereby correct those who erroneously claim that it is only a recent phenomenon among Latter-day Saints to sometimes refer to the Book of Mormon as a "revelation" rather than a "translation."

In a talk delivered during the April 2020 general conference of The Church of Jesus Christ of Latter-day Saints, Elder Ulisses Soares of the Quorum of the Twelve Apostles reaffirmed a core tenet of Latter-day Saint faith—that the early visionary experiences of Joseph Smith were real, and that the translation of the Book of Mormon was a miracle.[1] As Elder Soares affirmed on that occasion:

> This sacred ancient record was not "translated" in the traditional way that scholars would translate ancient texts by learning an

1. Ulisses Soares, "The Coming Forth of the Book of Mormon," *Ensign*, May 2020, 32–35.

> ancient language. We ought to look at the process more like a "revelation" with the aid of physical instruments provided by the Lord, as opposed to a "translation" by one with knowledge of languages. Joseph Smith declared that through God's power he "translated the Book of Mormon from [hieroglyphs], the knowledge of which was lost to the world, in which wonderful event [he] stood alone, an unlearned youth, to combat the worldly wisdom and multiplied ignorance of eighteen centuries, with a new revelation." The Lord's help in the translation of the plates—or revelation, so to speak—is also evident when considering the miraculously short time Joseph Smith took to translate them.[2]

Nearly six decades earlier, Elder Bruce R. McConkie, then a member of the First Quorum of Seventy, gave a talk in the April 1964 General Conference in which he stated something similar. After the First Vision, Elder McConkie taught, "in due course, amid testings and trials, other revelations came" to Joseph Smith. "The Book of Mormon was revealed, translated, and published as a new witness of Christ and his gospel—an inspired record of God's dealings with the ancient inhabitants of America. . . . New light and knowledge, new revelation, to meet all the challenges of a modern world, were added to the canon of scripture."[3]

Elder Soares's comment about the coming forth of the Book of Mormon—like Elder McConkie's before him—is just one recent example that highlights a persistent question at the heart of Joseph Smith's scriptural outpouring: is it better to speak of these textual productions as *revelations* or *translations*? At first glance, this question may appear superfluous. After all, Joseph Smith maintained throughout his prophetic ministry that he *translated* the Book of Mormon from ancient golden plates by the means of what he called "the gift and power of God."[4] This, indeed, is precisely how the Book of Mormon itself says it was to come

2. Soares, "The Coming Forth of the Book of Mormon," 33, citing Joseph Smith, History, 1838–1856, volume E-1 [1 July 1843–30 April 1844], 1775; Joseph Smith, Letter to James Arlington Bennet, 13 November 1843, 1, both online at josephsmithpapers.org.
3. Bruce R. McConkie, *Conference Report* (April 1964): 26–27.
4. Compare "Preface" in Joseph Smith, *The Book of Mormon: An Account Written by the Hand of Mormon, Upon Plates Taken from the Plates of Nephi* (Palmyra, New York: E. B. Grandin, 1830), [iii–iv]; Joseph Smith, Letter to Noah C. Saxton, 4 January 1833, JS Letterbook 1, 17; Joseph Smith, Journal, November 9–11, 1835, 25; "Church History," *Times and Seasons* 3, no. 9 (March 1, 1842): 707; Joseph

forth in the latter days: "To come forth by the gift and power of God unto the interpretation thereof—Sealed by the hand of Moroni, and hid up unto the Lord, to come forth in due time by way of the Gentile—The interpretation thereof by the gift of God" (Book of Mormon Title Page).[5] But precisely what kind of a translation the Book of Mormon is remains debated,[6] and the fact that Joseph produced the translated text by revelation (the "gift and power of God") and not conventional academic means is why this question remains an open one. Indeed, this lingering ambiguity can be seen not only in Elder Soares's remarks in General Conference, but also, for example, in the decision of the Joseph Smith Papers Project to categorize these two terms ("revelations" and "translations") together in their subdivisions of Joseph Smith's documents.[7]

This paper will present evidence that demonstrates how early Latter-day Saints, including Joseph Smith, understood the concepts of *revelation* and *translation* to be synonymous or nearly synonymous categories that fell under the broader umbrella of *seership*. Specifically, it will situate the language used by early Saints to describe the Book of Mormon in its historical context in order to address the question posed in this abstract. It will also thereby correct those who erroneously claim it is only a recent phenomenon among Latter-day Saints to sometimes refer to the Book of Mormon as a *revelation* rather than a *translation*.

Smith, Letter to James Arlington Bennet, 13 November 1843, 1[b]. All these sources are online at https://www.josephsmithpapers.org.

5. Compare Smith, *The Book of Mormon*, [i].
6. For samples of recent literature on the translation of the Book of Mormon, see Brant A. Gardner, *The Gift and Power: Translating the Book of Mormon* (Salt Lake City: Kofford Books, 2011); Michael Hubbard MacKay and Gerrit J. Dirkmaat, *From Darkness unto Light: Joseph Smith's Translation and Publication of the Book of Mormon* (Salt Lake City: Deseret Book; Provo, UT: Religious Studies Center, Brigham Young University, 2015); Stanford Carmack, "Joseph Smith Read the Words," *Interpreter: A Journal of Latter-day Saint Faith and Scholarship* 18 (2016): 41–61; Stan Spencer, "Seers and Stones: The Translation of the Book of Mormon as Divine Visions of an Old-Time Seer," *Interpreter: A Journal of Latter-day Saint Faith and Scholarship* 24 (2017): 27–98; Grant Hardy, "The Book of Mormon Translation Process," *BYU Studies Quarterly* 60, no. 3 (2021): 203–211.
7. The Joseph Smith Papers Project, on both its website and in its print series, combines "revelations and translations" together in a single category alongside the "documents," "journals," "histories" and other types of Joseph Smith papers. See https://www.josephsmithpapers.org.

Revelations Surrounding the Coming Forth of the Book of Mormon

A complete understanding of how Joseph Smith translated the Book of Mormon will, unfortunately, remain tenuous because the Prophet declined to give a full accounting thereof.[8] When asked for "information of the coming forth of the book of Mormon" at an 1831 church conference, Joseph declined, stating simply "that it was not intended to tell the world all the particulars of the coming forth of the book of Mormon."[9] However, one thing we know for certain is that the Prophet was adamant he received the translation of the text by revelation. Joseph once informed a crowd in 1840 how the Book of Mormon "was communicated to him, direct from Heaven." According to the record of this sermon, Joseph emphasized that "if there was such a thing on Earth, as the Author of it"—meaning the Book of Mormon—"then he (Smith) was the Author." But, Joseph added, "he wished to impress . . . that he had penned it as dictated by God."[10] One way we can confirm that this was the Prophet's understanding of the nature of the Book of Mormon translation is by turning to his revelations he received coterminous with it. These speak

8. Michael Hubbard MacKay, "The Secular Binary of Joseph Smith's Translations," *Dialogue: A Journal of Mormon Thought* 54, no. 3 (Fall 2021): 1–39, has recently suggested that part of the Prophet's inability or conscious decision not to fully describe the process of his scriptural translations lay in the "incommensurability" of the language needed to articulate the workings of a divine miracle.
9. See the minutes of the general conference held at Orange, Ohio, 25–26 October 1831, in Minute Book 2, 13, online at www.josephsmithpapers.org.
10. Joseph Smith, Discourse, 5 February 1840, [3], online at www.josephsmithpapers.org. Joseph's insistence that he was the "author" of the Book of Mormon appears to have been in response to claims circulating in anti-Mormon literature of the time that he either fabricated the text or pilfered it from another source. The 1830 first edition of the Book of Mormon indeed named Joseph as its "Author and Proprietor," but this was a mere legal technicality and does not contradict his claims to have been the book's inspired translator. See Miriam A. Smith and John W. Welch, "Joseph Smith: 'Author and Proprietor'," in *Reexploring the Book of Mormon: A Decade of New Research*, ed. John W. Welch (Provo, UT: FARMS, 1992), 154–157; Nathaniel Hinckley Wadsworth, "Copyright Laws and the 1830 Book of Mormon," *BYU Studies* 45, no. 3 (2006): 77–96; Royal Skousen, *Analysis of Textual Variants of the Book of Mormon, Part One: 1 Nephi – 2 Nephi 10* (Provo, UT: FARMS, 2014), 35–36. See also Oliver H. P. Cowdery to Cornelius C. Blatchly, November 9, 1829, in Larry E. Morris, ed., *A Documentary History of the Book of Mormon* (New York, NY: Oxford University Press, 2019), 374–375.

clearly of God granting him a "gift" as well as the "power" to translate that came by divine revelation and commandment.

Doctrine and Covenants 3

In July 1828, Joseph Smith received a revelation rebuking him for his part in the loss of the 116 pages.[11] This revelation is now canonized as section 3 of the Doctrine and Covenants. Verse 12 of this revelation speaks of Joseph having "sight and power to translate," which in verse 11 is designated a "gift" and in verse 14 a "privilege" given by God. This language reflects the revised 1835 first edition of the Doctrine and Covenants prepared under the Prophet's editorial direction.[12] Before, in the manuscript copy of the text, Joseph was instead said to have the "right to Translate."[13] In either case, the text makes it clear that this "sight and power" (or "right") to translate is clearly conditioned on God granting Joseph revelation. Only by repentance would this power be returned to him (v. 10). The language of the 1835 Doctrine and Covenants (also preserved in the current edition) of "sight and power to translate" unambiguously links the concepts of "translation" and "seership" in Joseph Smith's thinking.

Doctrine and Covenants 5

Another revelation received by the Prophet in March 1829,[14] now section 5 of the Doctrine and Covenants, speaks plainly of him having "a gift to translate the plates" of the Book of Mormon. This is said to have been the "first gift that [God] bestowed upon" young Joseph, who was instructed to "pretend to no other gift" for the simple reason that God would "grant unto [him] no other gift until [the translation of the plates] is finished" (Doctrine and Covenants 5:4). The seer stones used in the translation of the Book of Mormon were said to have been "entrusted" to Joseph for the purpose of translation, but they could also be withdrawn at any time (vv. 9, 31), meaning either they would be returned to the angel, or their power nullified. Joseph was even given the "command" only to

11. Revelation, July 1828, in Revelation Book 1, online at www.josephsmithpapers.org.
12. *Doctrine and Covenants of the Church of the Latter Day Saints: Carefully Selected from the Revelations of God, and Compiled by Joseph Smith Junior* (Kirtland, OH: F. G. Williams & Co., 1835), Section XXX:5, 157, online at www.josephsmithpapers.org.
13. Revelation, July 1828, 2.
14. Revelation, March 1829, online at www.josephsmithpapers.org.

"translate" at certain periods (v. 30), clearly indicating the Lord, and not Joseph, was ultimately the one who controlled the translation process.

Doctrine and Covenants 6

One month after this revelation, in April 1829, Joseph and Oliver Cowdery jointly received another revelation that again touched on the ability to translate.[15] In this text, Oliver is extended a "gift" to uncover "mysteries" and "the knowledge of the truth" (vv. 10–13). Later this is expanded to include the "gift . . . to translate," but only if Oliver "desired" it of the Lord (Doctrine and Covenants 6:25). This "gift" (clearly referring to some manner of revelatory power) is explicitly said to be "sacred" and "from above" (v. 10). Joseph and Oliver together were together granted "the keys of this gift" to translate the ancient records and receive revelation (v. 28).

Doctrine and Covenants 8

That same month, the Prophet and Oliver received another revelation, this one canonized as section 8 of the Doctrine and Covenants.[16] The revelation opens: "Oliver Cowdery, verily, verily, I say unto you, that assuredly as the Lord liveth, who is your God and your Redeemer, even so surely *shall you receive a knowledge of whatsoever things you shall ask in faith*, with an honest heart, believing that you shall *receive a knowledge concerning the engravings of old records, which are ancient*, which contain those parts of my scripture of which has been *spoken by the manifestation of my Spirit*" (Doctrine and Covenants 8:1, emphasis added). At the outset this section frames Oliver's knowledge of the Book of Mormon as a revelatory manifestation. From there it becomes even more explicit, calling this gift the "spirit of revelation" (v. 3). After a brief excursus on the nature of Oliver's ability to work a divining rod,[17] which

15. Revelation, April 1829–A [D&C 6]; *Doctrine and Covenants*, Section VIII, online at www.josephsmithpapers.org.
16. Revelation, April 1829–B [D&C 8], online at www.josephsmithpapers.org.
17. The current edition of the Doctrine and Covenants speaks of Oliver having the "gift of Aaron." The manuscript copy of this text calls it "the gift of working with the sprout," a clear reference to a divining rod. (See Revelation, April 1829–B [D&C 8], 13.) When this revelation was first printed in the Book of Commandments, the passage was emended to read that Oliver had "the gift of working with the rod." (*A Book of Commandments, for the Government of the Church of Christ* [Independence, MO: W. W. Phelps & Co., 1833], 19, online at

is likened unto Aaron's staff (vv. 6–8; compare Exodus 4:1–5; 7:1–13; 8:5–6, 16–17), the revelation instructs Oliver to "ask that you may know the mysteries of God, and *that you may translate and receive knowledge from all those ancient records* which have been hid up, that are sacred; and *according to your faith shall it be done unto you*" (v. 11, emphasis). The section thus ends how it begins by emphasizing that Oliver's "gift" to assist in the translation of the Book of Mormon (here conceptually envisioned as a divinatory activity akin to Aaron assisting Moses in his miraculous dealings in Egypt) can only come from God. It is thus not at all surprising that John Whitmer, as custodian of the Revelation Manuscript Book, hesitated on what to describe Oliver's "gift" so described, as seen in a revealing strikeout in his superscription attending this text: "A Revelation to Oliver [Cowdery] he being desirous to know whether the Lord would grant him the gift of ~~Revelation & the~~ Translation given in Harmony Susquehannah Pennsylvania April 1829."[18]

Doctrine and Covenants 10

Another revelation given to the Prophet at the time of the loss of the 116 pages is section 10 of the Doctrine and Covenants.[19] At the outset it speaks of Joseph having "the power . . . to translate by the means of the Urim and Thummim" (Doctrine and Covenants 10:1). Because of his transgression, the revelation reads, Joseph had "lost [his] gift" to translate (v. 2). It would, however, be "restored unto [him] again" if he remained "faithful," and thereby he could finish "the remainder of the work of translation as [he had] begun" (v. 3). The obvious point of this revelation is that Joseph only had any ability to utilize the Urim and Thummim in the translation of the plates by a divine gift. Without this power, the instruments were useless, and Joseph's had no ability to translate.

Doctrine and Covenants 20

The "articles and covenants" of the Church of Christ are now canonized as section 20 of the Doctrine and Covenants.[20] In what is one

---

www.josephsmithpapers.org.) An additional emendation for the 1835 Doctrine and Covenants changed it to the current reading: "the gift of Aaron" (*Doctrine and Covenants of the Church of the Latter Day Saints*, Section XXXIV.)

18. Revelation, April 1829, Revelation Book 1, 12.
19. Revelation, Spring 1829 [D&C 10]; *Doctrine and Covenants*, Section XXXVI.
20. *Doctrine and Covenants*, Section II.

of the earliest published accounts of the coming forth of the Book of Mormon, this section perfectly highlights the equivalence of *translation* and *revelation* in early Latter-day Saint parlance. As it reads in the earliest canonical version prepared by Joseph Smith:

> After it was truly manifested unto this first elder that he had received a remission of his sins he was entangled again in the vanities of the world; but after repenting, and humbling himself, sincerely, through faith God ministered unto him by an holy angel whose countenance was as lightning, and whose garments were pure and white above all other whiteness, and gave unto him conmandments [sic] which inspired him, and gave him power from on high, by the means which were before prepared, to translate the book of Mormon, which contains a record of a fallen people, and the fulness of the gospel of Jesus Christ to the Gentiles, and to the Jews also, which was given by inspiration, and is confirmed to others by the ministering of angels, and is declared unto the world by them, proving to the world that the holy scriptures are true, and that God does inspire men and call them to his holy work in this age and generation, as well as in generations of old, thereby showing that he is the same God yesterday, to-day, and forever.— Amen.[21]

This section speaks overtly of Joseph having "power from on high" and divinely prepared "means"—referring to the seer stones—"to translate the book of Mormon," which itself is said to have been "given by inspiration" and the ministration of an angel. There is no ambiguity in this text: the *translation* of the ancient record was accomplished by a *revelatory* power that God had bestowed upon the *seer* Joseph Smith.

From these examples we can see why the Prophet repeatedly affirmed that he "translated" the Book of Mormon "by the gift and power of God" and why he would tell a crowd in 1840 that the book was communicated to him "direct from heaven." We can also see why he would call the Book of Mormon "a new revelation" which he had "translated" by "the power of God" in his 1843 letter to James Arlington Bennet.[22] His own revelations use precisely that language and make that connection. They overtly collapse the categories of "revelation" and "translation" onto each other and assume that they operate under Joseph's capacity as a divinely ordained seer.[23]

---

21. *Doctrine and Covenants*, Section II:2.
22. Letter to James Arlington Bennet, 13 November 1843, 1[b].
23. See further Christopher James Blythe, "'By the Gift and Power of God':

How Early Latter-day Saints and Others Described the Book of Mormon

From the above, it is clear that Joseph Smith understood the Book of Mormon to be both a translation and a revelation. But how did the first generation of Latter-day Saints and other readers of the book understand or describe the text?

Diedrich Willers (Whitmer Family)

The Reverend Diedrich Willers was a minister in the Reformed German Church and a resident of Fayette, New York at the time of the publication of the Book of Mormon. He was also an acquaintance of the Peter Whitmer Sr. family. Shortly after the publication of the book and the founding of the Church of Christ by Joseph Smith, Willers composed one of the earliest receptions of the text just months after it became available to the public.[24] On June 18, 1830, Willers drafted a letter to Reverends L. Mayer and D. Young giving his impression on the new book and the claims of its translator. According to D. Michael Quinn, "Aside from its obvious and sometimes comical bias, the letter contains some important insights into the first months of" the restored Church of Jesus Christ. "His account of the manner in which Joseph Smith obtained and translated the Book of Mormon . . . is a fairly accurate version of the Mormon account of this matter." What's more, "A subtle but important insight provided by the letter concerns the method of translating the Book of Mormon. . . . Willers discusses the role of the Urim and Thummim in the translation . . . [and] records that although the Urim and Thummim was said to be indispensable, it was actually

Translation among the Gifts of the Spirit," in *Producing Ancient Scripture: Joseph Smith's Translation Projects in the Development of Mormon Christianity*, ed. Michael Hubbard MacKay, Mark Ashurst-McGee, and Brian M. Hauglid (Salt Lake City: University of Utah Press, 2020), 27–53, who maintains that the translation of scripture was conceptualized as a gift of the spirit among early Latter-day Saints.

24. See D. Michael Quinn, "The First Months of Mormonism: A Contemporary View by Rev. Diedrich Willers," *New York History* 54, no. 3 (July 1973): 317–333; Larry E. Morris, comp., "9.26 Diedrich Willer's Letter to Rev. L. Mayer and D. Young, June 18, 1830," in A Documentary History of the Book of Mormon (New York: Oxford University Press, 2019), 403–405.

the impressions of the Holy Ghost to Joseph Smith which provided the translation."[25] The relevant portion of the letter reads:

> The Angel indicated that the Lord destined him to translate these things into English from the ancient language, that under these plates were hidden spectacles, without which he could not translate these plates, that by using these spectacles, he (Smith) would be in a position to read these ancient languages, which he had never studied, *and that the Holy Ghost would reveal to him the translation in the English language.* Therefore, he (Smith) proceeded to Manchester township, Ontario County, and found everything as described, the plates buried next to the spectacles in the earth, and soon he completed the translation of this work.[26]

Although Willers does not appear to have been personally acquainted with Joseph Smith, he did know the Whitmer family, and it is from them whence he appears to have derived this understanding of how the book was produced.

Oliver Cowdery

Oliver Cowdery needs no introduction. As a firsthand participant in the translation of the Book of Mormon, Oliver's understanding of the nature of the text, while certainly not infallible, is nevertheless important. While on a mission in 1830 shortly after the organization of the Church, Cowdery preached in the vicinity of Hudson, Ohio (southeast of Cleveland). A local newspaper, the *Observer and Telegraph*, reported on his preaching activities and captured a sense of what Oliver was telling his listeners. According to one report, Oliver and his missionary companions had "brought with them copies of a Book, known in this region by the name of the 'Golden Bible,' or, as it is learned on its title-page, 'The Book of Mormon.' They solemnly affirm," the report continued, "that its contents were given by Divine inspiration." The account then relayed a summary of how Oliver described the coming forth of the Book of Mormon:

> They solemnly affirm, that . . . in or near the township of Palmyra, Ontario Co. N. Y. . . . an Angel appeared to a certain Joseph Smith residing in that place, who, they say, was a poor, ignorant, illiterate man, and made no pretensions to religion of any kind; . . . [The angel] directed him forthwith to dig up and

25. Quinn, "The First Months of Mormonism," 320–321.

26. Morris, *A Documentary History of the Book of Mormon*, 404–405, emphasis added.

> bring to light this precious record and prophecy. They affirm that the said Smith obeyed the heavenly messenger, when lo! a new Revelation—the Golden Bible was discovered!
>
> According to the narrative given by one of these disciples—Oliver Cowdery—at their late exhibition in Kirtland, this pretended Revelation was written on golden plates, or something resembling golden plates, of the thickness of tin—7 inches in length, 6 inches in breadth, and a pile about 6 inches deep. None among the most learned in the United States could read, and interpret the hand-writing, (save one, and he could decipher but a few lines correctly,) excepting this ignoramus, Joseph Smith, Jr. To him, they say, was given the spirit of interpretation; but he was ignorant of the art of writing, he employed this Oliver Cowdery and others to write, while he read, interpreted, and translated this mighty Revelation.[27]

As with Willer's account, the bias of this report is obvious, but it does capture with basic accuracy how Latter-day Saints, including Joseph Smith himself, described the coming forth of the Book of Mormon, and it is safe to assume it is a fairly accurate report of what Oliver had described in his preaching. The language of "revelation" and "inspiration" to describe the Book of Mormon in this retelling of Oliver's preaching and the power behind its production is unmistakable. That early missionaries were describing the Book of Mormon as a "revelation" to potential converts is further confirmed by other sources, such as Ezra Booth, who, after his disaffection from the Church in 1831, represented the language of the typical "Mormonite" missionary thus: "The Book of Mormon which I hold in my hands, is a Divine Revelation, and the very thing we need, to burst the cloud and remove the darkness, which has long surrounded the mysterious and degraded aborigines [of America]."[28]

Phineas Young (Samuel Smith)

Phineas Young, older brother to Brigham Young, was made aware of the Book of Mormon in 1830 through the missionary labors of Samuel

27. Morris, "9.10 Observer and Telegraph Articles, November 18, 1830," in *A Documentary History of the Book of Mormon*, 385.
28. Ezra Booth, "Mormonism No. VIII," *Painesville Telegraph* 3, no. 27 (December 20, 1831); rep. E. D. Howe, *Mormonism Unvailed* (Painesville, OH: The Author, 1834), 210–211. See additionally H. Michael Marquardt, "Ezra Booth on Early Mormonism: A Look at His 1831 Letters," *The John Whitmer Historical Association Journal* 28 (2008): 65–87.

H. Smith, younger brother to the Prophet and one of the Eight Witnesses. Almost three decades later, once Phineas had relocated to Utah with the Saints, he retold his experience of meeting Samuel and being presented with the Book of Mormon. "In April, 1830," he narrated,

> having received the Book of Mormon, as I was on my way home from the town of Lima, where I had been to preach, I stopped at the house of a man by the name of Tomlinson, to get some dinner; while engaged in conversation with the family, a young man came in, and walking across the room to where I was sitting, held a book towards me, saying, "There is a book, sir, I wish you to read;["] the thing appeared so novel to me that for a moment I hesitated, saying, 'Pray, sir, what book have you?' 'The Book of Mormon, or as it is called by some, the Golden Bible.' *'Ah, sir, then it purports to be a revelation.' 'Yes,' said he, 'it is a revelation from God.'* I took the book, and by his request looked at the testimony of the witnesses. Said he, 'If you will read this book with a prayerful heart, and ask God to give you a witness, you will know of the truth of this work.' I told him I would do so, and then asked him his name. He said his name was Samuel H. Smith. 'Ah,' said I, 'you are one of the witnesses.' 'Yes,' said he, *'I know the book to be a revelation from God, translated by the gift and power of the Holy Ghost, and that my brother Joseph Smith, jun., is a Prophet, Seer and Revelator.'*

Samuel's testimony proved so persuasive, in fact, that it wasn't long until Phineas himself was sharing the book with others and affirming that it "was a revelation from God, translated from the Reformed Egyptian language by Joseph Smith, jun., by the gift and power of God."[29] Although a later recollection, Phineas's account is still significant in how it interchanges "revelation" with "translation." While we perhaps cannot confirm that this is precisely how Samuel spoke on that occasion, we can see how Phineas—a devout Latter-day Saint who intended this account to be faith-promoting—had no problem at least attributing this language to both the missionary and to himself in his retelling. In any case, it highlights precisely how these terms—*revelation* and *translation*—were almost synonymous in the early Latter-day Saint religious parlance.

John Whitmer

John Whitmer was one of the Eight Witnesses of the Book of Mormon, a scribe in the translation of the Book of Mormon, a Church

29. "History of Brigham Young," *Deseret News* (February 3, 1858), 1, emphasis added.

leader in Missouri, and an early Church historian.[30] In 1836, he published an address to the public in the Church's periodical the *Latter Day Saints' Messenger and Advocate.* In it, Whitmer reaffirmed his printed testimony of the Book of Mormon as it appears in the Eight Witnesses' statement and reiterated his belief in the book's inspiration. Said he:

> It may not be amiss in this place, to give a statement to the world concerning the work of the Lord, as I have been a member of this church of Latter Day Saints from its beginning; *to say that the book of Mormon is a revelation from God, I have no hesitancy*; but with all confidence have signed my name to it as such; and I hope, that my patrons will indulge me in speaking freely on this subject. . . . Therefore I desire to testify to all that will come to the knowledge of this address; that I have most assuredly seen the plates from whence the book of Mormon is translated, and that I have handled these plates, and know of a surety that *Joseph Smith, jr. has translated the book of Mormon by the gift and power of God*. . . . [A]nd I know that the Bible, book of Mormon and book of Doctrine and Covenants of the church of Christ of Latter Day Saints, *contain the revealed will of heaven.*[31]

Here Whitmer exchanges phrases such as "revelation," "revealed," and "translated" in ways that are not only familiar at this point, but to be expected. That he freely associated the Bible, the Book of Mormon, and the Doctrine and Covenants all under the category of "the revealed will of heaven" punctuates the fluidity of the terminology used in describing these texts in the early Latter-day Saint canon. Indeed, Whitmer affirms in that same address that "the revelations and commandments given to us" (the manuscripts of which Whitmer was an early scribal custodian) "are, in my estimation, equally true with the book of Mormon, and equally neccessary for salvation."[32]

Orson Pratt

One final example worth looking at is Orson Pratt, an apostle and a significant thinker and writer in early Latter-day Saint history.[33] Orson

30. See Ronald E. Romig, *Eighth Witness: The Biography of John Whitmer* (Independence, MO: John Whitmer Books, 2014).
31. John Whitmer, "Address," *Latter Day Saints' Messenger and Advocate* 2, no. 6 (March 1836): 286–287, emphasis added.
32. Whitmer, "Address," 237.
33. Breck England, *The Life and Thought of Orson Pratt* (Salt Lake City: University of Utah Press, 1985).

left behind voluminous and hugely influential writings on the Book of Mormon, and so may be regarded as a representative orthodox figure for the purposes of this treatment. Only a few samples of Orson's writings will suffice to make my point, beginning with his 1848 *Divine Authority*, which argues for the truth of Joseph Smith's "account of the finding and translation of the Book of Mormon." This translation, readers are informed, was accomplished "through the inspiration of the Holy Ghost, by aid of the Urim and Thummim."[34] Appealing to passages such as Isaiah 29:11–12 and others, Orson affirmed, "The Book of Mormon comes testifying that the hour of these judgments is at hand.... [T]here is no circumstance mentioned by Isaiah, connected with *the revelation and translation* of the book he mentions, but what is connected with the Book of Mormon."[35] Elsewhere in this work Orson speaks of "the revelation of the record of Joseph, and its union with the Jewish record,"[36] and of "the revelation in the Book of Mormon, pointing out the location of many ancient cities,"[37] as well as of Moroni "reveal[ing] a book containing a beautiful and glorious system of salvation" to the young prophet.[38] At the same time, Elder Pratt mentions "the plates from which that book was translated," and how Joseph "was enabled to translate the book into the English language."[39] He writes of "Mr. Smith's translation of these records,"[40] how "the prophecy of Moroni was translated and printed in the Book of Mormon,"[41] and of the plates' "translation by the gift of God."[42]

Two years later saw the publication of Elder Pratt's *Divine Authenticity of the Book of Mormon*. It begins: "The Book of Mormon claims to be a divinely inspired record, written by a succession of prophets who inhabited Ancient America. It professes to be revealed to the present generation for the salvation of all who will receive it, and for the

34. Orson Pratt, *Divine Authority, or the Question, Was Joseph Smith Sent of God?* (n.p., 1848), 8.
35. Pratt, *Divine Authority*, 11, emphasis added.
36. Pratt, *Divine Authority*, 7.
37. Pratt, *Divine Authority*, 16.
38. Pratt, *Divine Authority*, 4.
39. Pratt, *Divine Authority*, 8.
40. Pratt, *Divine Authority*, 13.
41. Pratt, *Divine Authority*, 13.
42. Pratt, *Divine Authority*, 16.

overthrow and damnation of all nations who reject it."[43] This sets the tenor for the rest of Orson's treatment, who throughout speaks of the Book of Mormon and its message with the terms "revealed" and "revelation" as well as "translate" and "translated," to wit (emphasis added):

- "The Book of Mormon claims to be the sacred history of ancient America. . . . Mr. Smith, through the aid of the Urim and Thummim, and by the gift and power of God, *translated* this record into the English language. The *translation* contains about the same amount of reading as the Old Testament."[44]
- "These three men in company with Mr. Smith testify that, in answer to their prayers in the year 1829, they saw an angel of God, descend from heaven, clothed with glory, and that he took the plates from which the Book of Mormon was *translated*, and exhibited them before their eyes, so that they saw them distinctly, and also the engravings upon them; and they further testify, that while the angel was thus showing them the plates, they heard the voice of the Lord out of the heavens, declaring that they had been *translated* correctly."[45]
- "If [Joseph Smith] was sincere, then the Book of Mormon is a *divine revelation*, and this church must be 'the only true and living church of Christ upon the face of the whole earth,' and there is no salvation in any other. This is an immense conclusion, but we can come to no other, the moment we admit his sincerity."[46]
- "If, then, it can be proved by the Bible that such a book as the Book of Mormon was to be *revealed* in the last days, this would be an additional testimony to its truth, which none of the other inspired books have. Before we close this series, we shall show that the Bible has predicted that such a book, as the one now *revealed*, should be sent forth to fulfil the great events of the last days."[47]
- "The existence of the plates, filled with engravings, is proved by twelve eye witnesses: while the correctness of their *translation*

43. Orson Pratt, *Divine Authenticity of the Book of Mormon* (n.p., 1850), 1.
44. Pratt, *Divine Authenticity of the Book of Mormon*, 49.
45. Pratt, *Divine Authenticity of the Book of Mormon*, 50.
46. Pratt, *Divine Authenticity of the Book of Mormon*, 55.
47. Pratt, *Divine Authenticity of the Book of Mormon*, 57.

is proved by four eye witnesses, not only of the plates, but of the angel."[48]

- "After these plates had been exhibited to a sufficient number of witnesses, they were, by the commandment of God, hid up in charge of the heavenly messenger who first *revealed* them, and who had, from time to time, while they were being *translated*, directed Mr. Smith how to preserve them from the hands of his persecutors; for persecution was so heavy upon him that he had to flee from place to place to preserve his life. . . . The Book of Mormon informs us that the sealed portion of the plates contains a very great and sacred *revelation*, unfolding things from the beginning of the world unto the end thereof, and that it is hereafter to be *revealed* by the power of Christ. The plates, therefore, will no doubt be kept in charge of the heavenly messenger until the time arrives for the seal to be loosed, and for the remainder to be *translated*."[49]
- "This great manifestation of the power of God in contrast with the power of the evil one, must have given a knowledge to those who were present, that Joseph Smith was a great prophet and seer, and that the Book of Mormon was a *divine revelation*."[50]
- "As we have already stated, the Lord, in his great mercy, has condescended to give miraculous evidence to establish the Divine Authenticity of that *great and glorious revelation*—the Book of Mormon."[51]
- "The Latter-day Saints know that Joseph Smith is a true prophet, and that the Book of Mormon is a *divine revelation*, because God has confirmed the same unto them by the miraculous manifestations of his power."[52]

In other publications, such as an 1853 article in his periodical *The Seer*, Elder Pratt asked rhetorically, "Do you believe the Book of Mormon is a divine revelation?" to which he answered affirmatively and simply, "We do."[53] One year later he again spoke of "the revelation and transla-

48. Pratt, *Divine Authenticity of the Book of Mormon*, 57.
49. Pratt, *Divine Authenticity of the Book of Mormon*, 57.
50. Pratt, *Divine Authenticity of the Book of Mormon*, 63.
51. Pratt, *Divine Authenticity of the Book of Mormon*, 68.
52. Pratt, *Divine Authenticity of the Book of Mormon*, 78.
53. Orson Pratt, "Celestial Marriage," *The Seer* 1, no. 2 (February 1853): 30.

tion of the book of Mormon," which he deemed "a sacred history." Those who encountered this book had no alternative: "they must either embrace the Book of Mormon as a divine revelation, or be cut off by judgements from the land."[54] In 1856, he again avowed that Joseph's ability to translate ancient scripture was one of the gifts of the Spirit—specifically, "the gift of translation by the inspiration of the Holy Ghost." Being so "inspired by God," Joseph "translated the Book of Mormon from the original language of the ancient inhabitants of America," as well as "the Book of Abraham from Egyptian papyrus" and "a sacred revelation concerning the Apostle John," referring to section 7 of the Doctrine and Covenants.[55] And why not? After all, "The Spirit is perfectly acquainted with every language and tongue upon the earth," and can, accordingly, "speak words and sentences in an unknown tongue" as well as "speak the words of a new revelation."[56]

This manner of describing the Book of Mormon was not confined to Orson's printed works. In public discourses, such as that delivered on August 25, 1878, Elder Pratt conceptually merged the activities of *translation* and *revelation* to meet under the Prophet's use of the Urim and Thummim. "One of the first gifts bestowed by the Lord for the benefit of His people," said he on that occasion, "was that of revelation—the gift to translate, by the aid of the Urim and Thummim, the gift of bringing to light old and ancient records." Driving his point home, Elder Pratt mused, "What a wonderful thing the Book of Mormon is, to be brought forth by an angel sent from heaven to be translated from the ancient languages of this country into our English language, to have the Urim and Thummim given to the translator by which the words were translated."[57]

Conclusion

The preceding examination confirms the following: early Latter-day Saints understood that the ability of a *seer* like Joseph Smith to *translate* ancient scripture was due to *revelation* granted by God. Our sampling of the evidence reveals a consistent and unmistakable pattern in early

54. Orson Pratt, "Questions and Answers of Doctrine," *The Seer* 2, no. 2 (February 1854): 213, 215.
55. Orson Pratt, *Spiritual Gifts* (n.p., 1856), 71.
56. Pratt, *Spiritual Gifts*, 72.
57. Orson Pratt, "The Book of Mormon," *Journal of Discourses* (Liverpool: William Budge, 1880), 20:65, 69.

Latter-day Saint discourse that uses words such as *revelation*, *inspiration*, and *translation* interchangeably to describe Joseph Smith's scriptural texts—and specifically the Book of Mormon. For two centuries this has been so, as seen mostly recently with Elder Soares's remarks at the 2020 general conference. To somehow suggest that any of these figures reviewed in this paper were sheepishly conceding the historical authenticity or antiquity of the Book of Mormon by calling it a "revelation" in some instances instead of a "translation" is sheer folly and betrays a fundamental ignorance of the Latter-day Saint reception of the Book of Mormon.[58]

To answer, therefore, the question posed in the title of this paper: the Book of Mormon is *both* a translation *and* a revelation, not just one or the other. The two dwell together in a divine symbiosis that found its latter-day manifestation through Joseph the Seer. Well might we thus echo the declaration of William Appleby, who in 1856 exclaimed, "But thanks and praise be given to Him who rules on high and sways the destinies of men; He has spoken from the heavens in these days, raised up a Prophet, Seer, and Revelator, who has by commandment and the aid of the Urim and Thummim, and the power of inspiration, translated and brought back and restored '*the most plain and precious things*' that have been taken away by uninspired men, under the authority of a corrupt and apostate church, so that the Saints of Latter-days know, understand, and comprehend truth from error, and the inspiration of the Almighty from the wisdom of men."[59]

An earlier version of this paper was originally delivered at the Joseph Smith Papers Conference in Salt Lake City, UT on September 10, 2021.

58. See further Stephen O. Smoot, "Apologetics and Antiquity: Book of Mormon Reception, 1830–1844," *Journal of Mormon History* 48, no. 4 (October 2022): 1–31.
59. "Correspondence of Judge Appleby," *The Mormon* 2, no. 38 (November 8, 1856), [3], emphasis in original; cf. William I. Appleby, "Translations of the Bible," *The Latter-day Saints' Millennial Star* 18, no. 51 (December 20, 1856): 801–804.

11

Reconciling "All the Significant Geographic Details in the Book of Mormon"

Validating a New Book of Mormon Model

Laura B. Hathaway and Ronald D. Bracken

The internal geographic consistency of the Book of Mormon supports the possibility of a real-world setting. This paper uses an internal map created by John E. Clark to explore the potential value and limitations of applying such models, focusing on the Chesapeake Bay as one possible candidate. This model tentatively meets the Book of Mormon's criteria: a limited area with key features in correct relative positions, including a narrow neck of land, a north/south river flowing into the sea, hills, mountains, lands of "pure water," and a land of "many waters." A defining feature is the division between a "land northward" and "land southward," which would be geographically distinct in travel. In this model, the proposed division is marked by a geologic fall line separating the Piedmont from the coastal plains. The "land northward" lies between the Susquehanna and Delaware Rivers, with Lake Ontario corresponding to Ripliancum. The Chesapeake Bay model plausibly aligns with the text's features and illustrates both the promise and limits of using internal maps to evaluate geographical possibilities.

Introduction

> *"It has been my experience that most members of the Church of Jesus Christ of Latter-day Saints, when confronted with a Book of Mormon geography, worry about the wrong things. Almost invariably the first question that arises is whether the geography fits the archaeology of the proposed area. This should be our second question, the first being whether the geography fits the*

facts of the Book of Mormon—a question we all can answer without being versed in American archaeology. Only after a given geography reconciles all of the significant geographic details given in the Book of Mormon does the question of archaeological and historical detail merit attention. The Book of Mormon must be the final and most important arbiter in deciding the correctness of a given geography; otherwise, we will be forever hostage to the shifting sands of expert opinion."
– John E. Clark[1]

The purpose of this paper is to show how the Chesapeake Bay model (CBM) "reconciles all the significant geographic details given in the Book of Mormon."[2] Using John E. Clark's internal map as a starting point, we will show when that internal map is helpful and when it is not. Even where his understanding differs from the CBM, the work of Clark is beneficial because it allows us to critically evaluate whether our own interpretations are valid. This is also useful in moving towards a truer picture of Book of Mormon lands. Convincing counterarguments for differing interpretations are something that every Book of Mormon geography model must face. Below is a map showing the real-world model which will be used in comparison to Clark's internal map.

Clark proposes a geographical framework based on seven points, resulting in six transects (a line connecting two points). These transects are: (I) Hagoth to Bountiful, (II) Bountiful to Moroni, (III) Moroni to Seashore City, (IV) Seashore City to Hagoth, (V) Nephi to Zarahemla, and (VI) Bountiful to Cumorah.[3] This same proposed framework will be used to evaluate the Chesapeake Bay Model, supplemented when necessary with textual evidence from the Book of Mormon. Only the points where the CBM differs from Clark's explanation will be explored.

1. Clark, "Revisiting," 13–14.
2. Clark, "Revisiting," 14.
3. Clark, "Revisiting," 15.

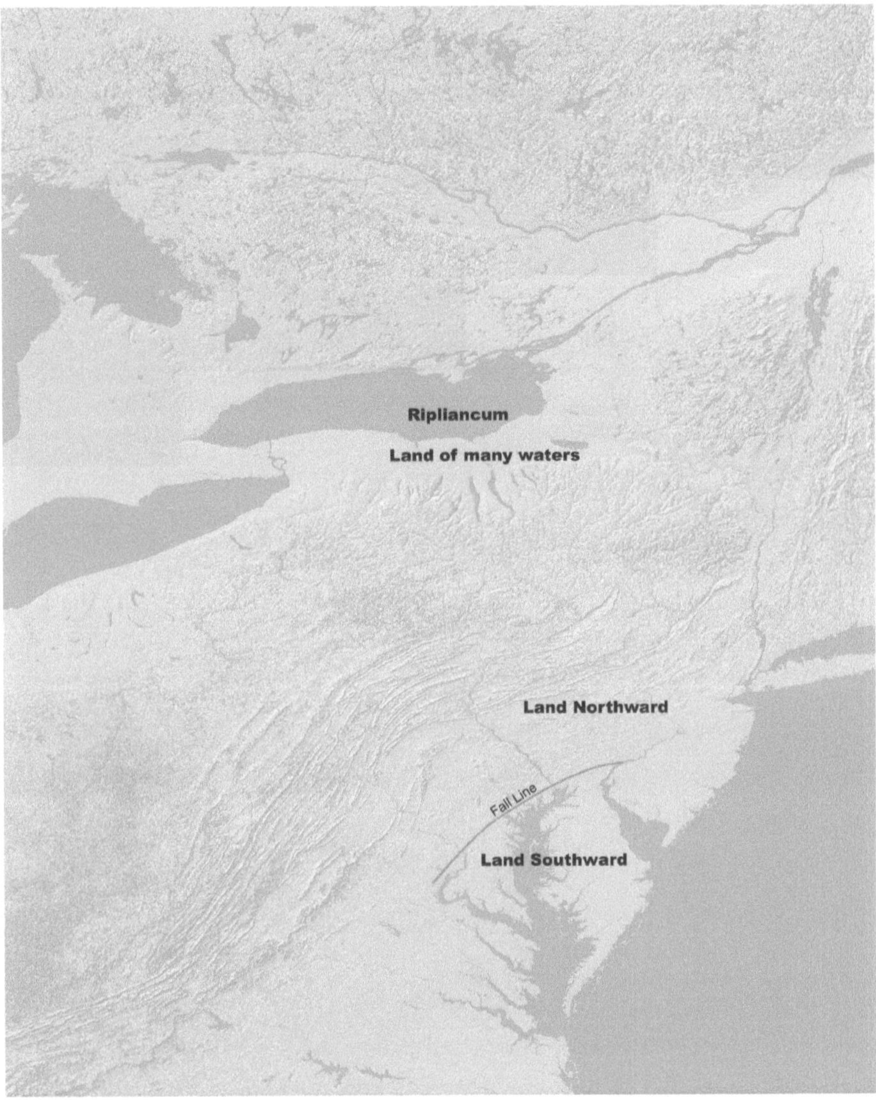

Overview of the Chesapeake Bay model. The land "southward" consists of the Delmarva Peninsula on the east of the Chesapeake Bay, as well as the land west of the Chesapeake Bay to the Potomac River. The land "northward" is the area sandwiched between the Susquehanna River and the Delaware River northward to Lake Ontario. Ripliancum is a Jaredite word meaning "large, or to exceed all."

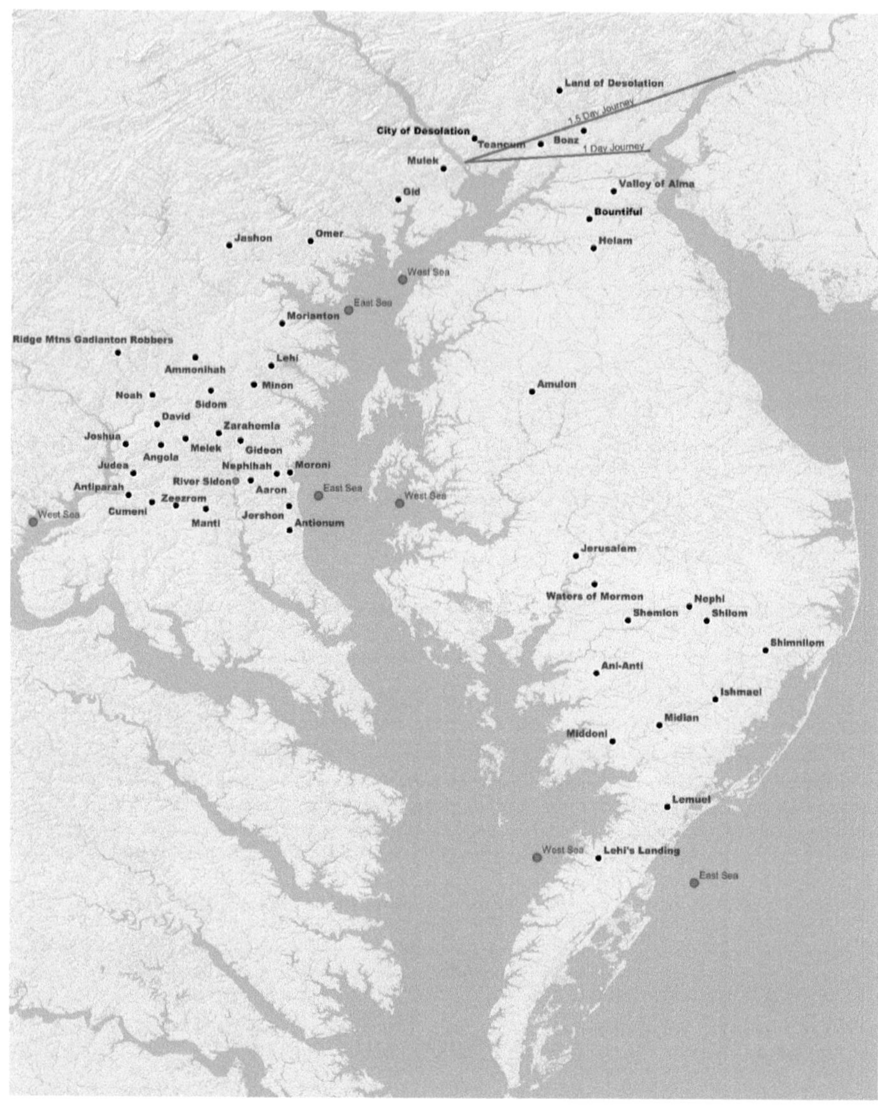

Possible locations of Nephite and Lamanite cities in the land southward. The distances between cities, as well as placement of geological features such as hills and rivers, are consistent with the description found in the Book of Mormon.

I. Hagoth to Bountiful[4]

Clark	*CBM*
The lands of Desolation and Bountiful meet in the narrow neck (Alma 22:30-32).	The lands of Desolation and Bountiful meet at the fall line (Alma 22:30-32).
A narrow pass or narrow passage led from the land southward to the land northward and was near the borders of the land of Desolation. The narrow pass was close enough to each sea that its location could be described by reference to both. This suggests that the narrow pass was near the center of the narrow neck of land (Alma 50:34; 52:9; Mormon 2:29; Mormon 3:5).	The narrow pass is not in the same location as the narrow neck. It is the way into the land northward from the western shore of the Chesapeake Bay; in other words, from the land of Zarahemla (Alma 50:34; Alma 52:9; Mormon 2:29; Mormon 3:5).
The city of Desolation was in the land of Desolation near the narrow pass and perhaps near the sea or a large river that led to the sea (Mormon 3:5, 8).	The city of Desolation was in the land of Desolation near the narrow pass and near the Chesapeake Bay, which was called the "sea that divided the land" (Mormon 3:5, 8, Ether 10:20).
The city of Bountiful was the northernmost fortification of the eastern border of Nephite territory during the days of General Moroni. Its purpose was to restrict access to the land northward and to keep the Nephites from getting boxed in by the Lamanites (Alma 22:29, 33; Alma 50:32-34; Alma 51:28-32; Alma 52:9; Helaman 1:23, 28; Helaman 4:6-7).	The city of Bountiful was not a city by the east sea, rather it was by a west sea (Alma 63:5). The purpose of the cities by the east sea were to defend the land of Zarahemla from Lamanites coming across the sea. (Alma 22:29,33; Alma 50:32-34; Alma 51:28-32; Alma 52:9; Helaman 1:23, 28; Helaman 4:6-7).
The "line" between the land of Bountiful and the land of Desolation ran "from the east to the west sea" and was "a day and a half's journey for a Nephite" (Alma 22:32; 3 Nephi 3:23). Since the east "sea" is not specified, maybe the travel distances were not meant to be from sea to sea, but from the west sea to a point to the east.	The "line" between the land Bountiful and the land Desolation followed the fall line from the Chesapeake Bay (west sea) to the Delaware river. (Alma 22:32; 3 Nephi 3:23)
A fortified "line" extended "from the west sea, even unto the east; it being a day's journey for a Nephite, on the line which they had fortified" (Helaman 4:7).	A defensive "line" from the west sea, even unto the east that is a day's journey would not need to follow the fall line and would be lower in the narrow neck (Helaman 4:7).

This northern boundary transect assumes that the place where Hagoth launched his ship into the west sea is the northwest corner of Nephite lands. There is textual evidence in the Book of Mormon suggesting that this may not be correct. For example, the Jaredites "built a great city by the narrow neck of land, by the place where the sea divides the land" (Ether 10:20). Clark suggests that this place where the sea divides the land is "perhaps a large river running into the east sea across the

4. Clark, "Revisiting," 17-19.

narrow neck of land, thus 'dividing the land.'"[5] He does not discuss why Mormon would call a river a sea, nor why it would be running into the east sea as opposed to the west sea. The CBM has the Chesapeake Bay as the "sea that divides the land." It is into this sea that Hagoth launches his ship. Zarahemla is on the west side of the Chesapeake Bay, west of where Hagoth launches his ship. Thus, "Hagoth" is not the westernmost part of the land of the Nephites.

Clark assumes an "hourglass" shape of the land, which comes from Mormon's description: "And now, it was only the distance of a day and a half's journey for a Nephite, on the line Bountiful and the land Desolation, from the east to the west sea; and thus the land of Nephi and the land of Zarahemla were nearly surrounded by water, there being a small neck of land between the land northward and the land southward" (Alma 22:32). This description of the narrow/small neck of land being between the land northward and the land southward corresponds well with the top of the Delmarva peninsula in the CBM, since the Nephites "land northward" is bordered by the Susquehanna and Delaware rivers. The description of "nearly surrounded by water" fits the Chesapeake Bay model more closely than any other currently available model.

One major point where CBM differs from Clark is in the placement of the narrow pass. Clark's description of the narrow pass being a passage through the narrow neck of land is understandable, since both lead into the land northward. However, the argument that the narrow pass is "close enough to each sea that its location could be described by reference to both" is inconsistent with his other statement that "the narrow neck had to have been wide enough that travelers going north-south could pass through without noticing both seas from one vantage point, including the narrow pass."[6] This last statement is also inconsistent with the Book of Mormon text, simply because a sea had to be close enough to the narrow pass to cast in dead bodies (Mormon 3:5-8). Having both the narrow neck and the narrow pass flanked by seas results in equating one with the other, which most models (including this one) do not accept. The CBM distinguishes the narrow pass (way into the land northward from the land of Zarahemla) from the narrow/small neck (way into the land northward from Bountiful).

5. Clark, "Revisiting," 40.
6. Clark, "Revisiting," 19.

II. Bountiful to Moroni[7]

Clark	*CBM*
Amalickiah attempted to break through the Nephites fortified line in Bountiful and gain access to the land northward (Alma 52).	Bountiful was not a city by the east sea.
Teancum fortified the city of Bountiful and secured the narrow pass (Alma 52:9).	The order from Moroni to Teancum to secure the narrow pass is so the Lamanites would not have access to the north side of Bountiful and ability to harass Bountiful "on every side" (Alma 52:9).
The sons of Helaman began their missionary travels at the city of Bountiful; they traveled to Gid and then to Mulek, visiting Gid and Mulek in reverse order of the Lamanite attack. This suggests that Gid was not directly in line with Mulek. (Helaman 5:14-15).	Gid can be accessed from Bountiful by crossing the sea. Lehi and Nephi could then travel north to Mulek.

This transect is the eastern boundary of the Nephite land. Clark's model places Bountiful near the east sea in order to account for it being within a day travel from Mulek, a city by the east sea. Notably, he does acknowledge that an east sea is never mentioned with Bountiful, only a west sea. For this reason, he places Bountiful slightly inland. Bountiful is never mentioned in the battles northwest of the land of Zarahemla, so the placement of Bountiful in the CBM is logical.

III. Moroni to Seashore City[8]

Clark	*CBM*
The land of Manti was located on the east and west of the Sidon, near the river's head-waters in the southern wilderness (Alma 16:6-7; Alma 22:27).	The land of Manti was located on the west of the river Sidon, near the head of Sidon (Alma 16:6-7; 22:27, Alma 43:32). The "head" of Sidon was near the sea (Alma 43:22; Alma 44:22).
Minon was southward from Gideon on a route that led to the land of Nephi (Alma 2:24).	Minon could have been northeast of the Valley of Gideon (Alma 2:24).

This south boundary transect consists of Moroni, Nephihah and Aaron to the east of the river Sidon and Manti, Zeezrom, Cumeni, Judea, Antiparah, and a city of unknown name by the seashore on the west side of Sidon. Clark places the land of Minon just to the east of Manti on the east side of the river Sidon and the Valley of Gideon to the east of Zarahemla on the east side of the river Sidon. This placement is due to his reading of Alma 2, where the Amlicites join Lamanites in the land of Minon,

7. Clark, "Revisiting," 19–22.
8. Clark, "Revisiting," 23–27.

"above the land of Zarahemla, in the course of the land of Nephi" (Alma 2:24). Since his "course of the land of Nephi" is south, he has Minon to the south. The CBM has the land of Nephi to the east of Zarahemla, across the Chesapeake Bay. Having Minon northeast of Gideon allows the Lamanites to cross the Bay, meet up with the Amlicites, and head southwest towards Zarahemla. This also is a foreshadowing of why the defensive cities by the east sea were later built in a time of war.

Clark refers to the head of Sidon as the "head waters." The 1828 Websters Dictionary gives one definition of "head" as a "body" or "conflux." Continuing, it defines conflux or confluence as a "flowing together; the meeting or junction of two or more steams of water."[9] Thus, when Joseph Smith was translating the record, the confluence of two streams of water could be considered as a "head" of the river. This is the definition that the CBM uses. This allows the river Sidon to flow from north to south past Zarahemla and have the "head" near Manti. This head is possibly located where the Western Branch of the Patuxent River flows into the Patuxent River. There are hills on both the east and west of the river near this head large enough for armies to hide behind (Alma 43:31-32). South of this point, the river is more sea-like as it widens and becomes tidal. This is an important feature because bodies thrown into the river Sidon were said to have been "buried in the sea" and not washed up on shore in route to the sea (Alma 3:3, Alma 44:22). This suggests a short distance to the sea.[10]

IV. Seashore City to Hagoth[11]

Clark	*CBM*
The land of Zarahemla had a northern wilderness area (not specifically described as such) that lay between Noah and the lower narrow-neck area (Alma 22:31; Mormon 3-5). It follows that Noah was still some distance from the narrow neck.	There is no evidence in the text for the narrow neck being directly north of Noah. The lack of mention of Bountiful in the land northwest of Zarahemla supports the idea that this area is not below the narrow/ small neck of land as the CBM shows.

This transect is the western border of the Nephite land. Although this

9. *Webster's American Dictionary of the English Language*, 1828 ed., s.vv. "head" and "confluence," accessed May 20, 2025, https://webstersdictionary1828.com/.
10. Theodore Brandley, "North American Book of Mormon Geography: The River Sidon," *Interpreter Foundation Blog*, May 26, 2016, online at interpreterfoundation.org.
11. Clark, "Revisiting," 27–31.

transect is labeled "Seashore City to Hagoth," Clark does not mention Bountiful in this section. This is unusual, since Hagoth launched his ship into the west sea on the borders of Bountiful. The Book of Mormon text describing the land northwest of Zarahemla does not mention the land of Bountiful. This suggests that (1) something prevents movement so far north on the west side of Zarahemla, or (2) like the Chesapeake Bay model predicts, Bountiful is not in this area. We know movement is not restricted, since at the end of the Book of Mormon the Nephites first retreat to the west sea then, uninhibited, they travel into the land northward.

The CBM does not have Hagoth as the northwest corner of the land of the Nephites as previously discussed. Only two cities on the western seashore are mentioned on the western side of Zarahemla: the city of unknown name and the city Joshua. Clark uses cities further inland to approximate distance of the western border. These inland cities are Melek, Noah and Ammonihah. He concludes that Noah is "some distance from the narrow neck" and thus the western border must be almost twice as long as the eastern border.[12] The Book of Mormon text does not implicitly suggest this discrepancy in lengths between the eastern boundary and western boundary and could be an example of bias in Clark's model.

V. Nephi to Zarahemla[13]

Clark	*CBM*
Mosiah granted sixteen strong men that they "might go up to the land of Lehi-Nephi, to inquire concerning their brethren" (Mosiah 7:2). After forty days they came to a hill north of the land of Shilom, and from there they went down to Nephi (Mosiah 7:5-6).	Travel to Nephi was always "up," except where they went "down" to Nephi from the hill north of Shilom. This hill is not named, even though it is mentioned multiple times in the Book of Mormon. This suggests there were not many, if any, other hills in that area.
Nephi was located in a highland valley; the wilderness to the north of the city of Nephi was "up" from the city.	Changes of elevation do not need to be dramatic (i.e., "highland valley"), but do need to be noticeable as one travels. This can be as simple as noticing how rivers flow.
The Limhi party obviously got to the land northward near the area of final destruction of the Jaredite people. They did not know the route to Zarahemla. They apparently passed through the narrow neck of land without realizing it.	CBM allows for the knowledge of passing through the narrow neck, but not knowing they should "bend their course" (Mosiah 22:11).

12. Clark, "Revisiting," 31.
13. Clark, "Revisiting," 31–35.

Clark	*CBM*
Alma and his followers fled eight days' journey into the wilderness" to escape the armies of King Noah who were searching for them in the land of Mormon, and they arrived in Helam (Mosiah 23:1-3).	The land of Mormon and the land of Helam were both lands of "pure water." Less than 10 miles from where the proposed location of the city of Nephi is a well-known spring, or "fountain of pure water." Approximately 70 miles north of this spring is a land of fresh ("pure") water that fits the description of the land of Helam.
The Lamanites could not follow Alma past the valley of Alma, owing to divine intervention (Mosiah 24:23).	The valley of Alma would be up at the top of the Delmarva. From there, one would need to bend their course and go through the narrow pass to reach Zarahemla. Without being "led," this would be hard to find.

The "land of Nephi" became a term that meant territory controlled by the Lamanites. This is seen when the Lamanites gained control of the city of Mulek for a time. Chief captain Moroni eventually "obtained possession of the city of Mulek, which was one of the strongest holds of the Lamanites in the *land of Nephi*" (Alma 53:6, emphasis added). Although the city of Nephi is on the eastern shore of the Chesapeake Bay, Lamanite territory was at one point to the east, south and west of the land of Zarahemla. Moroni saw a need to drive the Lamanites out of the eastern wilderness and established cities by the east sea to protect the land of Zarahemla.

VI. Bountiful to Cumorah[14]

Clark	*CBM*
We learn from the Jaredite account that the hill Cumorah was near the eastern seashore (Ether 9:3; Ether 14:12-13, 26).	The Jaredite account referenced does not name Cumorah, but says, "the place where the Nephites were destroyed." Although Cumorah was the last big stand, the word "destroyed" is not used for the battle itself, rather it is used in events before the battle as well as post battle (Mormon 5:7; Mormon 8:2), both which were south of Cumorah.

14. Clark, "Revisiting," 35–37.

Cumorah is in a land of "many waters, rivers, and fountains" (Mormon 6:4). This is an accurate description of the Finger Lakes region of the United States. Hill Cumorah, called hill Ramah by the Jaredites, is south of the waters of Ripliancum, a Jaredite word that means "large, or to exceed all" (Ether 15:8-11). Lake Ontario is a large body of water directly north of the land of many waters, rivers, and fountains and is a good candidate for Ripliancum. This large body of water explains why the remaining Nephites fled southward and not northward after the final battle in the land of Cumorah.

Conclusion

The use of an internal map can be helpful when attempting to validate a Book of Mormon geography; however, the Book of Mormon text itself must be the final authority. An internal map is useful as a starting place, but the user should be aware that bias will inevitably show up in the production of such map. The more deeply one studies the geography of the Book of Mormon, the more apparent it becomes that "anywhere" will not do. There are too many details that must be reconciled. The Chesapeake Bay model gives a rational and internally coherent explanation of the geography and reveals a new view of the land that is consistent with the text of the Book of Mormon.

Acknowledgements

Special thanks to Des. Isaías Baruch Peña Ramírez at Hall Labs for generously creating the maps.

FAIR takes no official position regarding the geography of the Book of Mormon. The specific model and views presented in this paper are those of the authors and do not constitute an endorsement by FAIR.

12

Second Nephi as a Legal Document

Martin Evans

Considering conventions of the ancient Near East, 2 Nephi can be understood as a collection of legal documents. Supporting this view are 1) Nephi's allusions to sealing the record and to a bar of judgment, 2) discussion of the law of witnesses, 3) components and formatting consistent with Neo-Babylonian depositions and plaintiff statements, 4) the presence of a conservative (in contrast to revisionistic) citation of Isaiah, and 5) rhetoric and vocabulary consistent with Judean legal genre. Nephi's references to judicial procedure are unmistakable and leave an impression on the reader. Many already understand Nephi's inclusion of Jacob and Isaiah's words as a witness, however, less straightforward is the structure of 2 Nephi which is consistent with legal documents and conventions of the time. This view understands 2 Nephi as collated texts that contain an agreement (2 Nephi 1-4), reaction (2 Nephi 4-5), three witness statements (2 Nephi 6-10, 12-24, 25-28) followed by a plaintiff statement (2 Nephi 33). Putting aside Nephi's design, I consider briefly that our current version of 2 Nephi is a harmonized text joining Nephite, Judean, early Christian, and early Protestant textual traditions.

Neo-Babylonian Depositions

There are several scholarly opinions on the book of 2 Nephi. Many have identified the first chapters as a covenantal agreement.[1] Our discussion will compare 2 Nephi with conventions in ancient Near East because research has shown conclusively cultures across Mesopotamia influenced neighboring legal systems.[2] In part due to necessity we turn

1. For a detailed overview of scholarly perspectives on the structure and interpretation of 2 Nephi, see Appendix A.
2. Raymond Westbrook and Bruce Wells, *Everyday Law in Biblical Israel: An Introduction* (Westminster John Knox Press, 2009), 23-24.

to surrounding nation's legal procedure as a surrogate for the legal procedure within Judea.

Four types of recorded depositions have been described in the ancient Near East. These include accusatory, testimonial, memoranda, and sworn depositions.[3] There are no identifying markings on court statements to identify them as depositions. This contrasts with Old Babylonian records when statements may begin with, "tablet of confirmation"[4] or "tablet with a sworn statement."[5] Official depositions include the speaker's name and a patronym or title. They list persons present that witness hearing the statement and often the scribe's name, date, and place of composition.[6]

Depositions are made before officials or a group of people. Some depositions were made outside of official buildings.[7] Shalom Holtz identifies depositions based on their content, inclusion in the legal archive, their references to the case, adjudicating authorities, or audience. Using Holtz's analysis as a guide it appears Jacob's, Isaiah's, and Nephi's words in 2 Nephi (2 Nephi 6-10, 12-24, 25-28 respectively) have features that are seen in formal witness depositions.

Components of Neo-Babylonian Depositions

2 Nephi 6 begins with an introduction similar to contemporary witness statements. For example, YOS 6,131 begins:

---

3. "Different text-types that record only statements: accusatory depositions, depositions of testimony, memoranda of depositions, depositions under oath. These text-types do not explicitly mention the activities of a court… Although these texts do not describe the entire dispute and decision, many of the statements seem to have been made as part of a larger legal process," see Shalom E. Holtz, *Neo-Babylonian Court Procedure* (Leiden, The Netherlands: Brill, 2009). 100–116.
4. Martha T. Roth, "Reading Mesopotamian Law Cases PBS 5 100: A Question of Filiation," *Journal of the Economic and Social History of the Orient* 44/3 (2001): 266-267.
5. Harry Hoffner, "Records of Testimony Given in the Trials of Suspected Thieves and Embezzlers of Royal Property," in *Context of Scripture Vol. III*, ed. William W. Hallo and K. Lawson Younger, Jr. (Brill, 2003): 57.
6. Depending on the type of deposition, the scribe may or may not be identified. As their name suggests, only sworn depositions document an oath taken by the speaker. Holtz, *Neo-Babylonian Court Procedure*, 101.
7. In Assyria "as a consequence of the fact that various administrative officials could act as judges, there was no specific court building." See Karen Radner, "The Reciprocal Relationship Between Judge and Society in the Neo-Assyrian Period," *MAARAV* 12/1-2 (2005): 43.

> The *mār banī*[8] in whose presence ^{m}Anim-aḫḫē-uṣur the messenger of the crown prince said thus to ^{m}Nabû-šarra-uṣur the ša *rēš* šarri[9] administrator of the Eanna:[10]

This excerpt uses formal titles and references the audience. Instead of an oath, depositions typically described the *audience* in front of whom the statement was made. The inclusion of the audience is a certifying feature. "A deposition could be taken before a local tribunal... It was recorded under the format: "These are the witnesses before whom ([personal name] stated...")."[11] Knowing this convention increases our understanding of the seemingly trivial words Nephi places in the superscription prior to Jacob's statement. He writes,

> The words of Jacob, the brother of Nephi, which he spoke unto the people of Nephi (2 Nephi 6:1).

The mention of the audience may be viewed as the inclusion of witnesses present at Jacob's statement and not merely a historical detail. This tradition was not limited to Babylon. When recording Egyptian "transcripts, the participants and onlookers were put down as witnesses."[12] Biblical superscriptions typically do *not* mention the audience.[13] Therefore, some information in the heading prior to Jacob's words is more characteristic of contemporary legal documents than scriptural text.

Another aspect comparable to that found in legal records is the term "brother of Nephi." Reference to a speaker's brother never occurs in biblical superscriptions. Biblical superscriptions typically use a patronym. Yet, Jacob is not referred to as "son of Lehi"; instead, he is the "brother of Nephi." Such titles, though uncommon, are found in Neo-Babylonian legal records. In YOS 7, 10 we read,

> Ḫašdaya, brother of Iddinaya, said thus in the assembly.[14]

---

8. Often translated as "citizens" or "freemen"; see Holtz, *Neo-Babylonian Court Procedure*, 54.
9. High ranking temple administrator.
10. Holtz, *Neo-Babylonian Court Procedure*, 106.
11. Joachim Oelsner, Bruce Wells, and Cornelia Wunsch, "Mesopotamia: Neo-Babylonian Period," in *A History of Ancient Near Eastern Law (2 vols)*, ed. Raymond Westbrook (Boston: Brill, 2003), 922.
12. Sandra Lippert, "Law Courts," *UCLA Encyclopedia of Egyptology*, 1/1 (Dec. 2012).
13. A notable rare exception is Deuteronomy 1:1.
14. Holtz, *Neo-Babylonian Court Procedure,* 103-104; Shalom E. Holtz, *Neo-Babylonian Trial Records* (Atlanta, GA: Society of Biblical Literature, 2014), 20-23.

If Nephi is using Jacob as a witness to a renewed covenant in 2 Nephi 1-4, we would expect Jacob to address the same issues. Jacob's words contain a preamble and titulary, historical overview, covenant speech, stipulations of the covenant, cursings, and blessings.[15] This is almost identical to the components Jan Martin identifies in 2 Nephi 1-4.[16]

Jacob's speech in 2 Nephi 6-10 can be viewed as a deposition because of its placement in the record (following a covenant), the formal title presenting Jacob, the mention of the audience, and the content supportive of the existing theme. Nephi also views Jacob as a witness.

Witnesses

The following parallelism shows Nephi sees Jacob's words in 2 Nephi 6-10 and Isaiah's in 2 Nephi 12-24 as witness statements:

> Wherefore, I will send [Jacob and Isaiah's] *words* forth unto my children to *prove*...that my words are true...
>
> Nevertheless, God sendeth *more witnesses*, and he *proveth* all his words. (2 Nephi 11:3)

Because Jacob is a witness, far from disjointed, the transition in 2 Nephi 6:1 could be *expected* (e.g., Martin wrote of the oddity no witnesses were identified at the end of what is clearly a suzerain covenant.[17])

The Law of Witnesses

A Latter-day Saint may believe the law of witnesses refers to multiple sources establishing spiritual truth. The law of witnesses as understood by those in the First Temple period is likely different. Amid a list of civil laws, the law of witnesses appears to be focused on protecting the accused

15. John S. Thompson, "Isaiah 50-51, the Israelite Autumn Festivals, and the Covenant Speech of Jacob in 2 Nephi 6-10." in *Isaiah in the Book of Mormon*, edited by Donald W. Parry and John W. Welch (Provo, UT: Foundation for Ancient Research and Mormon Studies, 1998): 123-150.
16. Jan Martin, "The Prophet Nephi and the Covenantal Nature of Cut-off, Cursed, Skin of Blackness, and Loathsome," in *They Shall Grow Together: The Bible in the Book of Mormon*, ed. Charles Swift and Nicholas Frederick (Provo, UT: Religious Studies Center, 2022), 107–141.
17. "Moses specified that the 'heavens' and the 'earth' were witnesses (Deuteronomy 32:1), and he directed that large, inscribed stones be set up on the banks of the river Jordan as witnesses to Israel's covenant renewal (see Deuteronomy 27:1-3). If Lehi did something similar with objects, Nephi did not record it on the small plates..." Martin, "*The Prophet Nephi*," 113.

from immediate consequences of violated civil laws.[18] Therefore, this law was used in judicial settings. Its implementation in the Second Temple period also suggests this view. The law of witnesses appears modified in Rabbinic literature and Qumran rules but still refers to civil law imposing immediate consequences.[19] With this background, it is no surprise some argue Paul's mention of the law of witnesses indicates he intends to "take disciplinary action" with "judicial proceeding[s]" upon his return.[20] Because the law of witnesses appears to be used in legal procedure in Judean culture, this is a potential interpretation of Nephi's meaning.

Sworn Depositions and Oaths

Returning to Neo-Babylonian convention we consider Nephi's deposition. When depositions were made under oath, surprisingly little notation was used. Typical notation is "they swore," saying: "indeed... (followed by the statement)." At times, the name of a deity was recorded as well. The following is an example from a case regarding a deposit of silver.

> (Lines 9–11) Rīmūt son of Šamaš-lē'i descendant of Arrabtu swore by Šamaš before the judges and [said] thus:
>
> (Line 11-12) "I and Ṣillaya are the creditors (with debts) owed by Iddin-[Marduk]. We did not know that silver was depo[sited] with Nabû-šuma-iškun."[21]

This statement depicts the two essential aspects of an oath which are a statement of sincerity (authenticating element) and the oath content.[22]

Nephi's rhetoric in 2 Nephi 25:4 and, to a lesser extent 2 Nephi 28:1 have features that are found in contemporary oaths. "Oaths are generally authenticated either by appealing to a precious entity outside oneself or

---

18. Deuteronomy 17:6 (KJV) states, "At the mouth of two witnesses, or three witnesses, shall he that is worthy of death be put to death; but at the mouth of one witness he shall not be put to death."
19. J. David Woodington, "A Precedented Approach: Paul's Use of the Law of Witnesses in 2 Corinthians 13:1," *Journal of Biblical Literature* 137/4 (2018): 1003–18.
20. David E. Garland, *The New American Commentary: 2 Corinthians* (Nashville: Broadman & Holman, 1999), 541; A. E. Harvey, *Renewal through Suffering: A Study of 2 Corinthians*, (Edinburgh: T&T Clark, 1996), 108.
21. BM 41663 in Holtz, *Neo-Babylonian Trial Records*, 138.
22. Blane Conklin, *Oath Formulas in Biblical Hebrew,* (Penn State University Press, 2011), 5:1–12.

by calling down a curse."[23] Documented oaths rarely include the corresponding apodosis.[24] Nephi writes:

Claim: I give unto you a prophecy

Authenticating element (precious entity): according to the spirit which is in me;

Claim restated: wherefore I shall prophesy according to the plainness which hath been with me from the time that I came out from Jerusalem with my father

When the apodosis is elided, the resulting consequence is not entirely clear. For example, despite numerous oaths that swear with the life of a deity, to call a potential curse on the respected third party has not been performed as far as we know.[25]

Nephi's stylized oath also appears functionally equivalent to Judean oaths.[26] Nephi makes an oath more typical of the time in 2 Nephi 25:20 but it does not appear to apply to the entire section.

NEO-BABYLONIAN LEGAL PROCEDURE AND PLAINTIFF STATEMENTS

Other legal aspects of Nephi's record are the plaintiff's statement and the promise of additional proof provided by the plaintiff. Mention of sealing the record and a judgment bar also appears to be an explicit reference to judicial activity.

---

23. Conklin., *Oath Formulas,* 46-59.
24. Johannes Hackl, *Der subordinierte Satz in den spätbabylonischen Briefen* (Munster, 2007), 72-73; See also Bruce Wells, F. Rachel Magdalene, and Cornelia Wunsch, "The Assertory Oath in Neo-Babylonian and Persian Administrative Texts," *Revue Internationale des droits de l'Antiquité* 107 (2010): 13-29.
25. Conklin, *Oath Formulas*, 24. Potential unstated consequences for Nephi may include death (i.e. for being a false prophet) or perhaps an acknowledgment the "spirit" is not "in [him]." These two scenarios are in no way comprehensive. Other consequences might include punishment by the spirit upon which he swore or to provide reparations of that which was lost due to Nephi's testimony. At the very least, it appears Nephi is staking all his credibility on his prophecy.
26. A comparable oath is found in 1 Kings 22:14, "Micaiah said, "As the LORD lives, I shall speak whatever the LORD tells me." For a discussion and examples of oaths containing only "As the Lord Lives" as an authenticating element please see: Yael Ziegler "'As the Lord Lives and as Your Soul Lives': An Oath of Conscious Deference." *Vetus Testamentum* 58/1 (2008): 117–30.

Again, due to the lack of records from Judean legal proceedings of necessity we turn to other ancient Near Eastern cultures to understand the conventions in Nephi's time and place.[27] This approach is reasonable, as some conventions were standardized over large regions.[28] After evaluating a series of legal proceedings from multiple cities contemporary to Nephi, Holtz wrote the most common format of plaintiff's statements[29] includes three components. These are:

A. *Opening* (mention of plaintiff and adjudicating authority)
B. *Quotation of the plaintiff's statement*
C. *Imperative to authority*

Plaintiff statements were common in legal cases.[30] Additionally, Isaiah uses a plaintiff's statement in a passage with an explicit allusion

27. It is clear that the civilizations in question had significant political influence on each other and the surrounding areas. Hebrew Bible attests to this influence, yet there is not a consensus on the degree of influence biblical law had on Judean state law. See Westbrook and Wells, *Everyday Law in Biblical Israel*, 3.
28. It appears there was a fair amount of standardization based on consistent practices across multiple regions. For example, plaintiff statements with imperatives were found primarily in decision records when cases originated in higher courts. Whereas records of cases originating in informal settings or in lower courts were less likely to contain a plaintiff statement with an imperative. This tendency was observed in the existing records composed in Babylon, Uruk, Tapsuhu, Sippar, and Bit-sar-Babil dating from approximately 560 BCE to ~550 BCE. Another tendency in the imperative is the wording. When the plaintiff appeared with the defendant the imperative was typically, "establish our decision". If the plaintiff appeared alone before the judge the imperative was usually, "Judge my case against [defendants name]." The latter decision records may result in a summons rather than a verdict. Similar notation used across multiple regions suggests a degree of standardization present in Neo-Babylonian times. Holtz, *Neo-Babylonian Court Procedure*, 226
29. Holtz, *Neo-Babylonian Court Procedure*, 227.
30. For example, the document YOS 19, 101, written in 545 BCE and discovered in Babylon discusses a decision record from a case that apparently pertains to a misappropriated shipment of dates. This document provides an example of a plaintiff statement. The first lines are translated as follows: *Opening:* (Lines 1–3): ^{m}Nergal-rēṣūa the slave of ^{m}Iddin-Marduk said thus to the judges of Nabonidus, king of Babylon.

Quotation of plaintiff's statement: (Lines 3-6) ^{m}Iddin-Marduk, my master, loaded a shipment of 480 *kur* of dates for transport from the hinterland on the boats belonging to ^{m}Amurru-natan, the boatman, son of ^{m}Ammaya. (Line 7) "He had him bear the responsibility for keeping the dates." (Line 8-10) "He brought the

courtroom activity.[31] His allusion to a courtroom suggest plaintiff statements indicate some specificity.

One may wonder if Nephi copies Isaiah's pattern here and, therefore, merely happens to copy a plaintiff's statement unknowingly. However, people from various backgrounds used the plaintiff's statement.[32] Further, cases in Israel could be held publicly with the citizenry acting as judges.[33] This suggests some aspects of legal proceedings were commonly understood. It does not appear accidental that Nephi writes a plaintiff statement near the end of his record. Nephi states:

> *Opening:*
>
> I, Nephi, cannot write all the things which were taught among my people; neither am I mighty in writing, like unto speaking; for when a man speaketh by the power of the Holy Ghost the power of the Holy Ghost carrieth it unto the hearts of the children of men… But I, Nephi, have written what I have written… And now, my beloved brethren, and also Jew, and all ye ends of the earth…
>
> *Quotation of plaintiff's statement:*
>
> [these] are the words of Christ…
>
> *Imperative to authority:*
>
> And if they are not the words of Christ, judge ye (2 Nephi 33:1-11).

Nephi mentions himself, the audience, and his claim before demanding a decision.[34] This language is consistent with that found in legal records.

---

boats to Babylon and he gave me mIddin-Marduk's message. 480 Gur of dates was written i[n it]." (Lines 11–12) I took account of the dates, and 47*gur* 1 *pi* were missing. (Lines 12–14) I raised a claim against mAmurru-natan concerning the missing amount of the dates and . . . (Line 24) Now, I have brought him before you.

Imperative to authority: (Line 25) "Establish our decision!" Holtz, *Neo-Babylonian Court Procedure*, 28-29.

31. Shalom E. Holtz, "Praying as a Plaintiff," *Vetus Testamentum* 61/2 (Jan. 2011): 258–79.
32. Including servants and slaves. See: A Boatman's Fraud HSM 890.4.8 in Holtz, *Neo-Babylonian Trial Records*, 80-82
33. In Judah, "the king, elders, priests, local assemblies of citizens, state officials and priests could function as judges"; see Wells, *The Law of Testimony*, 19.
34. A point of clarification regarding Nephi's relation to the reader. Nephi addresses the reader with what is termed a "plaintiff statement." In modern times the

An additional characteristic of ancient Mesopotamian court proceedings is the promise of additional proof provided by the plaintiff.[35] In modern times, all evidence must be presented before a judgement can be made.[36] Nephi does promises additional proof stating Christ will confirm his words (2 Nephi 33:11).

Nephi is not esoteric; he glories in plainness. Therefore he mentions the law of witnesses and alludes to a judgment bar. Altogether, Nephi's closing verse makes explicit reference to court proceedings. "For what I seal on earth, shall be brought against you at the judgment bar (2 Nephi 33:15)." All twelve mentions of the word "bar" in the Book of Mormon refer to a setting of judgment.

THE READER'S ROLE

The reader's position in this setting is initially ambiguous. Following the implications of this plaintiff's statement, Nephi posits the reader in an adjudicating role. It appears then that the words of Christ themselves are on trial. Conversely, unlike other prophets in the Book of Mormon, Nephi does not posit God as a judge. When the reader is the defendant, Nephi identifies Christ's words as the judge.[37] Therefore the reader and the written word assume the roles of both judge and defendant at different times.

Because of such prevalent legal terms, the context of contemporary legal systems must be considered to interpret Nephi's message.

---

plaintiff is a person or party wronged by the defendant. Thus, a modern reader might opine Nephi implies the reader has wronged him. However, this is not the convention anciently as state officials often brought suit against the defendant on behalf of the state.

35. Holtz, *Neo-Babylonian Court Procedure*, 135-165.
36. Holtz notes, "Most of the guarantees for testimony can be shown to be the result of the guarantor's accusations that must be substantiated. In these cases the accusations were made during formal hearings, after which the guarantor assumed responsibility for the testimony" (i.e., by providing another witness). Holtz, *Neo-Babylonian Court Procedure*, 148.
37. Nephi states, "[H]e shall bring forth [H]is words unto them, which words shall judge them at the last day." (2 Nephi 25:18). Restating the point, Nephi writes that the "nations who shall possess [the writings in question] shall be judged of them according to the words which are written (verse 22)."

Ancient Near East Judicial Structure

In Nephi's day, neighboring nations allowed for appeals. Prior to that era, appeals were generally not allowed. Leaders had embodied deities and judgments were immutable.[38] To appeal a judgement questioned the capability of the leader.[39] In stark contrast appeal was widely practiced in the Neo-Assyrian and Neo-Babylonian kingdoms.[40] The king was ultimately responsible for justice but he was less directly involved. This resulted in numerous letters directed to Neo-Assyrian kings complaining of injustice by appointed representatives and subsequently requesting appeals.[41]

---

38. The judge stands in the place of deity according to the general view prevailing in antiquity. If he fails in the proper discharge of his duties, he lowers the dignity of his office; and the deity, by permitting him to go astray, shows that he no longer desires the judge to speak in his name. Confidence in the probity and ability of the judge is the condition sine quo non of the execution of justice. Defective as this uncompromising attitude toward a judicial error may be from a modern standpoint in not recognising an appeal from a lower to a higher court, the ethical basis is both sound and of a high order. With such a provision… the integrity of the courts was firmly secured for all time." See Morris Jastrow Jr., *Aspects of Religious Belief and Practice in Babylonia and Assyria* (New York: The Knickerbocker Press, 1911), 396.
39. Even an attempt to appeal could result in punishment. Ronald A. Veekner, "An Old Babylonian Legal Procedure for Appeal: Evidence from the Ṭuppi Lā Ragāmim," *Hebrew Union College Annual* 45 (1974): 1–15.
40. F. Rachel Magdalene, Cornelia Wunsch, and Bruce Wells, "Chapter Six. On History and Theory: Administrative Law and Bureaucracy in Ancient Times" in *Fault, Responsibility, and Administrative Law in Late Babylonian Legal Texts* (University Park, USA: Penn State University Press, 2019), 175-262.
41. "The…way of addressing the ruler is rendered by the Akkadian expression… literally meaning «to present oneself to the king, » i.e., to bring a case to his attention. In messages of this type, supplicants sometimes explicitly ask the king for a judgment (denu epašu) or allude to cases previously decided by the ruler (denuparasu). For all that, it did not mean that the monarch himself pronounced a verdict… the king is never mentioned in [legal proceedings], which is at first sight surprising considering the relatively large number of letters asking for justice….All this seems to show that the Neo-Assyrian kings did not themselves pronounce the verdict in the cases submitted to them, but delegated this task to those whom they deemed competent for it. It is therefore understandable why the interventions of the ruler have not left any traces in the judicial documentation, whereas from the point of view of the petitioners, it was indeed the king who had rendered justice to them. Pierre Villard, "Degrees of jurisdiction and the notion

Further, appeals were likely needed due to what could be viewed as two legal systems in existence simultaneously. State administrators who were not legal professionals such as treasurers, eunuchs, and cup-bearers could adjudicate cases.[42] In contrast to the modern concept of mediator, these lower judges were state officials. "There also existed, alongside the notables acting as judges, a specialized judicial administration, directed by two of the highest figures in the state."[43] All derived their judicial authority from the king and acted as his representatives.[44] "Neo-Assyrian kings did not themselves pronounce the verdict in the cases submitted to them, but delegated this task to those whom they deemed competent for it... from the point of view of the petitioners, it was indeed the king who had rendered justice to them."[45]

Consistent with the tradition of his day, Nephi does not place God as a Judge. Rather, the *word* of God will judge and Christ will stand by and verify they are his words. In Nephi's judicially inflected writings, when the reader is at the judgement bar of God, the judge naturally should be a representative of God: in this case, the words of Christ. The Hebrew concept of "words" (*dabar*) carries the presumption that words contain their referents' essence or fundamental character. Therefore, the word of the Lord can represent the Lord. Additional meanings of *dabar* include "law" or "reality."[46] Nephi's imperative to the reader is to judge if his words are the words of Christ. It is an imperative to judge if 2 Nephi is

---

of appeal in the Neo-Assyrian period,"*Ash-Sharq: Bulletin of the Ancient Near East – Archaeological, Historical and Societal Studies* 6/2 (Nov. 2022): 113–126.

42. "Other state officials could take on judicial duties but are attested in this role much less frequently than the *sukalla* [vizier] and the *sartennu* [chief judge]. The *masennu* ("treasurer") assumed the role of the judge in a text from Assur (no. 22), and from the fact that he had a court clerk... at his disposal we can infer that also the *rab sa resi* ("chief eunuch") could pass judgment. The *rab saqe* ("chief cupbearer") was supposed to act as judge in the matter of an unsettled debt but somehow failed to do so; according to a memorandum from Nineveh, the king had been approached instead to speak justice." See Radner, "The Reciprocal Relationship," 57.
43. Villard, "Degrees of jurisdiction," 113–26.
44. Appeals for justice were made by seeking the word of the king. Małgorzata Sandowicz, "Nabonidus and Forty Thieves of Uruk: Criminal Investigation in Neo-Babylonian Eanna." *Iraq* 76 (2014): 245–61.
45. Villard, "Degrees of jurisdiction," 119.
46. Isaac Rabinowitz, *A Witness Forever: Ancient Israel's Perception of Literature and the Resultant Hebrew Bible* (Bethesda, MD: CDL Press, 1993), 8.

God's representative, His law and His reality. In the process, Nephi posits the revealed law, expressed in words, as subjugate to God, mirroring the relationship between judicial functionaries and the embodiment of legal authority, the king.

Differences Between Nephi's Record and Legal Records

It would be irresponsible to omit key differences between Nephi's writings in 2 Nephi and Neo-Babylonian trial records.

First, Nephi appears to be writing a verbatim record whereas extant contemporary records appear paraphrastic. Scribes did not act as transcriptionists but played an active role in legal proceedings.[47] The brevity depicted in Neo-Babylonian records is not ubiquitous in the ancient Near East. More detailed records (possibly verbatim) were found in Egypt.[48]

A second deviation between Nephi's writing is the lack of a list of persons present.[49] These persons could attest to the proceedings. Nephi does not list individual hearers. He does write the words were taught "among [his] people (2 Nephi 33:1)." Following the plaintiff's statement, Nephi does state Christ will show unto the reader that they are His words (2 Nephi 33:11). This does have a loose similarity with the legal convention of the time. Those listed at the conclusion of the record could attest to the veracity of the record.

---

47. Sara J. Milstein, *Making A Case: The Practical Roots of Biblical Law* (Oxford University Press, 2021), 35.
48. In the reign of Ramses II a surviving statement from a Theban court appears to include much more detail and may be more likely to be a verbatim recording. Cairo 65739 reads, "As for myself I am the wife of the district superintendent Simut, and I came to dwell in his house, and I worked in weaving, caring for my clothing. Now in the regnal year 15, in the seventh year of my having entered into the house of the district superintendent Simut, the merchant Raia approached me with the Syrian slave Gemniherimentet, while she was a young girl, and he said to me, "buy this young girl and give to me her price" – so he said to me. And I took the young girl and I gave to him her price. Now look, I am saying the price which I gave for her in the presence of the authorities ...[list of items]... And I gave them to the merchant Raia, without there being any property of the citizeness Bakemut among them and he gave to me this little girl and I called her Gemniherimentet by name. See Robert Ritner, "A Lawsuit Over a Syrian Slave," in *Context of Scripture Vol. III*, 31.
49. For example in Cairo 65739 the names of six persons who were present were listed.

Finally, following the list of names of those present there would often be a seal. Likewise, immediately after mentioning Christ as a witness of the record Nephi states he seals the record. If Nephi was speaking literally the seal may have been removed or the seal inscription wasn't included in translation. Many references in the Hebrew Bible to sealed legal documents appear literal (i.e., Jeremiah 32:11-15). The act of using a physical seal in ancient Israel is well-attested. Seals of the time typically had two lines which contained a name and a title or patronym.[50] Legal custom in the surrounding region was to make multiple copies of judicial records. The sealed copy would have the seal(s). Copies of the sealed document would include inscriptions of the seal(s).[51]

Regardless, that Nephi mentions sealing the document at the end of the record after naming a witness is certainly reminiscent of the contemporary legal practice we have been discussing. The paucity of books in the Hebrew Bible containing a seal and the simultaneous widespread use of seals in Judah and in legal records suggest a sealing reference is specific for legal records. Books in the Hebrew Bible, as they are presented today, do not contain a seal nor mention closing with a seal.[52] In this regard, Nephi's record is more similar to contemporary legal documents than religious writings.

The Language of Judean Legal Texts and Second Nephi

The language of extant Judean legal records is described in Sara Milstein's book, "Making a Case." She describes the legal rhetoric common to all early legal texts.[53] This includes root variations, colorful features, unusual legal situations, resonance with contracts, emphasis on social roles, repetitive language, and discussion of money or other penalties.

Certainly, in isolation, none of these features can identify a legal text or rhetoric. Scriptural text is filled with such writings. However, because

50. Jeffrey Tigay and Alan Millard, "Seals and Seal Impressions," in *The Context of Scripture. Canonical Compositions, Monumental Inscriptions, and Archival Documents from the Biblical World, Vol. 2,* ed. W.W. Hallo and K.L. Younger, Jr. (Leiden, Netherlands: Brill, 2000), 197-204.
51. Holtz, *Neo-Babylonian Trial Records*, 146.
52. A colophon found at the conclusion of a Septuagint Book of Esther serves a comparable function to a seal and could be considered the sole exception.
53. Specifically Milstein analyses early sections of the Covenant Code and select laws she terms "Hebrew legal fictions." See Sara Milstein, *Making a Case* (Oxford University Press, 2021), 20-158, also specifically page 72.

of their prevalence in Judean legal texts, these features reasonably form a *sine qua non* in such a text. If Nephi wrote 2 Nephi with legal proceedings and format in mind, he might have considered using the established legal rhetorical flourishes. These findings are present in 2 Nephi (Table 1).

Feature	*Verse*
Colorful language	And they shall be visited with thunderings, and lightnings, and earthquakes, and all manner of destructions, for the fire of the anger of the Lord shall be kindled against them, and they shall be as stubble, and the day that cometh shall consume them, saith the Lord of Hosts (2 Nephi 26:6).
Root variations[54]	Lehi counsels his sons to arise from the *dust* (*aphar*) and leave darkness and *obscurity* (*aphel*) (2 Nephi 1:21).[55] Nephi also uses permutations on Joseph's name. Following a prophecy by Joseph we read Laman and Lemuel choose to *increase* (*yasap*) in anger instead (2 Nephi 3-5), resulting in hatred and rejection of the suzerain covenant and freedom.[56]
Unusual legal situations	For the atonement satisfieth the demands of his justice upon all those who have not the law given to them (2 Nephi 9:26).
Resonance with contracts	And they sell themselves for naught; for, for the reward of their pride and their foolishness they shall reap destruction (2 Nephi 26:10).
Emphasis on social roles	They rob the poor because of their fine sanctuaries; they rob the poor because of their fine clothing. (2 Nephi 28:13).
Repetitive language	Wo unto the liar, for he shall be thrust down to hell. Wo unto the murderer who deliberately killeth, for he shall die. Wo unto them who commit whoredoms, for they shall be thrust down to hell (2 Nephi 9:34-36).
Discussion of money or other penalties	For the time speedily cometh that the Lord God shall cause a great division among the people, and the wicked will he destroy; and he will spare his people, yea, even if it so be that he must destroy the wicked by fire (2 Nephi 30:10).

Table 1: Features in most Judean legal texts are also seen in 2 Nephi. *While many of these features are seen throughout the Book of Mormon, it is essential to demonstrate their presence in 2 Nephi is essential to confirm contemporary legal rhetoric was used.*

54. Milstein also noticed extensive wordplay in the HLFs. Some root variations are only observed in the Hebrew case laws suggesting scribes would intentionally seek uncommon words if needed when writing in this genre. Milstein, *Making a Case*, 81.
55. Jeff Lindsay, ""Arise from the Dust": Insights from Dust-Related Themes in the Book of Mormon (Part 1: Tracks from the Book of Moses)," *Interpreter: A Journal of Mormon Scripture* 22 (2016): 179-232.
56. Matthew Bowen, "Their Anger Did Increase Against Me": Nephi's Autobiographical Permutation of a Biblical Wordplay on the Name Joseph," *Interpreter: A Journal of Latter-day Saint Faith and Scholarship* 23 (2017): 115-136.

Nephi's Conservative and Revisionistic Citations of Isaiah

Nephi's adaptive citations of Isaiah are well described. Scholars note Nephi's writing, "makes additions...omits material in others, transposes, [and] makes grammatical changes"[57] "as might be expected of a truly ancient and authentic record."[58] In contrast, it is not clear that Nephi adapts the text in 2 Nephi 12-24, which appears to be a much more conservative citation. I propose this is because he has a formal extrinsic purpose for the record (i.e., it serves as a deposition).

Much of Nephi's Isaiah-centric writing can fairly be described as exegetical.[59] This is not to say that he exceeded his remit as a scribe. Exegetical techniques of the period were accepted and expected as core scribal activities.[60] These included manipulation, harmonization, paraphrasing, allusion, and, in some cases, the addition of new material to expand on existing themes.[61]

To accurately characterize texts from that era, it is helpful to classify them according to scribal intervention. Accordingly, textual reproductions may be categorized broadly as conservative or revisionistic.[62] Such classifications help us more fully appreciate the process by which each text was recorded, and can avoid anachronistic labelling. Of course, not all texts fall neatly into any given category in their long histories. Some manuscripts may come down to us as the result of a mixed treatment.[63]

George Brooke describes five aspects of text written by scribes when

---

57. Sharp, "Except Some Man Should Guide Me," 338.
58. Sharp, "Except Some Man Should Guide Me," 338.
59. Grant Hardy, "Prophetic Perspectives and Prerogative: How Lehi and Nephi Applied the Lessons of Lehi's Dream," in *The Things Which My Father Saw: Approaches to Lehi's Dream and Nephi's Vision*, ed. Daniel Belnap, Gaye Strathearn, and Stanley A. Johnson (Salt Lake City: Deseret Book, 2011), 199–213; Hardy, *Understanding the Book of Mormon*, 61-65.
60. Sidnie White Crawford, *Rewriting Scripture in Second Temple Times* (Grand Rapids, MI: William B. Eerdmans Publishing, 2008), 4.
61. Crawford, *Rewriting Scripture*, 80.
62. The latter may also be described as a "free" or "creative" scribal approach. See Sidney White Crawford, "Understanding the Textual History of the Hebrew Bible: A New Proposal," in *The Hebrew Bible in Light of the Dead Sea Scrolls*, edited by N. David et al. (Gottingen: Vandenhoeck & Ruprecht, 2012), 60-69.
63. Dres Lingacre, "A Contextualized Approach to the Hebrew Dead Sea Scrolls Containing Exodus," (University of Birmingham, 2014).

performing exegesis (he uses the term "rewritten scriptural text").[64] His criteria make clear only 2 Nephi 12-24 in Nephi's writing does not qualify as rewritten.[65] One indication that 2 Nephi 12-24 is not exegetical is that it is introduced as an explicit citation of Isaiah (2 Nephi 12:1).

Examples of Nephi's Literary Technique

To get a sense of the fidelity with which Nephi treats 2 Nephi 12-24, we can compare it to a corresponding section in 2 Nephi 30. Fortunately, we have a section of Isaiah that Nephi cites twice (Table 2). While acknowledging the limits of textual criticism across translated texts, if we assume the English translation has *any* degree of correlation with the base text, then it does appear that these two passages appeared differently as Nephi wrote them.

---

64. 1. The source is thoroughly embedded in its rewritten form not as explicit citation but as running text. 2. The dependence of a rewritten scriptural text on its source is also such that the order of the source is followed extensively. 3. The dependence of a rewritten scriptural text on its source is also such that the content of the source is followed relatively closely without very many major insertions or omissions. 4. The original genre or genres stays much the same. 5. And finally, the new texts are not composed to replace the authoritative sources which they rework. G J. Brooke, "The Rewritten Law, Prophets and Psalms: Issues for Understanding the Text of the Bible," in *The Bible as Book: The Hebrew Bible and the Judaean Desert Discoveries*, ed. E. D. Herbert and Emmanuel Tov (British Library, 2002), 32.
65. Some consider 1 Nephi 20-21 a citation, but that view imposes our modern conventions on the text. Indeed, 1 Nephi 20-21 meets all scholarly criteria for its classification as a *rewritten* scriptural text. Most notably, without a superscription it cannot be considered an explicit citation. This leaves modern scholars at something of a loss as to where Isaiah's words actually start (c.f. Brooke's criterion 1). Additionally, Nephi never states that his copy can directly replace Isaiah's words (criterion 5). In contrast, prior to the citation of 2 Nephi 21 Nephi suggests his text may replace Isaiah's words (as a copy). He writes, "And now I write some of the words of Isaiah, that whoso of my people shall see these words may lift up their hearts and rejoice for all men. Now these are the words…" (2 Nephi 11:8). "As Nephi quoted this Servant Song to his brothers, he included several lines of text in the first verse not found in other current versions of the Old Testament. It is not clear whether these additional lines were in the ancient text of Isaiah that Nephi knew, or if these lines are his own commentary." Terry B. Ball, "Isaiah's 'Other' Servant Songs," in *The Gospel of Jesus Christ in the Old Testament* (Provo, UT: Religious Studies Center, Brigham Young University, 2009). See also John A. Tvedtnes, *The Isaiah Variants in the Book of Mormon* (Provo, UT; Foundation for Ancient Research and Mormon Studies, 1981), 73.

Isaiah 11:4-6	*2 Nephi 21:4-6*	*2 Nephi 30:9-12*
but with righteousness shall he judge the poor and reprove with equity for the meek of the earth and he shall smite the earth with the rod of his mouth and with the breath of his lips shall he slay the wicked	but with righteousness shall he judge the poor and reprove with equity for the meek of the earth and he shall smite the earth with the rod of his mouth and with the breath of his lips shall he slay the wicked	**and** with righteousness shall **the Lord God** judge the poor and reprove with equity for the meek of the earth and he shall smite the earth with the rod of his mouth and with the breath of his lips shall he slay the wicked
		for the time speedily cometh that the Lord God shall cause a great division among the people, and the wicked will he destroy; and he will spare his people, yea, even if it so be that he must destroy the wicked by fire.
and righteousness shall be the girdle of his loins and faithfulness the girdle of his reins	and righteousness shall be the girdle of his loins and faithfulness the girdle of his reins	and righteousness shall be the girdle of his loins and faithfulness the girdle of his reins
the wolf also shall dwell with the lamb and the leopard shall lie down with the kid and the calf and the young lion and the fatling together and a little child shall lead them	the wolf also shall dwell with the lamb and the leopard shall lie down with the kid and the calf and the young lion and the fatling together and a little child shall lead them	**and then** shall the wolf dwell with the lamb and the leopard shall lie down with the kid and the calf and the young lion and the falling together and a little child shall lead them

Table 2: Selected Examples of Nephi's Citation of Isaiah. *From Royal Skousen, The History of the Text of the Book of Mormon and The Book of Mormon: the Earliest Text. These excerpts appear to demonstrate Nephi's use of conservative and revisionistic scribal techniques.*

Nephi values Isaiah's words, but his children do not understand Isaiah (2 Nephi 25:1-3). And yet, Nephi seeks to preserve Isaiah's words for his people (2 Nephi 11:8). An easy way to resolve this dilemma would be to modify Isaiah's words. Nephi has the tools to do this, but Nephi appears not to do so in 2 Nephi 12-24. The data in Table 2 suggest that Nephi needed both to *comment* on this text and *change* a few words. Instead Nephi re-writes these verses in a later section. Such fidelity, we would expect with a document with a formal extrinsic purpose,[66] such

66. Supporting the notion 2 Nephi has a more formal purpose is the introduction of words attributed to others as well. We discussed 2 Nephi 6:1 states, "The words of Jacob, the brother of Nephi." This verse serves no important narrative purpose: we have already read about Jacob in 1 Nephi 18, 2 Nephi 2 and 2 Nephi 5. The reader knows Jacob is Nephi's brother. While we can never be sure of Nephi's reason for reintroducing Jacob, his choice connotes a level of formality not previously

as a certified copy or a verbatim deposition. Given the textual freedom enjoyed by scribes in Nephi's day, it seems clear that they copied text verbatim as a deliberate choice.

To understand 2 Nephi the question is not limited to the existence of a *lengthy* Isaiah citation, or to an en bloc decrease in *rate of variants*.[67] We must also ask why Nephi's only ***firmly non-exegetical*** text is found in 2 Nephi.

Second Nephi 4–5: Reactions to the Covenant Renewal

The events following covenant renewals are often recorded.[68] Similarly, following 2 Nephi 1-4 Nephi details his own commitment as well as Laman and Lemuel's rejection. All parties had grievances and had anger with each other at one point.

In Nephi's psalm we read that Nephi was angry. He asks, "Why am I angry because of mine enemy?" (vs. 27). Nephi resolves to "not anger again" (vs. 29). Nephi chooses God. In attestation Nephi writes, "My voice shall forever ascend up unto thee, my rock and mine everlasting God" (vs. 35). In marked contrast the end of Nephi's psalm states, "But behold, [Laman and Lemuel's] anger did increase" (2 Nephi 5:2). The anger of Laman and Lemuel will eventually lead to hatred, a breach of the covenant, and curse. Martin reminds us the term "curse" is covenantal language and signifies Laman and Lemuel made and broke a covenant (a curse can only apply if the covenant is made and breached).[69]

Nephi's Record as a Modern Harmonized Text

Setting aside how *Nephi* viewed his record we need to discuss what the text means to us today. Harmonization is a process described by Dead Sea Scroll scholars to account for the incorporation of multiple textual

---

apparent in his writings. Nephi did not introduce his father's visions or blessings with such formality. This sudden formality is unusual for someone modern readers have described as a guide. Joseph Spencer, *1 Nephi: A Brief Theological Introduction* (Neal A Maxwell Institute for Religious Scholarship, 2020), 110-113. See also Gardner, "Labor Diligently to Write," 161, 169, 245. Another example of such formality is 2 Nephi 12:1 and 23:1.

67. Martin Evans. *Comparing Nephi's Citation of Isaiah,* 2023, online at shipsofhagoth.com.

68. For example, following the Mosaic covenant, the elders of the people saw God and ate (Exodus 24:11). After a covenant renewal performed by Jehoiada, the people "slew Mattan the priest of Baal (2 Kings 11:17-18)."

69. Martin, "The Prophet Nephi," 117

traditions into a single text.[70] Because the KJV is based on Masoretic textual tradition; ultimately the Book of Mormon incorporates Judean textual traditions (e.g., Deutero-Isaiah). Further, because of the integration of early Protestant language and themes[71] that textual tradition is also incorporated. Finally early Christian traditions are incorporated by including Pauline phrases as well.[72] The translation of 2 Nephi we have access to can be viewed as a harmonized text incorporating Nephite, Judean, early Protestant and early Christian textual traditions.

Sealed Records

If Nephi did intend 2 Nephi as a legally permissible record it is ironic the text we have today is harmonized (though that doesn't necessarily delegitimize it). However, we have not fully considered the cultural practices associated with legal documents. Legal documents of that day were written at least twice. One copy was for public view and another for safe keeping to be opened in need of court proceedings.[73] "The second part of many double documents was not [always] a verbatim repetition of the first part."[74] Unsealed portions contain as little as a quarter of the sealed copy's text. Before Hellenistic influence in Judah the "controlling docu-

70. As an example, in the production of 4Q175 a scribe incorporated both proto-Masoretic and pre-Samaritan textual traditions. Such harmonized scriptures were "considered valid scripture passages since they were used in phylacteries." See Crawford, *Rewriting Scripture in Second Temple Times*, 34-36.
71. Royal Skousen, "Tyndale Versus More in the Book of Mormon," *Interpreter: A Journal of Mormon Scripture* 13 (2015): 1-8. All of this quoting from the King James Bible is problematic, but only if we assume that the Book of Mormon translation literally represents what was on the plates. Yet the evidence...argues that the Book of Mormon translation is tied to Early Modern English, and that even the themes of the Book of Mormon are connected to the Protestant Reformation, dating from the same time period. What this means is that the Book of Mormon is a creative and cultural translation of what was on the plates, not a literal one See Skousen, "The History of the Text of the Book of Mormon. *BYU Studies Quarterly* 59/1 (2020).
72. Frederick writes that Pauline phrases have been "carefully integrated" into the Book of Mormon. Nicholas Frederick, "The Language of Paul in the Book of Mormon," in *They Shall Grow Together*, 206.
73. Welch, "Doubled, Sealed," 391–444.
74. Welch, "Doubled, Sealed," 244. Welch also states, "some of the double documents have a "greatly abridged [*stark verkümmerter*] scriptum interior" from Elisabeth Koffmahn, *Die Doppelurkunden aus der Wüste* Juda (Leiden: Brill, 1968), 13.

ment" was the sealed portion.[75] Regardless, our lack of access to Nephi's entire body of work, and perhaps even to a literal translation of his writings, is analogous to long-standing limitations on access to full, sealed records.[76] If this is the case our copy of 2 Nephi was never intended (by Nephi) to be the controlling or primary document. Rather, it points to another sealed document. David Whitmer referred to additional sealed records of Nephi. It is not clear he meant an analog of 2 Nephi (or that he was using the term "sealed" to mean a duplicate document).[77] Returning

---

75. Welch, "Doubled, Sealed," 244.
76. Inaccessible sealed records appear to be common to all gospel ages. The Israelites did not have access to the tablets containing the Ten Commandments, as they were sealed in the Ark of the Covenant. Further designating their authoritative status, [the tablets] were effectively sealed in the Ark of the Covenant. Official records were generally sealed by the scribe and a second unsealed version was made available for viewing. There was a "'double-document' convention in ancient Near Eastern scribal practice, where an official version remains sealed (or otherwise inaccessible) while a public copy could be consulted, examined, and studied." Mark Leuchter, "Sacred Space and Communal Legitimacy in Exile: The Contribution of Seraiah's Colophon (Jer 51: 59–64a)," in *The Prophets Speak on Forced Migration*, ed. Mark J. Boda et al. (Atlanta: SBL Press, 2015), 77-100. Rather, the people were only able to directly view copies that were man-made and likely less visually impressive. The tablets in the Ark do "not come out again.... From now on, the words inscribed in the tablets of stone are hidden words"; see G. J. Venema, *Reading Scripture in the Old Testament: Deuteronomy 9-10; 31 - 2 Kings 22-23 - Jeremiah 36 - Nehemiah 8* (Leiden/Boston: Brill, 2004), 36-44. Welch mentions long-held tradition that even King David had not read the sealed book of the law (thus implying that he was missing aspects of the law). Sealed documents, including much of what Moses wrote, were never distributed. "In Jubilees 1:5–29, Moses was given two stone tablets and was shown a vision of "what was in the beginning and what will occur in the future" (compare Moses 1...). He was instructed to write a book containing everything the Lord would tell him on the mountain so that it might serve as a testimony in the future against the people. While the Testament of Moses and the book of Jubilees do not say that this eschatological and prophetic book of Moses would be sealed, the authors of those works presume that those writings of Moses would be preserved until the final day of judgment." See Welch, "Doubled, Sealed," 391–444.
77. Decades after his estrangement from the church, David Whitmer—who saw the golden plates from which the Book of Mormon was translated in the presence of an angel and multiple witnesses—commented on the sealed portion, emphasizing that there remained sealed records "of Nephi" that will come "when the time comes." That certainly may refer to other sealed records of Nephi (i.e., not a sealed version of 2 Nephi). As quoted in Lyndon W. Cook, *David Whitmer Interviews:*

to our original thesis, if we consider 2 Nephi as a legal text, it also follows that a second version - likely lengthier - exists.[78]

Conclusion

The Book of Mormon was translated without punctuation or extensive formatting. This lack of formal features can sometimes make it difficult to know *what* we are reading. Second Nephi contains an agreement (2 Nephi 1-4), a record of participant reactions (2 Nephi 4-5), a collation of witness statements (2 Nephi 6-10, 12-24, 25-28), and a plaintiff statement (2 Nephi 33).

Nephi's allusion to sealing the record, bar of judgement, law of witnesses, reference to Isaiah and Jacob as witnesses, formatting and verbiage consistent with Neo-Babylonian deposition and plaintiff statements, legal rhetoric, and inclusion of non-exegetical text are idiosyncrasies of 2 Nephi that suggest it is best seen as a legal document.

An edited version of this paper was published as "Second Nephi as a Legal Document," in Interpreter: A Journal of Latter-day Faith and Scholarship *60 (2024): 253–312.*

A Restoration Witness (Orem, Utah: Grandin Book Company, 1991), 20–21.

78. Discussing other sealed and doubled documents Welch writes, "the abridged text served as a working summary or general identification of the main contents of the transaction, so the shortened text would only prevent falsification of the main document in a limited number of cases. In any event, "both texts are always formatted in the same way and written in the same hand." Welch, "Doubled, Sealed," 391–444.

Appendix: Scholarly Perspectives on the Structure and Interpretation of 2 Nephi

As noted in the main text, 2 Nephi has long invited diverse readings; this appendix compiles significant perspectives on its literary design and spiritual purpose.

The second book of Nephi has confounded and intrigued readers for more than a century. Elder Jeffrey R. Holland emphasized its spiritual significance, describing the writings in 2 Nephi as "standing like sentinels at the gate of the [B]ook [of Mormon]," and added that they "admit us into the scriptural presence of the Lord."[79] Despite this high praise, some readers perceive 2 Nephi as a compilation of instructive yet disconnected incidents, doctrines, and prophecies.[80]

Scholars have offered a wide array of interpretations. Grant Hardy, for instance, describes 2 Nephi as containing "undated, contextless excerpts, along with reflections."[81] Benjamin McGuire similarly portrays it as a commentary interwoven with scripture.[82] Brant Gardner argues that Nephi begins with narrative intentions but shifts course, ultimately composing a sermon.[83] Frederick Axelgard, by contrast, offers a holistic reading, suggesting that the spiritual themes of 2 Nephi parallel the historical structure of 1 Nephi, with corresponding themes presented in the same order.[84] This structural parallelism is further explored by Gardner, who also emphasizes Nephi's evolving authorial intent.[85]

Joseph M. Spencer identifies Isaiah's theophany (2 Nephi 16) as the structural and theological center of the book. He argues that Nephi

79. Jeffrey R. Holland, *Christ and the New Covenant: The Messianic Message of the Book of Mormon* (Salt Lake City: Deseret Book, 1997), 34–36.
80. Frederick Axelgard, "1 and 2 Nephi: An Inspiring Whole," *BYU Studies Quarterly* 26, no. 4 (1986): 53–65.
81. Grant Hardy, *Understanding the Book of Mormon: A Reader's Guide* (Oxford: Oxford University Press, 2010).
82. Benjamin L. McGuire, "Nephi: A Postmodernist Reading," *Interpreter: A Journal of Mormon Scripture* 14 (2014): 49–78.
83. Brant Gardner, "Labor Diligently to Write: The Ancient Making of a Modern Scripture, Chapters 6–8," *Interpreter: A Journal of Latter-day Saint Faith and Scholarship* 35 (2020): 107–166.
84. Axelgard, "1 and 2 Nephi," 58.
85. Brant Gardner, *Second Witness: Analytical and Contextual Commentary on the Book of Mormon: Second Nephi through Jacob* (Salt Lake City: Greg Kofford Books, 2007), 20–35.

employs this episode as a paradigm for divine-human interaction and suggests that when Nephi refers to "more sacred things" (2 Nephi 19:5), he is referencing much of the material found in 2 Nephi itself.[86] Spencer also proposes that a major structural division in the book precedes 2 Nephi 6:1, a suggestion that Noel B. Reynolds critiques.[87] Reynolds instead contends that 2 Nephi is organized around a chiastic structure centered on chapter 11, positioning the book primarily as a witness of Christ.[88] He argues that this structure reorients traditional understandings of Abrahamic and Lehitic covenantal promises toward a Christ-centered theology.[89]

Terryl Givens offers yet another approach, emphasizing how 2 Nephi constructs a new Nephite identity in the wake of Jerusalem's fall. Drawing on the example of Jewish responses to the Babylonian exile—such as the formation of the Torah—Givens suggests that Nephi's people, similarly disoriented, turned to scripture and covenant to forge a renewed theological identity. In this view, 2 Nephi affirms the establishment of a new land of promise.[90]

Taylor Halverson and John W. Welch both highlight the legal and covenantal structure of the early chapters of 2 Nephi. Halverson describes Lehi's final address as his "last will and covenantal speech,"[91] while Welch analyzes it through the lens of ancient Near Eastern legal traditions, arguing that the text functions as Lehi's will and testament. This legal discourse establishes Nephi as a leader, formally adopts Zoram, and provides a constitutional framework for Nephite society.[92]

---

86. Joseph M. Spencer, "Lecture XV: Nephi's Comments on Reading Isaiah," in *The Vision of All: Twenty-five Lectures on Isaiah in Nephi's Record* (Salt Lake City: Greg Kofford Books, 2016), 167.
87. Joseph M. Spencer, *An Other Testament: On Typology* (Salt Press, 2016), 34–35.
88. Noel B. Reynolds, "On Doubting Nephi's Break Between 1 and 2 Nephi: A Critique of Joseph Spencer's 'An Other Testament,'" *Interpreter: A Journal of Mormon Scripture* (2017): 85–102.
89. Noel B. Reynolds, "Chiastic Structure of Large Texts: 2 Nephi as a Case Study," in *Chiasmus: The State of the Art*, eds. John W. Welch and Donald Parry (Provo, UT: BYU Studies; Springville, UT: Book of Mormon Central, 2020), 177.
90. Terryl L. Givens, *2nd Nephi: A Brief Theological Introduction* (Provo, UT: Neal A. Maxwell Institute for Religious Scholarship, 2019), 4–6.
91. Taylor Halverson, *The Covenant Path in the Bible and the Book of Mormon* (Springville, UT: Line of Sight Publishing, 2020), 228.
92. John W. Welch, "Lehi's Last Will and Testament: A Legal Approach," in T*he*

Jan Martin builds on this covenantal framework by suggesting that the destruction of Jerusalem—so central to First Temple theology—may have prompted the division between 1 and 2 Nephi. She identifies the opening chapters of 2 Nephi as a structured suzerain covenant, comprising standard components such as a preamble, historical prologue, stipulations, blessings and cursings, and instructions for record-keeping and remembrance. However, she notes that the typical inclusion of covenant witnesses appears absent at first glance.[93]

Taken together, these perspectives demonstrate the richness and complexity of 2 Nephi's structure and purpose. Far from being a loose collection of disconnected teachings, the book has been variously understood as a sermon, a covenant, a theological reorientation, and a Christ-centered chiasm—each reading contributing to our understanding of Nephi's literary and prophetic aims.

Book of Mormon: Second Nephi, the Doctrinal Structure, eds. Monte S. Nyman and Charles D. Tate Jr. (Provo, UT: Religious Studies Center, Brigham Young University, 1989), 61–82.

93. Jan Martin, "The Prophet Nephi and the Covenantal Nature of Cut-off, Cursed, Skin of Blackness, and Loathsome," in *They Shall Grow Together: The Bible in the Book of Mormon*, eds. Charles Swift and Nicholas J. Frederick (Provo, UT: Religious Studies Center, 2022), 107–141.

13

Vengeance is Mine

Retributive Rhetoric in the Book of Mormon and Early Latter-day Saint History

Tyler J. Andersen

From 1846 to 1927, Latter-day Saints made temple covenants to obey the Law of Retribution. This "oath of vengeance" is presumed to come from Revelation 6:9-11, however, a close reading of the Book of Mormon finds numerous passages employing similar wording. In this paper, I argue that a full accounting of early Latter-day Saint rhetoric involving oaths or prayers of vengeance must also include teachings from the Book of Mormon and other Restoration scripture. I contend that the Book of Mormon is essential to understanding the Law of Retribution's origins, as well as its eventual removal from Latter-day Saint temple ceremonies. While some early Latter-day Saints used scripture to justify their own acts of retribution—most notably the Mountain Meadows Massacre—the Book of Mormon clarifies that justice, mercy, judgement, and vengeance belong to the Lord.

As a text sacred to The Church of Jesus Christ of Latter-day Saints, the Book of Mormon purports to be an ancient record of ancient people. Like the Bible, it contains several teachings on the topic of justice, and by extension divine vengeance. While the Book of Mormon does mention instances of righteous retribution, its overall message follows a similar pattern to the New Testament, emphasizing forgiveness, mercy, and turning away from the desire for personal vengeance. By attempting a general hermeneutical approach to these passages, I will provide a rhetorical analysis of early Latter-day Saint understandings of the Law of Retribution, and how they may have shaped modern Latter-day Saint views about justice and atonement.[1]

1. By general hermeneutics, I rely on the definition provided by Virkler as "the study

The Law of Retribution was an element of the temple endowment for nearly eight decades. Known colloquially as an "oath of vengeance" or "prayer of vengeance," it set in motion several ideas outlined in the Book of Mormon and other Latter-day Saint scripture. From its inception following the deaths of Joseph and Hyrum Smith, to its official cessation in 1927, the Law of Retribution called for those receiving their temple endowments to petition divine justice upon those responsible for killing the Lord's anointed. David Henry Cannon, who served as president of the St. George Temple from 1893 to 1924, described the oath's language for proxy ordinances as coming directly out of Revelation 6:9-11, with initiates supplicating God to "avenge the blood of martyrs shed for the testimony of Jesus."[2] However, a close reading of the Book of Mormon finds numerous passages utilizing similar key elements and language, suggesting the Law of Retribution's origin could just as likely come from Restoration scripture.

Though oaths on behalf of the dead apply the apocalyptic language of John the Revelator, the purported wording for living ordinances is also paralleled in nearly a dozen references in the Book of Mormon. Nephi's foreboding prophecy about the eventual destruction of the Nephites alludes to the crying blood of the saints "ascend[ing] up to God from the ground against [the wicked]" who stoned and killed the prophets.

> And after the Messiah shall come there shall be signs given unto my people of his birth, and also of his death and resurrection; and great and terrible shall that day be unto the wicked, for they shall perish; and they perish because they cast out the prophets,

---

of those rules that govern interpretation of the entire biblical text. It includes the topics of historical, cultural, contextual, lexical-syntactical, and theological analyses." See Henry A. Virkler, *Hermeneutics: Principles and Processes of Biblical Interpretation* (Grand Rapids: Baker Book House, 1981), 16.

2. Devery S. Anderson, *The Development of LDS Temple Worship, 1846–2000: A Documentary History* (Salt Lake City: Signature Books, 2011), 164. Cannon cites the ninth chapter of Revelation as the wording basis for proxy ordinances, though this is likely in error. The quotation being cited was, in all likelihood, Revelation 6:9-11. The use of these verses as the basis for the oath in living ordinances is also referenced in Kathleen Flake *The Politics of American Religious Identity: The Seating of Senator Reed Smoot* (Chapel Hill: The University of North Carolina Press, 2004), 143; Michael H. Paulos, *The Mormon Church on Trial: Transcripts of the Reed Smoot Hearings* Salt Lake City: Signature Books, 2008), 438; and David J. Buerger, *The Mysteries of Godliness: A History of Mormon Temple Worship* (Salt Lake City: Smith Research Associates, 1997), 134.

	Slain martyrs/prophets	*Blood/souls crying*	*Divine vengeance*
2 Nephi 26:3	X	X	
2 Nephi 28:10	X	X	
Alma 20:18	X	X	X
Alma 37:30	X	X	X
Alma 41:11	X	X	
Alma 60:10		X	X
3 Nephi 9:11	X	X	X
Ether 8:24	X	X	X
Mormon 8:27		X	
Mormon 8:40-41	X	X	X

> and the saints, and stone them, and slay them; wherefore the cry of the blood of the saints shall ascend up to God from the ground against them. (2 Nephi 26:3)
>
> And the blood of the saints shall cry from the ground against them. (2 Nephi 28:10)

The most reliable first-hand accounts of the latter-day oath of vengeance all feature the Saints asking God to avenge the blood of the prophets – presumably Joseph and Hyrum Smith – as well as a charge for initiates to instruct their posterity regarding the law.

Most scholars attempting to discern the original wording of the oath cite former Brigham Young Academy professor Walter M. Wolfe, who during the Reed Smoot hearings outlined the oath as follows:

> You and each of you do covenant and promise that you will pray, and never cease to pray, Almighty God to avenge the blood of the prophets upon this nation, and that you will teach the same to your children and your children's children unto the third and fourth generations.[3]

Whether the prayer actually contained the phrase "upon this nation" remains the subject of controversy, as well as whether the act of avenging the martyred prophets was the responsibility of God, or of those taking the oath.

Richard Turley and Barbara Jones Brown note that "Latter-day Saints had varying interpretations of what avenging the blood of the prophets meant. The people of Nauvoo did not use violence to avenge

3. See *Smoot Hearings* 4:6–7.

the Smiths' deaths." Brigham Young, on the other hand, "believed God would command his people to avenge the blood of the prophets before the world's end, though he did not exactly know how or when."[4]

The language of this prayer, absent from the current endowment ceremony, clearly appealed to the participants' *pathos*. By applying a metaphoric image of innocent blood crying from the ground for justice, initiates solidified their familiarity with the developing persecution narratives.[5] Their supplication for divine recompense enabled them to serve as arbiters of alleviation – prevailing against the enemies of God as "saviors of men."[6]

Samuel Brown's work on the early Latter-day Saint conquest of death, highlights the way the image of spilt blood shaped Latter-day Saint discourse in the years following the deaths of Joseph and Hyrum Smith:

> To claim that blood has stained the earth is to describe a disruption of cosmic order that cannot persist. Rather than decomposing with the rest of the body, blood alters the composition of the earth, creating a permanent mark of a life stolen prematurely. The blood within the ground had a voice for Mormons, and it cried from the dust with great urgency.[7]

The allegorical theme of vociferate blood[8] is perhaps best illustrated in the words of Moroni, who vehemently criticized the clandestine murders of reticent societies and corrupt governments:

> And whatsoever nation shall uphold such secret combinations, to get power and gain, until they shall spread over the nation, behold, they shall be destroyed; for the Lord will not suffer that the blood of his saints, which shall be shed by them, shall always cry unto him from the ground for vengeance upon them and he avenge them not (Ether 8:22).

Moroni's aesthetic delivery in the eighth chapter of Ether resonates closely with Abinadi's warning to the priests of Noah that God would

4. Richard E. Turley Jr. and Barbara Jones Brown, *Vengeance is Mine: The Mountain Meadows Massacre and its Aftermath* (New York: Oxford University Press, 2023), 9.
5. Doctrine and Covenants 103:24-28.
6. Doctrine and Covenants 103:6-9.
7. Samuel M. Brown, *In Heaven As It Is On Earth: Joseph Smith and the Early Mormon Conquest of Death* (New York: Oxford University Press, 2012), 291.
8. See for example, Alma 14:11, Alma 20:18, Alma 37:30, Alma 60:10, 3 Nephi 9:11, Ether 8:24, Mormon 8:27, Mormon 8:40-41.

execute "vengeance upon those who destroy his people" (Mosiah 17:18). In fact, Abinadi's final testimony can be read almost in its entirety as a prayer for vengeance, especially his prophecy that Noah himself would suffer death by fire.[9]

At the very heart of the discussion of retributive justice is the means by which it is enforced. Paul's epistle to the Romans warned the early Christian proselytes not to take matters of vengeance into their own hands, but to allow reprisals at the discretion of God. Moroni essentially repeats this wording in Mormon 8:20 that "man shall not smite, neither shall he judge," for judgment and vengeance came from heaven. This language thus implies that either God would perform the act of retribution personally, or authorize someone to do it on his behalf.

Aside from an aesthetic reading of characters mourning for vengeance – abundant with metaphor and a repulsion of ugliness – is its use for an epistemic end. Moroni's conclusion to the eighth chapter of Ether typifies the Book of Mormon's rhetorical tactic of bringing the lost to Jesus Christ. Emblematic images of martyrs crying from the ground for justice served to persuade readers to "do good continually," that evil would be thwarted, that they might "come unto the fountain of all righteousness and be saved."[10] Likewise, Nephi's execution of Laban[11] can be read as a divinely sanctioned act of retribution contrived for the salvation of an entire nation – a political, utilitarian act of civic virtue.[12]

In light of the Book of Mormon's relatively frequent promises of vengeance upon the wicked, early Latter-day Saints were largely reluctant to enact their own vengeance upon their enemies, consistent with the Savior's admonition in 3 Nephi 12:38-39, that "ye shall not resist evil, but whosover shall smite thee on thy right cheek, turn him the other also."

The Book of Mormon consistently emphasizes the central role of Jesus Christ in providing salvation and mercy. It teaches that through faith and repentance, individuals can access the mercy of God, which satisfies the demands of justice. It encourages people to seek repentance

9. Mosiah 17:10-19.
10. Ether 8:26.
11. 1 Nephi 4:1-18.
12. I am hardly the first to argue that Laban's death was an act of utilitarianism. However, an excellent overview of Laban's utilitarian death in light of the Divine Command Theory can be read in Ross D. Baron, *Social Ethics of The Church of Jesus Christ of Latter-day Saints* (Saarbrücken: VDM Verlag, 2008), 57–59.

rather than vengeance. While the Book of Mormon promotes forgiveness and turning the other cheek, it also recognizes instances where self-defense or defense of one's people may be necessary. Alma 60:10 illustrates that righteous individuals may resist wickedness, but the emphasis is on defending oneself and others, not on seeking vengeance:

> And now behold, we will resist wickedness even unto bloodshed. We would not shed the blood of the Lamanites if they would stay in their own land.

By August 1833, Joseph Smith introduced a revelation that would set in motion a series of theological explanations and justifications for Mormon retribution. Section 98 of the Doctrine and Covenants implored the Saints to avoid revenge, even if the same offense against them had been committed three times. It was on the fourth offense that Latter-day Saints could justifiably enact self-defense,[13] even by preemptive means.[14]

It was at the dedication of the Kirtland Temple in March 1836 that latter-day prayers for vengeance began to take a palpable, organized form. Joseph Smith called upon attendees to "enter into a covenant to give [themselves] no rest until [they were] avenged of [their] enemies to the uttermost."[15] The inherent lack of civic justice following the expulsion of the Saints from Missouri during the winter of 1838–39 prompted Latter-day Saints to further reiterate their heavenward pleas for recompense.

The death of the Prophet and Patriarch at Carthage Jail on June 27, 1844, gave rise to relatively common prayers for divine justice among the Latter-day Saints.

Chief prosecutor Josiah Lamborn, doubtlessly influenced by Latter-day Saint cries for justice, outlined the following in his opening argument during the trial of the Smiths' assassins.

> The guilt of this crime, hangs over you [the jury] as a blight, and curse, which is destroying your character, and gnawing at the root of your prosperity, it is a blood stain upon your character, and a foul blot, which cannot be erased, but with vengeance, and rigour (sic), to deal out the law, as the law is, As you respect,

13. Doctrine and Covenants 98:23-37.
14. Doctrine and Covenants 103:1, 26, 28, 34. See also D. Michael Quinn, *The Mormon Hierarchy: Origins of Power* (Salt Lake City: Signature Books, 1994), 82–85.
15. Dean C. Jessee, *The Personal Writings of Joseph Smith* (Salt Lake City: Deseret Book Company, 1984), 193.

> and fear your God, as you respect, and fear God, and not man, do your duty, for it is better that truth and righteousness prevail, and that even handed Justice, be dealt out to the full, than to suffer the guilty to go free, and escape the merited punishment due to their deeds.[16]

A December 1845 journal entry from Heber C. Kimball noted that "seven to twelve persons [had met] together ever since Joseph's death," covenanting and never resting "until those men who killed Joseph and Hyrum [had] been wiped out of the earth."[17] By 1846, the Law of Retribution became a requisite element of the temple endowment.[18]

Stories of acts of revenge almost immediately began circulating in the months after the martyrdom.[19] In September 1845, "Porter Rockwell shot and killed several anti-Mormons, including Frank A. Worrell, one of the guards who had allowed the mob to kill the Smiths at Carthage Jail."[20] Rockwell was acquitted the following August on grounds that he was acting under the direction of "Jack-Mormon" Sheriff Jacob B. Backenstos.[21] William W. Phelps, who served as a scribe and confidant to the Prophet prior to his murder, penned a poem for the *Times and Seasons* implicating the state of Illinois, whether directly or indirectly, for the deaths of Joseph and Hyrum. Later adapted to the haunting tune of "Star in the East," Phelps' poem warned that the martyrs' blood would "Stain Illinois" while the earth lauded the Prophet's fame.[22]

Even after the largest body of Church members began their mass migration to the Great Basin in the spring of 1846, the Law of Retribution shaped how Latter-day Saints reacted to outsiders, especially through their first decade in Utah. Decades after the Mountain Meadows Massacre occurred, some perpetrators of the attack questionably

---

16. Josiah Lamborn, Opening Statement for the Prosecution, reproduced at "The Carthage Conspiracy Trial," UMKC School of Law Famous Trials Project, accessed June 19, 2022, online at law2.umkc.edu. See also Dallin H. Oaks and Marvin S. Hill, *Carthage Conspiracy: The Trial of the Accused Assassins of Joseph Smith* (Urbana: University of Illinois Press, 1975), 114–115.
17. Buerger, 135.
18. Quinn, 179.
19. Oaks and Hill, 67
20. Quinn, 180–181.
21. Oaks and Hill, 200.
22. Brown, 293.

claimed[23] that members of the Fancher train had "boasted openly and defiantly that they had helped to kill Joseph Smith and his brother Hyrum,"[24] incensing them enough to fulfill their obligations to avenge the blood of the prophets.

The role the Law of Retribution may have played in the Mountain Meadows Massacre is debatable, as some participants retroactively pointed to it to justify their actions. John D. Lee later claimed he was fulfilling his obligation to avenge the martyrdom of Joseph and Hyrum, recalling Isaac C. Haight telling the perpetrators that "they had been privileged to keep a part of their covenant to avenge the blood of the prophets, and suggested that if the army came into the state, or if the one that was threatened marched upon them in California, they would likely be called to fight under much different circumstances."[25] Though some of the massacre's participants may very well have assumed that their actions were divinely sanctioned, deliberation prior to the massacre prompted Haight to send an express rider to Brigham Young for advice.[26] The law didn't give the Saints an arbitrary endorsement to kill anyone suspected of being involved in the persecution of early settlers. Young, they assumed, would give them the answer they were looking for.

Upon receiving Young's reply, Haight reportedly "sobbed like a child."[27] Failing to wait for Young's answer, Haight assumed that Young would give the necessary stamp of approval to enact vengeance upon hostile Gentiles. Instead, Young told Haight to "not interfere with them untill (sic) they are first notified to keep away. You must not meddle with them."[28] The massacre likely initiated a shift in thought about the limits of retribution. In its evolution in the years leading up to the Reed Smoot hearings, initiates placed less emphasis on their own acts of divine justice.

23. Turley, Walker, and Leonard call the veracity of these stories into question, noting that they were "written down many years after the massacre, some by men who played key roles in the massacre, making the claims suspect." Ronald Walker, Richard E. Turley Jr., and Glen M. Leonard, *Massacre at Mountain Meadows* (New York: Oxford University Press, 2008), 125.
24. Juanita L. Brooks, *The Mountain Meadows Massacre* (Norman: University of Oklahoma Press, 1950), 53.
25. Juanita L. Brooks, *John Doyle Lee: Zealot, Pioneer Builder, Scapegoat* (Logan: Utah State University Press, 1992), 221.
26. Turley, Walker, and Leonard, 162–163.
27. Turley, Walker, and Leonard, 226.
28. Turley, Walker, and Leonard, 184.

Rather than seeking approval from God to take action on their own, Latter-day Saints assumed that the Almighty hand of vengeance would take all action necessary. Whether in this life or the next, those guilty of persecuting the Saints would receive their reward. This increasing pacifism was reflected by a general shift toward moderating perceived radical doctrines. The phasing out of polygamy beginning with the 1890 Manifesto, coupled with a deemphasis of violent rhetoric and other peculiarities, demonstrated the Church's desire for a possible shift toward the ecclesiastical mainstream.

The scrutiny regarding the Church's early practice of the Law of Retribution came to a climax during the Reed Smoot hearings, where dozens of current and former Latter-day Saints were questioned about whether the oath's wording conflicted with their loyalty to the government.[29] Most witnesses called to testify before Congress had never known Joseph Smith, and many were two or three generations removed from their first Latter-day Saint ancestors. Unlike early settlers who had experienced the persecutions of Missouri and Illinois firsthand, the new generation was less apt to seek vengeance upon an enemy they had only known through the tenor of folk rhetoric.

Early twentieth-century Latter-day Saints grew uncomfortable with historical narratives seeking retribution. Revisions to the temple endowment beginning with the administration of Heber J. Grant prompted Church leaders to reconsider whether vengeance had a place on the path toward modernization. In June 1924, St. George Stake President Edward H. Snow, who would later serve as president of the St. George Temple, expressed his feeling that the prayer for vengeance had "been answered and [was] no longer necessary."[30] Following a December 1926 meeting with the Church's Temple Committee, Apostle George F. Richards recorded that the "question of Retribution took considerable time."[31]

Even the earliest accounts of the Law of Retribution's wording implied that the law was temporary, rather than remaining a permanent fixture in the temple endowment. Nauvoo temple patrons purportedly pledged to teach the law only "unto the third and fourth generation." This phrasing is also reflected in Abinadi's final vengeance sermon that the jealous God of Abraham would "[visit] the iniquities of the fathers

29. Buerger, 133–136.
30. Buerger, 140.
31. Buerger, 139.

upon the children, unto the third and fourth generations of them that hate [him]."[32] Thus the Book of Mormon may provide a theological justification for both instituting and ultimately removing the Law of Retribution from temple ceremonies. Edward Snow's suggestion to eliminate the Law of Retribution altogether became a reality on 15 February 1927. At the direction of the First Presidency, temple presidents were asked to "Omit from the prayer in the circle all references to avenging the blood of the prophets" and to "Omit from the ordinance and lecture all reference to retribution."[33]

Unlike their predecessors, who saw innocent blood crying from the ground as an invitation to petition God for vengeance, Latter-day Saints three or four generations removed from the martyrdom of Joseph and Hyrum had no direct connection to it. Though praying for divine retribution had brought solace to a religious community mourning the loss of their leader simultaneously decrying a failed judicial system, its ambiguity left a vacuum that some Latter-day Saints believed would excuse general acts of violence against "Gentiles." It also challenged the very place of Mormonism in American culture. As the Church began to expand its core membership outside the confines of the Great Basin, its general identity and exclusivism was internally challenged by a rising generation that had never known Joseph or Brigham, and who instead saw themselves as part of a rapidly advancing era of innovations and ideas. It is in that tradition – and perhaps by Mormonism's inherent capacity to allow change through latter-day revelation – in which the modern Church continues to shape itself.

32. Mosiah 13:13.

33. Anderson, 218.

About the Contributors

Richard Lyman Bushman is Gouverneur Morris Professor Emeritus of History at Columbia University and the author of many books, including *Joseph Smith: Rough Stone Rolling* and *Mormonism: A Very Short Introduction.* He has received fellowships from the American Council of Learned Societies, the Charles Warren Center, the John Simon Guggenheim Foundation, the National Endowment for the Humanities, the Huntington Library, the Shelby Cullom Davis Center, and the American Antiquarian Society. He co-founded and is chairman of the Board of the Center for Latter-day Saint Arts.

Matthew Roper (MA, Brigham Young University) has been a research scholar at the Neal A. Maxwell Institute for Religious Scholarship and is currently a researcher and writer at Scripture Central. He has published in *Literary and Linguistic Computing*, *BYU Studies Quarterly*, *Mormon Studies Review*, *Interpreter: A Journal of Latter-day Saint Faith and Scholarship* and the *Journal of Book of Mormon Studies.*

Joshua Gehly is an ordained Evangelist of The Church of Jesus Christ—headquartered in Monongahela, Pennsylvania—and has preached the everlasting gospel of Jesus Christ domestically, on indigenous reservations and on multiple continents. He independently hosts and produces the Book of Mormon History Podcast, which interviews scholars about the Book of Mormon in order to provide easy access to current research for personal study. He has presented lectures regarding the historicity of the Book of Mormon to many different religious affiliations both within and outside the Restoration Movement.

Neal Rappleye is currently working as a researcher for the Ancient America Foundation. His primary research interests include ancient

Jerusalem, ancient Arabia, the ancient Near East, pre-Columbian Mesoamerica, the 19th century witnesses to the discovery and translation of the Book of Mormon. His work has been published by The Interpreter Foundation, BYU Studies, Religious Educator, Book of Mormon Central, Greg Kofford Books, and Covenant Communications, and he has presented at several conferences. He was previously at Scripture Central (2015–2025) where he wrote over 200 KnoWhy and Evidence articles, and oversaw and contributed to a number of other research projects as the director of research.

Morgan Deane is a freelance writer, military historian, and former U.S. Marine. He earned history degrees from Southern Virginia and Norwich University and studied Chinese military history at Kings College London. He has authored numerous books and articles on a variety of topics ranging from ancient history to the Russian invasion of Ukraine. But his passion remains the Book of Mormon, and his latest manuscript explores the interactions between the Book of Mormon and Just War Theory.

Brent J. Schmidt earned degrees in history and classics from the University of Utah and a Ph.D. in classics from the University of Colorado-Boulder. He teaches in the religion and humanities departments at BYU-Idaho. He specialized in Greek and Latin moralistic literature and he wrote and later published his dissertation on ancient utopian communities. He has published works on Biblical subjects including word studies about grace and faith. He is an author and editor of the BYU New Testament Commentary series. He enjoys reading, especially the Book of Mormon and Bible, gardening, collecting ancient coins, world travel, skiing and learning ancient and modern languages. For fifteen years now he has read at least one academic book a day. He and his wife, Judith, are the parents of one son.

Spencer Kraus graduated from Brigham Young University with a Bachelor's degree in Computer Science, Modern Hebrew, and Ancient Near Eastern Studies. He is a researcher for the Ancient America Foundation and works with Lincoln Blumell on topics relating to early Christianity and the Greek New Testament.

Spencer R. Marsh graduated from Brigham Young University with a Bachelor's Degree in philosophy and a minor in business. Spencer has plans to pursue graduate studies in law and business. He has done extensive volunteer writing and producing for organizations such as Scripture Central, the Interpreter Foundation, and FAIR.

Charles Dike served in the United States Navy for six years from 1967 to 1973. Most of his service was on a submarine so he is familiar with boats that are "tight like unto a dish" and concerns with CO 2 buildup in those boats. He spent some time on a surface ship and was tossed upon the waves of the sea in storms and observed and experienced challenges involving seasickness in fairly large populations. Later he enjoyed sailing on a small dinghy with a hole in the bottom – its functionality being unfamiliar to most Book of Ether readers. After being discharged from the navy he attended BYU and received an MSEE in 1984 while researching and designing integrated circuits. After retirement in 2015 he began writing technical papers dealing primarily with the Book of Mormon. His first religiously themed published article is *"A Comet, Christ's Birth and Josephus's Lunar Eclipse."*

Jacob Billings is an artificial intelligence engineer and computational linguist. He obtained a B.A. in Middle Eastern Studies with an emphasis on Biblical Hebrew from the University of Utah. He received an M.A. in Linguistics from Francisco Marroquin University in Guatemala City focusing on the K'iche' Mayan language and early colonial texts of the K'iche' Maya and early mendicant preachers. Presently, he is a Ph.D. candidate at Complutense University in Madrid, Spain, in the Department of Prehistory and Archaeology where his studies involve the use of artificial intelligence and quantitative methods to recreate Mesoamerican language families in order to trace migrations and influence throughout prehistory. He is specifically focused on the influence of Mix-Zoque-speaking people on other Mesoamerican cultures.

Jacob's academic pursuits encompass a variety of interests, including artificial intelligence algorithms within historical linguistics and epigraphy, morphosyntax in Mesoamerican and Mesopotamian languages, the linguistics of the Book of Mormon, and the early members of the Latter-day Saint faith movement in the 19th century.

Stephen O. Smoot is a doctoral candidate in Semitic and Egyptian Languages and Literature at the Catholic University of America. He previously earned a master's degree from the University of Toronto in Near and Middle Eastern Civilizations, with a concentration in Egyptology, and bachelor's degrees from Brigham Young University in Ancient Near

Eastern Studies, with a concentration in Hebrew Bible, and German Studies.

Laura B. Hathaway graduated from Utah State University with a Bachelor of Science in Chemistry. She then moved to the "land of many waters," where she worked in a chemistry lab at Cornell University. She returned to Utah and completed a second bachelor's degree, this time in Horticulture and worked in the Pharmacology/Toxicology department at the University of Utah. Her analytical mind naturally led her to a desire to understand the details of Book of Mormon geography. After spending years studying, she has concluded that the large number of geographical references and the internal consistency in the Book of Mormon suggests a real-world setting. She believes that finding the true location is found in reconciling all the details. She currently divides her time studying Book of Mormon geography, raising four children (and a husband), and running her own tax firm.

Ronald D. Bracken (1943–2023) held a degree in accounting from Brigham Young University and had a lifelong interest in scriptural studies, with a particular focus on patterns, symbolism, and the geography of the Book of Mormon. After a successful career in business and construction in southern Utah, he dedicated his later years to intensive study of the scriptures, spending over 15,000 hours exploring questions such as the timing of the Savior's birth and the structure of sacred texts. He was especially known for his research into Book of Mormon geography, advocating for alternative interpretations outside the commonly held models. Ron passed away in 2023, leaving behind a legacy of faith, intellectual curiosity, and deep devotion to his family and religious community.

LTC Martin Evans, D.O. is the Military Director of the Kombewa Clinical Research Center in Kenya, affiliated with the Walter Reed Army Institute of Research. A U.S. Army physician and clinical researcher, Dr. Evans has led investigations into immunomodulators, vaccines, and treatments for conditions such as sepsis, Long COVID, malaria, and Venezuelan equine encephalitis. He holds an osteopathic medical degree from A.T. Still University and completed fellowships in Allergy and Immunology as well as Clinical Pharmacology. A recipient of the BG Theodore C. Lyster Flight Surgeon of the Year Award and the Meritorious Service Medal, he is also an Assistant Professor of Medicine at the Uniformed Services University. He and his wife, Anne-Marie, have two children.

Tyler J. Andersen is an instructor of Speech and Film at Tarrant County College and a remote adjunct instructor of Communication for Brigham Young University–Idaho Online. He holds an M.A. in Rhetorical Studies from Idaho State University. His research interests include Latter-day Saint rhetoric, American religious discourse, and the intersection of faith and public memory. Tyler and his wife, Kacey, are the parents of four children.

Image Credits

Cover: "Praying at Cumorah" by Patrick Spencer, used by permission.

page 17: Pyramid of Life. Created by Matt Roper, used by permission.

page 29: Wheeled Mayan figurine. Photo taken by John Sorenson, used by permission.

page 141: Cropped image from page 100 of Old Testament Revision 2 from the Joseph Smith Papers website. © By Intellectual Reserve, Inc. Used by permission.

page 165: Modified image, originally from Wikimedia Commons.

page 167: Modified image, originally from Wikimedia Commons.

page 173: Drawing by Charles Dike, used by permission.

page 174: Drawing by Charles Dike, used by permission

page 181: Photograph by Charles Dike, used by permission.

page 181: Figure adapted by Charles Dike, inspired by Figure 5.1 from Britton Ward, "The hydrodynamics of sailboat bailing devices", 57.

page 182: Modified figure (Figure 2.3) from Britton Ward, "The hydrodynamics of sailboat bailing devices", 23.

page 184: Drawing by Charles Dike, used by permission.

page 215: Overview of the Chesapeake Bay model by Des. Isaías Baruch Peña Ramírez. Used by permission.

page 216: Possible locations of Nephite and Lamanite cities in the land southward by Des. Isaías Baruch Peña Ramírez. Used by permission.

www.ingramcontent.com/pod-product-compliance
Ingram Content Group UK Ltd.
Pitfield, Milton Keynes, MK11 3LW, UK
UKHW041635190726
13854UKWH00006B/2512